underbelly

The authors

John Silvester has been a crime reporter in Melbourne since 1978. He worked for *The Sunday Times* Insight team in London in 1990, and has co-authored many crime books, including the *Underbelly* series, *Leadbelly* and *The Silent War*. He is currently senior crime reporter for *The Age*.

Andrew Rule started in journalism in 1975 and has worked in newspapers, television and radio. He wrote *Cuckoo*, the inside story of the 'Mr Stinky' case, since re-issued in the collection *Sex, Death and Betrayal*, and has co-written, edited and published several other books, including the *Underbelly* series. He became deputy editor of *The Sunday Age* in 2007.

underbelly

THE
GANGLAND WAR

JOHN SILVESTER AND ANDREW RULE

SLY
Ink..

Published by Floradale Productions Pty Ltd and Sly Ink Pty Ltd
January 2008

Reprinted February 2008 (three times), March 2008, April 2008 (twice), May 2008,
June 2008, August 2008, February 2009

Distributed wholesale by Gary Allen Pty Ltd
9 Cooper Street
Smithfield, NSW
Telephone 02-9725 2933

Underbelly: The Gangland War
ISBN   0 9775440 6 0

Cover design, typesetting and layout: R.T.J. Klinkhamer

Front cover image of Vince Colosimo as Alphonse Gangitano
in the Channel Nine drama series *Underbelly* courtesy of
Greg Noakes Photography
www.gregnoakes.com
Back cover image of Carl Williams being arrested courtesy of
Angela Wylie, *The Age*

....

'Here we go again,
fasten your seatbelts.'

CARL WILLIAMS MINUTES AFTER HIT MAN
ANDREW VENIAMIN WAS SHOT DEAD.

CONTENTS

. . . .

'For the salvation of the
good, the destruction of the
evil-doers, and for firmly
establishing righteousness.'

HINDU PROVERB: PURANA

1

GUT REACTION

'He became the most dangerous
gangster in Australia.'

THE bloodiest underworld war in the history of Australian crime began with both a bang and a whimper in a tiny park in the western suburb of Gladstone Park, near Melbourne Airport.

A gunman, drug dealer and notorious hothead called Jason Moran made two decisions — one premeditated, the other off the cuff — that started the vicious vendetta which would wipe out his crime family, including himself and his closest male relatives.

The longest journey starts with a step, and the path towards death, destruction and lifetime detention began simply enough. Moran and his half-brother, Mark, had arranged to meet amphetamines manufacturer Carl Williams to discuss their mutual business interests. Williams liked to talk in parks and public places to avoid police listening devices, and the Morans were happy to meet in an open space where they thought they would not be ambushed.

The Williams and Moran families had trafficked drugs for years and while they were sometimes associates, they were never close.

They did deals and begrudgingly co-operated when it suited, but they also competed with each other for a slice of the obscenely lucrative illegal pill market.

While there were reasons for their hostility, none was pressing enough for them to go to war. Business was booming. Demand had increased ten-fold as amphetamines became a mainstream 'party drug'. All they had to do was keep a low profile, source their pills and count the cash.

But there were niggles. The Morans, always quick to take offence, began to stew.

At first it was a simple domestic matter: Carl Williams' wife, Roberta, had previously been married to Dean Stephens, a friend of the Morans, and there was lingering ill-feeling over the broken relationship.

The next was competition: Williams was undercutting his rivals, selling his pills for $8, compared with the Morans' $15.

The third was business: Williams had supplied the Morans with a load of pills, but he had not used enough binding material and they were crumbling before they could be sold.

The fourth niggle was greed: the Morans claimed ownership of a pill press and said Williams owed them $400,000. Carl disagreed.

The problems could have been settled, but the Morans, known for short tempers and long memories, tended to use unreasonable violence to achieve what they believed were reasonable outcomes.

All of which meant that the meeting at the Barrington Crescent park, no bigger than two suburban blocks and bordered by houses on three sides, gave the Moran brothers the perfect

2

opportunity to remind Williams where he stood — before they shot him off his feet.

It was 13 October 1999, Carl Williams' birthday. He was 29.

Williams was unlikely to have sensed danger. The mid-week meeting was to be held in the afternoon in the open — hardly the ideal place to pull a double cross. But soon after they arrived, Jason Moran pulled a gun, a .22 Derringer. A woman nearby heard a man cry out, 'No, Jason!' and then a single shot.

It showed the Morans' arrogance. It was broad daylight in suburbia, not some dark alley or an isolated spot in the bush. They simply did not believe they could be stopped.

But this time the gunman showed uncharacteristic restraint. Mark Moran urged his half-brother to finish the job, but Jason said they needed Williams alive if they were ever to get their money. That hasty decision to shoot him — but not to kill him — would destroy the Moran clan, and many who were close to it.

The brutal truth was that if they had killed Williams, he would have been just another dead drug dealer and the case would probably have remained unsolved. Instead, the wounded Williams turned into an underworld serial killer determined to exterminate every real or imagined rival he could find.

From the day he was shot, Williams refused to co-operate with police. He was young but had started life in Richmond and prided himself on being an old-school crook. When detectives interviewed him in hospital, he said he had felt a pain in his stomach as he was walking, and only then realised he had been shot. It was straight out of the painters and dockers rulebook.

Much later Williams told the author he did not see his attacker. 'I have no idea who shot me and I've never asked ... I don't know who did it. Police told me who they think did it, but that's their business.' When the author suggested they had nominated Jason Moran, he smiled and said, 'You'd better ask them.'

Roberta Williams gave more away in a later conversation, but denied the shooting was drug-related. 'Mark was yelling, "Shoot him in the head," and Jason then shot him in the stomach,' she said.

If the Morans thought shooting Williams would frighten him off, they were wrong. The wound soon healed but the mental scar remained. The drug dealer began planning his revenge, setting off an underworld war that would catch police, the legal system and politicians unprepared.

Williams, with his plump, pleasant face, his shorts and T-shirts, did not look like an influential crime boss who could and would order a death with a phone call. As a strategist he would appear more a draughts man than a chess player. Perhaps that is one of the reasons he flew under the police radar for many months. By the time they realised who and what he was, he had become the most dangerous gangster in Australia.

At first, police knew he was part of his family's drug business but they assumed the former supermarket packer was a worker — not the foreman.

Like the Morans, police underestimated Williams and his power base. He was ruthless, cashed-up and had recruited a loyal gang of reckless young drug dealers driven by pill money, wild dreams and illegal chemicals.

His team went from underworld try-hards to big players in a matter of months. Guns, drugs and rivers of cash can do that. At one point his family drug business was turning over $100,000 a month.

Williams' reputation and power grew with every hit. He began to refer to himself as 'The Premier' because, he smirked, 'I run this fucking state'. But to detectives, he was just 'The Fatboy'.

Police say Williams was connected to ten underworld murders and would have kept killing if he had not finally been jailed.

He will never face charges over many of the murders he arranged because he cut a deal with police that gives him some chance of release one day. His only hope is that he will die a free old man, rather than in jail.

Williams' rise from middle-ranked drug dealer to heavy-weight killer should never have happened. His plans for revenge and control of a big drug syndicate should have collapsed when he was arrested in slapstick circumstances six weeks after the Morans shot him.

For Broadmeadows police, it began as a low-level fraud investigation and ended as a $20 million drug bust. The fraud involved an enterprising local family running up credit card debts with no intention of paying, then changing their names to obtain new cards to repeat the scam.

On the morning of 25 November 1999, police arrived at a Housing Commission house in Fir Close, Broadmeadows, to serve warrants, but no-one was home.

Later that day, Detective Sergeant Andrew Balsillie was passing, and noticed two cars at the house. He recalled his team to issue the warrants and, after bursting in, found a pill press, 30,000 tablets (almost certainly the Moran pills that had been returned to be re-pressed) and nearly seven kilograms of speed valued at $20 million. Williams was found hiding in a bed fully dressed and his father, George, was found between a bed and the wall in another room, in which a loaded Glock semi-automatic pistol was later found.

Local police rightly chose to run the investigation but called in the amphetamines experts from the drug squad. They were not to know that the two drug squad detectives — Malcolm Rosenes and Stephen Paton — were corrupt and would later be jailed. While there was no suggestion Rosenes and Paton interfered with the investigation, the Supreme Court later decided that several drug cases, including Williams', should be delayed until the detectives' prosecutions were completed.

It was while Williams was on bail for those (and other) drug charges that he organised the underworld murders.

If the drug cases had not been delayed, Williams would have been jailed for at least four years, unable to carry out a homicidal vendetta.

All of which means that police corruption led, at least indirectly, to the underworld war that shocked Australia.

WHILE in jail on remand for close to two months, Williams began to plan his first attack. First, he recruited the team he believed would kill for him.

One of the first to join was Andrew 'Benji' Veniamin, the former kick boxer and gunman who once idolised Carlton identity Mick Gatto, who has cast a giant shadow in Melbourne's underworld for years. Williams saw Gatto, who was loosely affiliated with the Morans but not involved in the squabble over drugs, as a potentially powerful enemy.

Williams thought that if he killed the Moran brothers immediately, it meant established underworld figures, including Gatto, would seek revenge. He decided his best chance of survival was not to jump at shadows but to cast a bigger one, so he launched a hostile takeover.

Initially, Williams was outnumbered and in no position to take on the Morans, let alone contemplate plans for gangland domination. Then, by a stroke of perfect timing, he was finally bailed on his drug charges on 22 January 2000. Three days later, Jason Moran was jailed for affray and sentenced to twenty months jail. That meant Mark Moran had lost his closest ally and was now dangerously exposed.

Five months later, on 15 June, Mark Moran was killed outside his Aberfeldie home. More driven than Jason, but less erratic,

Mark had managed to keep a lower profile than his half-brother — until then.

When his death was first reported, he was referred to as a local football star rather than an underworld identity. But police immediately knew it was a gangland hit.

They also knew Mark Moran was entrenched in crime as much as the rest of his family, who had always considered honest work a personal affront.

Moran lived in a house valued at $1.3 million at a time when most western suburban houses were worth much less than half that. His occupations had been listed as personal trainer and unemployed pastry chef, neither of which would explain how much dough he had.

Four months before his murder, on 17 February 2000, police noticed Moran driving a new luxury hire car. When they pulled him over and opened the boot, they found a high-tech handgun fitted with a silencer and a laser sight. They also found a heap of amphetamine pills that had been stamped through a pill press to appear as ecstasy tablets.

His days as a battling baker were long gone.

In the hours before his death, Mark Moran had been busy. First he had passed drugs to a dealer at the Gladstone Park shopping centre, a few hundred metres from where he and his brother had shot Williams the previous year.

The dealer was short of cash and Moran agreed to give him credit. It was no problem. Few people were stupid enough to try to rip off the Morans.

Moran drove home, but soon decided to leave again for another meeting. He was blasted with a shotgun as he stepped into his Commodore.

Police later established that Williams had been waiting only ten minutes for Moran to leave the house. It smelled of an ambush based on inside information.

Moran's natural father, Leslie John Cole, had been shot dead in eerily similar circumstances outside his Sydney home eighteen years earlier. But Mark's stepfather, Lewis Moran, was very much alive and drinking in a north-western suburban hotel when he first heard of the shooting.

He immediately called a council of war at his home.

The Moran kitchen cabinet discussed who they believed was responsible, and how they should respond. The Morans, never short of enemies, narrowed the field to three. Williams and his team were by no means the favourite. 'We still didn't know we were in a war,' a Moran insider later said.

For Williams it was the beginning, and for the Morans it was the beginning of the end.

Much later, Lewis Moran, said to still hold the first dollar he ever stole, tried to take out a contract on Williams, first at $40,000 and later at $50,000. Lewis's idea of a hit fee hadn't kept up with inflation. There were no takers.

There were seven men at the meeting at Moran's home. Five are now dead.

Police suspected Carl Williams from the start for Mark Moran's murder, so much so they raided his house next day. But internal police politics terminally damaged the investigation. Members of the drug squad, who had worked on the Morans for years, deliberately concealed information from the homicide squad because they believed their long-term investigation was more important than a murder probe they thought was doomed to fail in any case.

Their prediction was self-fulfilling.

Jason Moran was allowed special leave from prison to speak at Mark's packed gangland funeral (one of many repeated in Melbourne in the following few years). Mourners later said he spoke with real emotion, but the death notice he placed in the *Herald*

Sun worried police. It read: 'This is only the beginning; it will never be the end. REMEMBER, I WILL NEVER FORGET.'

But nor would Carl Williams.

Police, and the underworld, expected that when Jason Moran was released he would make good his implied promise of vengeance. But by the time Moran was freed on 5 September 2001, Williams was back inside on remand, having been charged in May with trafficking 8000 ecstasy tablets.

The parole board let Moran go overseas because of fears for his life, while Williams continued his private recruiting drive from a small area filled with potential killers — Port Phillip Prison.

AS is customary when important business deals are sealed, the main players celebrated with a quiet drink. But when the man we will call 'The Runner' decided to accept Carl Williams' offer, the drink was smuggled alcohol and the venue was the aptly-named Swallow Unit of Port Phillip Prison, Victoria's top security jail.

According to The Runner, it was there that Williams first asked him to kill Jason Moran. Moran — who had been spotted in London by one of the Williams' team ('The Lieutenant') — had decided to return, even though he must have known his life was still in danger.

Williams was not content with one hit team and continued to recruit inside and outside prison. While he was not a great student of history, he knew that in a war there would inevitably be casualties and prisoners. He looked to relatives, close friends and hardened gunmen whose loyalty he thought he could demand, or buy.

Williams knew that The Runner, no pin-up boy for prisoner rehabilitation programs, was soon to be released after serving a sentence for armed robbery. He was good with guns, and ruthless.

In March 1990, The Runner had escaped from Northfield Jail in South Australia, where he had been serving a long sentence for armed robberies. The following month he was arrested in Melbourne and questioned over four stick-ups. As he was being driven to the city watch house he jumped from the unmarked police car and bolted, much to the chagrin of the sleepy detective escorting him. He wasn't caught until January 1991 – in Queensland.

Police claim The Runner carried out 40 armed robberies in Victoria, South Australia and Western Australia over seven years. In 1999 he was again arrested after he tried to rob a Carlton bank.

Why 'The Runner'? His trademark was to run into a bank, pull a gun, demand large denomination notes and then run up to 500 metres to his getaway car. His gun-and-run method earned him a reputation as a long-distance runner among police and criminals.

Williams believed this running talent could prove useful in ambushes that might have to be carried out on foot. When he popped the question, The Runner did not hesitate.

On 17 July 2002, Williams was bailed, despite having twice been arrested on serious drug charges. But the courts had no choice, Williams' case (and those involving six others) was indefinitely delayed while prosecutions against corrupt drug squad detectives were finalised.

Five months later, The Runner was released and within weeks he was going out with Roberta Williams' sister, Michelle. He may not have been blood family, but he seemed the next best thing.

The Runner and Carl Williams met daily, and Williams asked his new right-hand man to find Moran. He said Moran was aware he was being hunted and had gone to ground.

'Carl told me that he still wanted Jason dead and that he

wanted me to locate Jason so he could kill him. We did not discuss money at this point but I was to start surveillance on Jason Moran.'

Williams' ambitions and his desire for revenge were growing. No longer did he want only to kill Jason. 'Carl developed a deep-seated hatred of the Moran family ... there is no doubt it was an obsession with him. Carl told me on numerous occasions that he wanted everyone connected with the Moran family dead.'

The Runner began to track Moran. With every report Williams would peel off between $500 and $1000 for the information. His former prison buddy was also paid to deliver drugs and collect money, and set up in a Southgate apartment that Williams sometimes used as a secret bachelor pad.

The Fatboy may have been prepared to wage war in the underworld but he was still frightened of Roberta, whom he had married the previous year when she was heavily pregnant with his baby.

The Runner would tell police he was not the only one spying on Moran. Williams also received information from convicted millionaire drug trafficker, Tony Mokbel, and soon-to-be-deceased crime middleweight, Willie Thompson.

Williams and The Runner regularly swapped cars — a black Ford, a silver Vectra, a grey Magna and Roberta Williams' Pajero.

But finding Moran was one thing, killing him quite another. They began to discuss how — and the schemes ranged from the imaginative to the innovative to the idiotic.

One was to hide in the boot of Moran's silver BMW and spring out, another involved lying beneath shrubs outside the house where Moran was believed to be staying. Williams even considered hiding in a rubbish bin. It would have had to have been a big bin.

Another plan was to lure Moran to a park so The Runner, dressed as a woman and pushing a pram, could walk past and shoot him. They even bought a shoulder-length brown wig before ditching the idea. Just as well. The Runner had a distinct five o'clock shadow and hairy legs.

Killer? Yes. Drag Queen? No.

Finding Moran proved difficult. He was an expert in counter-surveillance and teamed with a man who appeared to be a bodyguard. He quit his flamboyant lifestyle, rented a modest house in Moonee Ponds and kept on the move.

Also, The Runner had never met Moran and Williams did not provide him with a picture.

They finally spotted him in late February at a Red Rooster outlet in Gladstone Park. Williams was not armed. They followed him and an unidentified female driving a small black sedan.

As a surveillance operative, Carl made a good drug dealer. He grabbed a tyre lever and a screwdriver from inside his car and followed at a distance of only twenty metres. According to The Runner, 'The rear of the hatch of the car opened up and Jason shot several shots at us from the back of the car.' Which is when Williams lost interest, saying: 'We will get him another time'.

Williams and the Runner went to pubs and clubs where they might find Moran. They may have ended up full, but they came back empty. They thought about a hit at the docks where Moran was said to work occasionally, but fears of terrorism had prompted tight security that made it impossible to hang around without attracting suspicion.

Williams started to get desperate. If he couldn't get to Jason he would kill those close to him, he thought. He told The Runner to start surveillance on Moran's oldest family friend, Graham Kinniburgh, and another associate, Steve (Fat Albert) Collins.

Kinniburgh was a semi-retired gangster, well-known in police and underworld circles and close to Jason's father, Lewis Moran.

Williams finally figured that even an erratic man like Moran must have some family routine. He and Moran were linked by more than greed, drugs and hatred — their children all went to the same private school in the Essendon area.

Williams finally put a bounty on Moran's head in April 2003. Veniamin and The Runner would get $100,000 each. The pair, armed and masked, hid in the back seat of a rented car outside the school expecting Jason to drop his children off. But he did not show. Next time, Roberta Williams picked a fight with Jason's wife, Trish, outside the school in the hope she would call her husband to come and support her. Still no Jason.

Williams wanted Veniamin (who was still associating with Gatto and the Carlton Crew) to set up Moran for an ambush, but Benji was frightened Big Mick would realise he was working for Williams.

'Carl was becoming wary of Andrew and told me that he was concerned that Andrew was more in the Moran camp than in ours,' The Runner later told police.

In fact, Williams believed Moran was trying to persuade Veniamin to become a double agent and kill Carl.

When Benji failed to deliver Moran to a planned ambush at the Spencer Street taxi rank near *The Age* building, Williams started to doubt his number one killer.

'From then on Carl would only meet Andrew on his own terms. That way Carl could be sure of his own safety. He did not trust Andrew any more,' The Runner said.

Certainly Williams was jumpy. An interstate AFL spy wanted to check out the Essendon team at Windy Hill, but because it was a locked training session he had to drive to one end of the ground where he hoped to use binoculars to study the opposition.

He lost interest in sport when Williams, whose mother lived nearby, fronted him, believing the spy was trying to follow him.

The spy waved a *Football Record* at him, stuttering that his interest in sharp shooters was limited to Essendon's star full forward, Matthew Lloyd. It is thought to be the only time the *Football Record* has been used to save a life.

The Williams team learned that Moran took his children to Auskick training every Saturday morning in Essendon North, near the Cross Keys Hotel. Williams had eased Veniamin out of the hit team and replaced him with the getaway driver from the Mark Moran murder.

The Runner and his new partner, 'The Driver', inspected the football oval and planned an ambush. On 14 June 2003, armed and ready, they watched the football clinic but did not see Jason. They agreed to try again the next week.

Williams had another plan. He wanted not only to kill Moran, but to make a statement no-one could mistake. He told The Runner he wanted Jason ambushed on 15 June, the anniversary of Mark's murder, at Mark's grave at Fawkner Cemetery.

It was too late to do the necessary homework and on the assigned day it took the hit team more than an hour to find the grave. By then the window of opportunity had shut. When they arrived, they found a card signed by Jason. They had missed their mark, but only just. As they left, they saw a car fly through a red light. It was probably Moran.

During the following week, the team repeatedly went to the Cross Keys ground to fine tune their planned hit. The Runner would be dropped at the hotel car park where Moran would be parked; he would run up, shoot Moran in the head then run over a footbridge to the getaway van.

At the precise moment of the hit, Williams was committed to spilling blood but in an environment far more sterile than the grubby murder scene. He had organised a blood-test for that morning, giving him an alibi.

On the Saturday morning they collected guns stashed at a

safe house, and fitted stolen number plates on the white van to be used in the getaway.

Williams' lieutenant, a man who could source chemicals for amphetamines and who cannot be named, then advised The Runner to, 'Get Jason good and get him in the head'.

The Lieutenant later disputed this when he became a police witness. He claimed he told The Driver to do the killing away from the kids at Auskick — 'Hey, I'm no monster.'

As they sat near the park, The Runner spotted a man he thought was Moran. Williams and The Lieutenant drove past and nodded to confirm the target's identity, then headed off to set up their alibi at the medical clinic.

As the football clinic ended, the hit team watched Moran walk to a blue van. Williams' men drove to the rear of the car park for The Runner to get out before the driver headed around the block to wait for him.

The Runner put on a balaclava. He had a shotgun and two revolvers. He ran to the driver's side of the blue van, aimed the shotgun at Moran and fired through the glass.

He dropped the shotgun and fired at least three shots with a revolver, then ran off.

The man sitting with Jason was Pasquale Barbaro, a small-time crook who often worked for Moran. The Runner later said he didn't see Barbaro, let alone intend to kill him.

Williams received news of the hit with the message that 'the horse...had been scratched'.

Later, Williams and The Lieutenant congratulated The Runner on a 'job well done' and gave him $2500 cash. At first he was promised $100,000, and then a unit in Frankston as payment, but neither happened. The killer was short-changed and it would prove a short-sighted decision. But if it worried the hired gunman it didn't show — hours after killing two men and scrubbing off gunshot residue, he attended a birthday party at a North Melbourne restaurant.

Murder, it would seem, can sharpen the appetite.

Another person was clearly pleased with the news of Moran's death. Roberta Williams was picked up on a bug shortly after the murders saying, 'I'll be partying tonight.'

EVEN though Williams was the obvious suspect, his blood-test alibi was standing up. The shotgun found at the scene had not been traced and those around the Williams camp said nothing.

There had been eleven underworld murders since 2000 and all remained unsolved. Police initially treated each crime individually, despite it being obvious that some (but not all) of the murders were connected.

Senior homicide investigator, Phil Swindells, was frustrated by the lack of results and began lobbying for a taskforce. He reported that Andrew Veniamin was suspected of three murders and a taskforce was necessary to target his group. Senior police finally acted and the Rimer task group (later renamed Purana) was established in May 2003, with Detective Senior Sergeant Swindells in charge.

Many believed it was doomed to fail. 'We had no intelligence and we didn't know anything about many of the major players,' Swindells would recall. Assistant Commissioner Simon Overland would later admit that police 'dropped the ball'.

Swindells knew there would be no early arrests and there might be more murders. He also knew police had to go back to the start and build up dossiers on all the players. Only then would they be able to try to isolate the weak links.

Politicians, self-proclaimed media experts and cynical old detectives thought Purana would self-destruct. A lack of success would result in bitter infighting and no results. The underworld code of silence would never be broken, they said.

To keep up morale during the years of investigation, the task-force called on Essendon coach and long-time AFL survivor Kevin Sheedy to motivate Purana investigators. Believe in yourselves and your team mates and don't worry about the scoreboard, he said. Do the planning and the results will come.

In October 2003 the taskforce was enlarged to 53 staff, including nine investigative groups, with Detective Inspector Andrew Allen in charge.

From the start no-one really doubted that Williams was behind the killing, but there was no hard evidence. Several names were nominated as the shooter, including The Runner, but names without facts were little use.

The initial homicide squad team was convinced The Runner was the gunman and had identified others who would later be shown to be part of Williams' hit squad.

The initial work of the homicide squad cannot be underestimated. But the better-resourced Purana team was able to make vital breakthroughs — eventually.

It was months before the first strong lead emerged from the double murder. Near the Cross Keys Hotel in Moreland Road is a public telephone and detectives eventually checked the calls made from there around the time of the murder.

On a long list, a series of numbers stood out. On Friday 20 June, the day before the double murder, someone rang Williams' mobile phone from the telephone box. Roberta Williams' mobile had also been called, and then The Runner's. It was clear to police that one of the hit team was checking out the layout for the ambush planned for the following day.

But the next call on the list was not a known suspect. When police tracked down the man who received the call he told them he had been rung that day by a mate. That friend was The Driver. It did not take long to find out that The Driver was a thief, drug dealer and close friend of Williams. He sold speed and had a lucrative sideline in stolen Viagra. He was still selling the remains of 10,175 sample packs lifted from a Cheltenham warehouse in April 2000.

Detectives went to The Driver's house. Sitting in the driveway was a white van, the same type as one captured on closed-circuit video depositing a masked gunman in the car park just before Moran and Barbaro were killed.

It was a breakthrough — but not *the* breakthrough. It would take police fourteen months before they could lay charges. Meanwhile, the murders kept happening.

PURANA detectives knew the Williams team would eventually make a mistake, but wondered how many would die before they found the weak link.

In October 2003 police learned that The Driver, Williams' trusted associate, had sourced an abandoned sedan rebuilt by a backyard mechanic — a perfect getaway vehicle.

Police placed a listening device in the car and waited. But The Driver, having collected the car and driven it a short distance, noticed the brake light was on. He checked it and found the bug, which he ripped out.

He immediately told The Runner, 'we're hot' and wanted to cancel the job. But The Runner had lost his sense of risk and insisted they push on, a decision he later admitted was 'sheer stupidity' caused by the pressure on him to get the job done.

That night they met Williams separately in Flemington for new instructions but Williams' growing sense of invincibility lulled him into making a massive misjudgement. The one-time suburban drug dealer with gangster boss dreams ordered his hit team to carry on regardless.

Inexplicably, The Driver decided to use his own car (a silver Holden Vectra sedan once owned by Williams) to drive to the scene. But it, too, was bugged with recording and tracking devices.

Police knew that The Runner and The Driver planned a major crime in a square kilometre block of South Yarra but did not know what it would be.

For a week, the pair repeatedly drove around the same streets. Police suspected they were planning an armed robbery and guessed potential targets could be the TAB at the Bush Inn Hotel or two luxury car dealerships.

A week later, on Saturday 25 October, the Purana chief, Detective Inspector Andrew Allen, was catching up on paperwork when he got the call from police monitoring the car.

The suspects had been talking about guns, getaways and something 'going down'. But the tracker failed (they drop out in the same manner as mobile phones) so police could not identify the car's location. Detectives could only sit back and listen, as they still did not know the men's intended target. They could hear muffled gunshots and the suspects driving off. It wasn't until police received calls that a man was lying in Joy Street, South Yarra, that they knew what had happened. Michael Ronald Marshall, 38, drug dealer and nightclub hotdog salesman, was dead.

Marshall had just got out of his four-wheel drive, his five-year-old son still in the vehicle. The Runner later told police that he shot the drug dealer four times in the street before escaping.

Later The Runner rang Williams to give him the usual crudely coded message: the job was done.

Williams understood — but so did the listening police. Within hours, The Runner and The Driver were arrested. The walls were starting to close in on 'The Premier'.

Police knew who had killed Marshall and who ordered the hit, but it would be more than two years before they learned why.

THREE days before Christmas 2003, Carl Williams and Andrew Veniamin met Mick Gatto at the Crown Casino to have what were supposed to be peace talks. It was only days after Gatto's close friend, Graham Kinniburgh, had been gunned down outside his Kew home.

Kinniburgh was an old-time gangster who had made his name as Australia's best safebreaker. For three decades he had been connected with some of Australia's biggest crimes. He was known to be the mastermind behind the magnetic drill gang, which had pulled some huge jobs. Kinniburgh had put his children through private school and was semi-retired, but he was a friend of Jason Moran's father, Lewis, and therefore Williams saw him as an enemy. In what would prove to be Kinniburgh's final few months he had become downright morose. A shrewd punter and expert numbers man, he knew the odds were that his would come up. He told a friend, 'My card has been marked' and began to carry a gun. He was shot dead on 13 December 2003, carrying groceries from his car to his house.

Next day, Williams told one of the authors he was not involved.

NINE days after Kinniburgh's murder three edgy men met at Crown Casino. They were Carl Williams, Andrew Veniamin and Mick Gatto. It was an open secret that Gatto was on Williams' death list and this was a last chance to stop the killings.

'It's not my war,' Gatto warned the two upstarts from the western suburbs. His words, later deciphered by a lip reader from security footage, were carefully chosen but the meaning was clear: if anything happened to Gatto or his crew, retribution would be swift. 'I believe you, you believe me, now we're even. That's a warning,' the big man said.

For perhaps the first time Williams wavered. Later, he went to see The Lieutenant for a second opinion. Should he trust Gatto and declare a truce?

The Lieutenant advised him to ask Veniamin because he knew Gatto better. Veniamin had no doubts. 'Kill him,' he said, thereby effectively passing his own death sentence.

Gatto would shoot Veniamin dead in a Carlton restaurant just three months later, on 23 March 2004, and subsequently be acquitted on grounds of self-defence.

And eight days after Veniamin died, Williams hit back.

LEWIS Moran was shattered by the death of his stepson, Mark, and his natural son, Jason. But it was the death of his best friend, Kinniburgh, that destroyed his will to live.

Lewis, a former skilled pickpocket, tried carrying a gun after Mark and Jason were murdered, but arthritis meant he couldn't handle it properly. Moran had little formal education but, as an experienced SP bookmaker, he could calculate odds in a flash. After Kinniburgh was killed he knew his own survival was a long shot.

Williams denied the existence of a death list and told the author: 'I've only met Lewis once. I haven't got a problem with Lewis. If he thinks he has a problem with me I can say he can sleep peacefully.' Not only was Williams a murderer but he was also, it would seem, a terrible fibber.

Police knew Moran was a sitting duck and they successfully applied to have a court-ordered bail curfew altered so his movements would not be easily anticipated by would-be hit men.

Detective Senior Sergeant Swindells gave evidence at the bail hearing in the forlorn hope he could save Moran's life.

He said Moran's 'vulnerability relates to a perception by the taskforce that if the curfew remains between 8pm and 8am ... it is possible for any person to be lying in wait for Mr Moran to return to his home address'.

But Lewis no longer cared. He knew that if he stuck to a routine he was more vulnerable but he continued to drink at the Brunswick Club — where he was shot dead by two contract killers on 31 March 2004. The killers were allegedly paid $140,000 cash. They were supposed to be paid $150,000 but were short-changed.

As a friend said, 'Lewis died because he loved cheap beer.'

POLICE knew they needed a circuit breaker and that the best way to do it would be to jail Williams. It was the self-styled 'Premier' himself, always so cautious about phones, who handed them the damning evidence. He told his wife in one call that if Purana Detective Sergeant Stuart Bateson raided their house she should 'grab the gun from under the mattress and shoot them in the head'.

In a prison phone call The Runner complained of his treatment and Williams talked about chopping up Sergeant Bateson's girlfriend.

Bateson was not one to be intimidated. He received the Valour Award in 1991 after wrestling a gunman to the ground and disarming him after the offender had forced another policeman to his knees at gunpoint.

The tape of Williams' threats was the break police needed. On 17 November 2003, the Special Operations Group grabbed Williams in Beaconsfield Parade, Port Melbourne.

The arrest was captured brilliantly by ace *Age* photographer Angela Wylie, who snapped an image of the man who thought he was beyond the law lying helplessly on the ground with detectives standing over him. It was a sign that times were changing.

Purana police believed they had enough to hold Williams, but he was bailed for a third time. It meant he was able to organise at least another three murders, police suspect.

In the two weeks before he was bailed, Williams befriended another would-be tough guy who was keen to be fast-tracked when he got out of prison. He was an alleged heroin trafficker and amateur boxer with a big mouth and he would finally bring the big man down.

ONE of the most boring jobs in a long investigation is to monitor police bugging devices. The Purana taskforce virtually dominated the technical capacity of the entire crime department with many detectives in other areas quietly grumbling that their investigations were put on hold because Simon Overland had ordered that the gangland detectives get first priority.

During the investigation Purana would log half a million telephone conversations — most consisting of the inarticulate ramblings of would-be gangsters. They used listening devices to bug suspects for 53,000 hours and conducted 22,000 hours of physical surveillance.

Police on the case found that listening to the Williams family was cruel and unusual punishment. 'It was like being subjected to the Jerry Springer Show 24 hours a day,' one said.

At one stage Roberta was talking to Carl when the son from her previous marriage distracted her. 'Put it down,' she said, and then told Carl in a matter-of-fact voice what 'it' was. 'He's got the tomahawk,' she said.

In another conversation she was talking to Greg Domaszewicz, the 'babysitter' accused of killing Jaidyn Leskie at Moe in 1997.

Roberta was complaining how difficult it was to look after the children while Carl was in prison. Domaszewicz suggested he could pop around and look after them if she needed a break. After a pause, she responded: 'You're fucking joking, aren't you?'

Carl Williams always assumed his phone, house and cars were bugged. When he wanted a business discussion he chose open parks or noisy fast food restaurants. This also suited his appetite, as he had a weakness for chicken and chips.

For police, trying to trap the Williams crew through bugging operations was like looking for the proverbial needle in the haystack.

But in late May 2004 they found it. Two of Williams' soldiers, sitting in what they thought was a clean car, discussed killing a close friend of Mick Gatto and key member of the so-called Carlton Crew, Mario Condello.

The two men in the car reminded each other of the importance of their mission. 'We're not just doing a burg,' one said to the other.

Williams saw Condello as the money man of the team he was determined to destroy. He also thought the lawyer-turned-gangster would find the money to take out a contract on him if he did not move first.

Condello and Gatto were close, so close that when Big Mick was in jail waiting for his trial over the Veniamin killing, he told Mario to keep one eye on business and the other in the back of his head.

The Williams' team had done their homework. They knew Condello was a creature of habit and took his small dog for an early morning walk past the Brighton Cemetery most week days.

It was the perfect place for an ambush. Police agreed, but their plan was to ambush the hit team before they could strike.

It was the beginning of a secret police high risk/high reward operation, codenamed Lemma. Detective Inspector Gavan Ryan was in charge of the 170 police needed to surround the area without spooking the hit men.

The would-be killers might have been committed but they weren't punctual. Twice when they were supposed to kill Condello they slept in. The second time, one of the team had chatted up a woman and preferred a hot one-night stand to a cold-blooded early morning killing.

Finally, they moved. They were still using the car that police had bugged and detectives could hear them preparing for the murder. But police also knew Condello had left the family home and moved into a city apartment. He also had heard he was on the hit list and moved out of his house to protect his family.

But then Ryan heard one of the team spot a big man walking his small dog near the cemetery. One of the gunmen was clearly heard asking, 'Is that the man, is that the man?'

By coincidence, another local with a similar build to Condello was walking a small dog on exactly the same route.

'He shouldn't bother buying Tattslotto tickets. I think he used all his luck that morning,' the then Director of Public Prosecutions Paul Coghlan said later of the dog walker.

With would-be hit men getting jumpy, Ryan knew it was time to move. Police arrested two men at the scene. They also seized two pistols, two-way radios and a stolen getaway car.

They then arrested Williams at his mother's home in Primrose Street, Essendon, and Williams' cousin Michael Thorneycroft in an outer eastern suburb.

Thorneycroft would later tell police he had been offered $30,000 to be the driver in the hit team and the shooter stood to make $120,000.

For police, it was a major breakthrough. But for Mario Condello it was only to be a delay. After the attempt on his life he was interviewed on Channel Nine and publicly addressed the

Williams team: 'My message is stay away from me. I'm bad luck to you people. Stay away. Don't come near me, please.'

He also expressed a poetic wish that the violence stop 'and everything becomes more peaceful than it has over the last however many years, because after all we are not going to be here forever.'

He was right.

Mario Condello was shot dead as he returned to his East Brighton home on 6 February 2006. He was on bail charged with, among other things, incitement to murder Carl Williams.

But the arrest of the hit team outside the Brighton Cemetery was the beginning of the end of Melbourne's underworld war. It meant that after five years of trying, police were finally able to put Williams inside jail on charges that guaranteed he would not be bailed.

For Gavan Ryan, the arrest was the moment that police finally seized the initiative — four years after Williams declared war with the murder of Mark Moran. 'For us (Operation Lemma) it was the turning point. It was the first time we were in front of the game.'

CARL Williams had previously done jail time easily. But this time he was in the highest security rating and locked up 23 hours a day. In one video link to court his lawyers argued that Williams had not been able to hold or touch his young daughter since being in maximum security.

No-one mentioned the feelings of the children of the men he'd had murdered in the previous five years.

Williams knew he was in trouble. He knew some of his troops were starting to waver and the wall of silence was starting to crack. He started to threaten and cajole his team to keep them staunch, working on those he thought most susceptible.

But he always assumed that The Runner, the career armed robber and willing killer, was unbreakable. This was a man who had never co-operated with police. When forensic experts took a swab from his gums in prison after the Marshall murder they were disgusted to find a 'brown substance' in his mouth. The substance, intended to compromise the test, was not officially identified, but it was definitely not breath freshener.

But the case against The Runner was compelling. Marshall's blood was found on his pants and police had the bugged conversations and had positive identifications.

At first The Runner wanted to fight. On legal advice, he put on 30 kilograms to try to beat eye-witness descriptions, and he wanted Williams to fund a Queen's Counsel for his case.

But Williams knew The Runner was doomed and decided to cut him free so Williams could save himself. He wanted his loyal soldier to plead guilty and cop a life sentence. The cash flow stopped and The Runner was left to the mercy of legal aid while his boss continued to employ the best lawyers drug money could buy.

Williams didn't want to be sitting in the criminal dock with The Runner as the evidence was put to a jury. He believed he still stood a chance if he managed to get a separate trial. The loyal hit man knew he was gone. He asked a lawyer to tell Williams and Mokbel to send The Runner's elderly mother some money and he was assured she would be looked after. Yet again the hit man was short changed. The old lady got barely $1500.

It wasn't a smart move.

IN early 2006 Crown Prosecutor Geoff Horgan, SC, returned from his summer break to find a letter from prison. It was The Runner and he wanted to talk. The note was non-committal but the message was clear. The soldier was ready to mutiny.

'To us it was unbelievable. He was seen as one of the hardest men in the system,' Horgan said.

Gavan Ryan, who was by then the head of Purana, went to see The Runner. 'He didn't need persuading, he was ready to talk. None of us imagined he would roll over.'

The Runner was removed from prison and for nearly 30 days exposed the secrets of Melbourne's gangland murders, sinking any hopes for Williams in the process.

Inspector Ryan, Detective Sergeant Stuart Bateson, and senior detectives Nigel L'Estrange, Mark Hatt and Michelle Kerley questioned him for weeks. A stream of Purana detectives questioned him on individual murders.

Police guarded him, fed him and did his washing as he exposed all Williams' dirty laundry. Crims who roll over often want rock star treatment but after he had completed his statements The Runner politely asked for one simple indulgence: a vanilla slice. Police immediately found the nearest bakery to satisfy his craving. It was the least they could do.

He told them about the crimes they knew he had committed but also implicated himself in ones they didn't know about.

He told them he was part of the hit team that killed drug dealer and standover man Nik 'The Bulgarian' Radev, shot dead in Coburg on 15 April 2003.

As five of Williams' closest allies turned on him and became police witnesses, Purana detectives discovered more about his crimes.

They were told Williams had offered the contract to kill Jason Moran to others, including notorious killer, drug dealer and armed robber Victor George Peirce, shot dead in Bay Street, Port Melbourne on 1 May 2002.

Peirce was paid $100,000 in advance and was to pocket a

further $100,000 if and when Moran was killed. But Peirce changed sides and warned Moran. And he didn't return the $100,000 advance.

Another career criminal was shot after he refused to carry out a contract to kill Moran. Convicted murderer Mark Anthony Smith supposedly agreed and then refused to kill Moran. So Smith was shot in the neck in the driveway of his Keilor home on 28 December 2002. He recovered and fled to Queensland for several months.

So was Peirce killed because he refused to kill Moran?

The trouble with criminals like Victor Peirce is they always have more than one set of enemies who want to see them dead.

His best friend was Frank Benvenuto, son of the late Godfather of Melbourne, Liborio. Peirce had worked in the fruit and vegetable market for Frank Benvenuto during a heavy power struggle in the business. Peirce was not there to lug turnips. He once arrived at work armed with a machine gun.

But for Benvenuto, having Peirce on his side was not enough. On 8 May 2000 Benvenuto was shot dead outside his Beaumaris home. The shooter was Andrew Veniamin. But who paid for the hit and why? Certainly not Carl Williams.

Veniamin knew that Peirce suspected he was the gunman. The two killers met to try and establish a truce. According to Victor's widow, Wendy, 'They met in a Port Melbourne park. He wanted to know if Victor was going to back up for Frank.'

According to Mrs Peirce her husband assured Veniamin there would be no payback. But Benji was not convinced.

Police say Veniamin was the gunman who shot Peirce in Port Melbourne but *why* he shot him is not so clear. Because although Benji worked for Williams he also did freelance work for anyone that would pay.

While Williams had reasons to punish Peirce for not carrying out the contract on Moran, Veniamin had his own reasons to want him dead.

And there was a third possibility: whoever paid Veniamin to kill Benvenuto would also have been relieved when Peirce was no longer a living threat.

Perhaps the key to the mystery rests with whoever it was Peirce planned to meet at Bay Street when he was shot dead — a man who had known Frank Benvenuto all his life. Also of interest to police is the man who rang Peirce to tell him of Frank's murder shortly after the ambush. The question is, how did he know so soon?

Jason Moran was a prominent mourner at Peirce's funeral. The next year he would also be shot dead.

FOR Purana investigators to crack the underworld code of silence they needed to offer deals that were too good to refuse. In doing so, they have changed the model of plea bargaining in Victoria forever.

Purana police had previously refused to do deals with trigger men but senior police and legal strategists in the Office of Public Prosecutions decided it was more important to nail the underworld generals that ordered the killings than the soldiers who carried them out.

From early in the investigation police had two main targets, Carl Williams and Tony Mokbel. They knew one was behind the killings and they suspected the other.

Paid killers can expect life in prison with no chance of release. Their crimes are not based on passion or psychological problems but greed.

But under the Purana model some of Melbourne's worst

gangsters were offered a chance of freedom if they turned on Williams and Mokbel.

Men who had spent decades in jail and had never talked were courted. By now they were middle-aged and the thought of never being released was too much to contemplate.

The Purana taskforce used the proven US tactic of turning alleged hit men into star witnesses. The most notorious of these was Salvatore 'Sammy the Bull' Gravano, a former underboss of the New York Gambino family.

The first to do a deal was The Driver. He was sentenced to eighteen years with a minimum of ten for his role in the murder of Michael Marshall and he was never charged with his involvement in the killings of Mark Moran, Jason Moran and Pasquale Barbaro.

It was a dream deal for a man who could have faced a life sentence — and for the police, because he was the domino who made the others fall.

'Without him we wouldn't have been able to move on Cross Keys (the Jason Moran and Pasquale Barbaro murder),' Horgan said later.

But it was The Runner's confessions that finally tipped the balance — implicating Williams in six murders and exposing Mokbel's alleged role in the underworld war.

The Runner was moved from his prison in Victoria and is believed to be interstate. He was sentenced to a minimum of 23 years for the murders of Marshall, Barbaro and Jason Moran. He will be in his early 70s before being eligible for release.

Police were confident they could make a case against Tony Mokbel for murder. So, it would seem, was Mokbel.

Days before being found guilty of cocaine trafficking in March 2006 Mokbel jumped bail and disappeared. But police say it was not the fact that he would be sentenced to a manageable term (a minimum of nine years) for drug trafficking that made him run.

In the week before Mokbel disappeared a lawyer had given him The Runner's secret statements, tipping him off he was likely to be charged with murder.

On 20 March, he fled. But the Purana taskforce was always confident he would surface and began to dismantle his financial empire. In February 2007 Mokbel was charged with Lewis Moran's murder. And in June, despite being disguised with a bad wig, he was arrested in Greece and a few weeks later charged with the murder of Michael Marshall. Leaving aside his drug convictions and his decision to jump bail, juries will judge his guilt or innocence on the fresh charges at a later date.

Once The Runner made his statements, Williams knew there was no chance he could beat the mounting charges. Williams was convicted of the Marshall murder and sentenced to a minimum of 21 years. The verdict was suppressed because he had multiple trials pending, including the murders of Mark Moran and the murders of Jason Moran and Pasquale Barbaro.

For months, Williams secretly tried to negotiate a deal that gave him some chance of release and in February 2007, on the eve of his trial for the murders of Jason Moran and Barbaro, he finally pleaded guilty.

By August 2006 the manipulator who once had teams of hit men prepared to kill for him knew he was facing the rest of his life in jail. Several of his trusted offsiders had cut deals with prosecutors, leaving him increasingly isolated.

He knew if he pleaded guilty he would be entitled to a discount. Aged 35, he wanted a chance to be out of jail at 70.

But the first tentative approaches were not encouraging. His team floated a prison sentence of around twelve years. 'They were looking for a ridiculous bargain basement sentence,' Paul Coghlan, QC, would recall.

As the trial date came closer, so too did the negotiators. In February the two sides spent ten days talking. Then the apparently promising talks collapsed.

Coghlan: 'We were very cross. We thought Williams had been fooling around and was never serious. He was wasting our time because they came up with various proposals that were absolutely laughable."

On Wednesday 28 February at midday the court process began before Justice King with pre-trial discussions.

It was legal tent-boxing with a few slow punches thrown and none landing.

First, Williams' team asked for an adjournment because of pre-trial publicity, but the same argument had been tried before and failed. Next gambit was a suggestion of judicial bias — another move doomed to fail.

Then it was agreed the star protected witnesses could give video evidence for security reasons. There would be a few more pre-trial details to be cleared up then a jury would be selected.

On Monday, 5 March, Geoff Horgan was scheduled to begin his opening address to declare that Williams organised the murders of Jason Moran and Pasquale Barbaro.

Once the jury was empanelled any chance of a deal for Williams would be over.

It was 2.10pm on 28 February when Horgan received a call in his chambers from Williams' barrister, David Ross, QC. The message was brief: 'We may have a deal.'

A message was passed to Justice King's associate Helen Marriott and a decision made to reconvene the court that day.

But Williams had left the court and was heading down the Princes Freeway to Barwon Prison. Then Justice King intervened and ordered the bus back.

This was no sweetheart deal. The prosecutors agreed they would make no recommendations on a jail sentence although they acknowledged Williams should be set a minimum due to his decision to plead. 'His sentence will be totally up to the judge,' Horgan said.

The charge sheet was quickly typed, documents signed and Williams led back into court.

But the crime deal of the decade that resulted in Williams pleading guilty to three murders was teetering on the point of collapse when Justice Betty King reconvened her court after being told of his decision.

While it had taken nearly seven months of secret negotiations to get Williams to the point of being prepared to admit his guilt, the final deal was nearly derailed in the final minutes.

The man linked to ten underworld killings had just told his relieved lawyers he would plead to the murders of Lewis Moran, Jason Moran and Mark Mallia and conspiracy to murder Mario Condello. (He did not plead over Barbaro, arguing he had not ordered his death and the victim was killed accidentally. The Mark Moran murder charge was dropped.)

But the agreement was worth nothing until he said the words, 'I plead guilty', in open court.

He had been brought up from the court cells to sign a document instructing his defence team of his intentions to enter guilty pleas.

Outside the court, members of the police Purana taskforce stood waiting. One nervously said, 'I won't believe it until I hear him say it.'

Williams' mother, Barbara, and father, George, were also there and were allowed in to see their son before the hearing began. While George remained quiet, Barbara was animated. She pleaded with her son not to plead.

George Williams didn't apply any pressure. He was then still facing drug trafficking charges himself and part of the deal was that he would plead guilty if the prosecution would not demand a jail sentence. Carl's hope that his 61-year-old father would get a suspended sentence persuaded him to plea to the extra three murders but the final decision was always going to be Justice King's, as Williams senior would find out many months later.

While the Crown honoured its end of the 'bargain' by not pushing for a jail sentence for George in late 2007, Justice King would reject the sweetheart deal and sentence him to a minimum twenty months prison, regardless of his heart condition.

But that would be later. Meanwhile, it was Carl's big day in court. According to an insider, he began to waver as his mother begged him to change his mind. The observer said the deal was 'within a hair's breadth' of collapsing. 'If we had lost him then maybe we would have lost him forever.'

But the court convened in front of Justice King and three times Williams 'nodded' — admitting his guilt. A decision that saved millions of dollars in trial costs and sent a message to the underworld that no-one was above the law.

Before Williams would agree to any deal he wanted to pass a message to a man on the outside. He desperately wanted him to know that no matter what, he wished him no harm. That man was Mick Gatto.

Postscript

* The Runner, The Lieutenant and The Driver cannot be identified by name as they have been given protected witness status. All are in jail.

* Williams' cousin, Michael Thorneycroft, 32, also became a protected witness but he couldn't use his second chance in life. The first to turn on Williams and tell police he was prepared to give evidence, Thorneycroft was arrested with three others on 9 June

2004 and charged with conspiracy to murder Mario Condello. He soon agreed to plead guilty and make a prosecution statement. In return he was given a three-year suspended sentence.

He was offered a new identity but decided to live with his mother in Melbourne's east and although he was given a new name he always knew that Williams could have reached out if he wished.

Police urged him to move and start a new life but he told them he was determined to stay in the area where he lived and maintain a low profile.

He sought and received assurances from a Williams relative that there would be no payback.

Thorneycroft returned to playing suburban football under his new name but lost his battle with drug addiction.

He was found dead in his Boronia home in May 2007 of a suspected drug overdose. Police say there were no suspicious circumstances.

❊ Phil Swindells has been promoted to inspector and works in the Ethical Standards Department. Andrew Allen was promoted to Superintendent and became officer in charge of Geelong police before transferring to Ballarat. Detective Inspector Jim O'Brien was appointed head of Purana. He masterminded the destruction of the Mokbel drug syndicate and retired shortly after Tony Mokbel was arrested. Detective Inspector Gavan Ryan was picked to head a taskforce into the Hodson murders before returning to run Purana and in 2007 was awarded the Australia Police Medal in the Queen's Birthday Honours.

Stuart Bateson was promoted to work as a crime strategy expert and Assistant Commissioner Simon Overland was promoted to Deputy Commissioner.

* Members of the Purana taskforce, initial homicide investigators, Special Operations Group, bugging experts and surveillance police received commendation awards from Chief Commissioner Christine Nixon at a private dinner in 2006.

Ryan sang a duet with Chief Commissioner Christine Nixon and the police show band at the function, proving beyond reasonable doubt he is a better detective than nightclub crooner.

* Mick Gatto lost 30 kilograms while in jail. On his release he put the weight back on and runs his successful crane company. His portrait has been painted for the Archibald Prize.

* Roberta Williams split from Carl Williams and was seeing someone else. She says she considered converting to Islam and was dubbed for a short time 'Roberka'. Carl Williams' new girlfriend was in court to see him plead guilty. Wearing a new engagement ring, she is called a 'glass-widow' — a woman who visits her partner in prison but never has to touch him. Taped prison phone calls indicate their conversations can be quite risqué.

* Tony Mokbel was arrested in Athens in June 2007. He was charged with drug trafficking and the murders of Lewis Moran and Michael Marshall. A Greek court ordered his extradition but he was sentenced to first serve 12 months for the local offence of entering the country on a false passport.

THE HOUSE OF MOKBEL

Mokbel was the drug dealer
from central casting.

IT was just a little stumble that spilt the tin that caused the fire
that led to the explosion that brought the firemen who called the
police who found the amphetamine laboratory that Tony built.

The lab, in a quiet residential street in the Melbourne suburb
of Brunswick, had proved a virtual goldmine, pumping out speed
until the day Paul Edward Howden kicked over a bucket of sol-
vents that ignited and burnt the house down in February 1997.
Police didn't have far to look for their main suspect. They found
Howden at the Alfred Hospital being treated for severe burns to
30 per cent of his body.

Police also discovered the lab had produced at least 41.25 kilograms of pure methylamphetamine with a potential street value
of $78 million. Prosecutors claimed the clandestine operation
had produced enough speed for 1.3 million users. 'It is the largest seizure of methylamphetamine in Victoria and it's the largest

detected manufacture of methylamphetamine in the state,' the County Court was told. Even the seasoned trial judge, Graeme Crossley, seemed impressed. 'I can't believe how big it is,' he declared.

Howden's barrister, the energetic and multi-skilled Con Heliotis QC, told the court his client was just a minor player who agreed to the plan out of loyalty to a friend — the godfather to one of his three children — identified only as, 'Tony'. For Howden's work in the massively profitable enterprise, Heliotis claimed, he was paid just $10,000 — and even that wasn't cash. It was cut out in home renovations.

Police agreed that Howden, a plumber by trade, was the stooge of the operation and Heliotis helpfully added that his client was 'just short of stupid'. When he jailed Howden for four years, Judge Crossley took into account his minnow status: 'You were a factory roustabout rather than the managing director.'

The managing director was Godfather Tony — who was never formally identified in court — but police needed only to look over the badly charred side fence to solve the mystery. The house next door was one of many owned by a tight-knit family with unlimited ambitions and unexplained incomes — the Mokbel clan. It was purchased for just $161,000, but the Mokbels were to be enthusiastic home improvers.

Tony Mokbel was said to have lost millions when the lab was discovered, but he was a master at finding advantage in adversity. While the court was told Howden was the official owner of the speed lab house, the property was soon absorbed into the growing Mokbel Empire. The extended Mokbel family knocked down the burnt shell to enlarge their garden, planting a mature palm worth $15,000 to go with their sparkling new swimming pool.

The furnishings were another matter. A policeman who raided the property described the décor as 'Franco Cozzo on angel dust'. Long before Tony Mokbel had become the public face of drug dealing in Victoria, children in the street began to refer to the million-dollar property as 'the drug house'.

The $1.1 million Brunswick property would be used as bail surety for Tony Mokbel when he was charged with cocaine trafficking in 2002.

The property was listed as being owned by Mokbel's sister-in-law, Renate Lisa Mokbel, but police believe the house was financed through Mokbel's prodigious drug activities.

But Howden, the burnt patsy, would never tell detectives who funded the initial venture — and 'Tony' would not forget his loyalty. During Howden's sentence, Mokbel would regularly drive to the jail to visit, even persuading prison officers to let him take his friend for an unauthorised trip to a local McDonald's for a break from prison food.

It would not be the only time Mokbel tried to lift the spirits of inmates with fast food.

In June 2004, he visited a friend at the Melbourne Custody Centre who complained about his bland dinner. Mokbel — who had once owned an Italian restaurant — immediately spoke to a guard and peeled off $350 to pay for pizzas and soft drink from La Porchetta in North Melbourne.

The obliging officer popped out to collect 40 large pizzas for all inmates and staff.

It was typical of Mokbel, whose seemingly impetuous generosity was calculated to build long-term loyalty. Police say he would hand over $10,000 on a whim for a friend to have a bet, with a casual, 'Pay me back if you win'.

One associate said he was known as the 'softest touch in town'. Any sob-story resulted in Mokbel handing over $5000, but in return he expected total support and the money repaid on demand.

Tony's reliance on fast food rewards for his team backfired when Howden, 36, died of heart disease in December 2001. Mokbel placed a death notice in the *Herald Sun* that read, in part, 'You will always be in my prayers and I will never ever forget you. I promise to you my friend to be there for your family till the day I die.' It was another Mokbel trademark — never forget a friend or an enemy.

While police had known for years that Mokbel was involved in drug manufacturing, it was the Brunswick lab fire that showed the businessman on the make had become a big underworld player. And it would be another decade before they were able to trace his shadowy financial network and prove he was one of Australia's richest — and nastiest — men.

Of course, by the time Mokbel was finally sentenced to a minimum of nine years in prison for cocaine trafficking in early 2006, he had jumped bail and become Australia's most wanted man.

ANTONIOS Sajih Mokbel was one of the sharper students at Coburg's racially diverse Moreland High School in the late 1970s, but he was never going to push on to tertiary study. He had no desire to spend years as a poor undergraduate, although he would later employ university chemistry students in his drug enterprises.

The school was divided into three sub-schools and the teenage Mokbel stayed in the Zeta stream of nearly 100 students until he was old enough to leave.

He might not have immediately embraced the school motto of *Sapere Aude* ('Dare to be Wise') but outside the classroom the apprentice wise guy was keen to excel.

The Kuwaiti-born boy with rich Lebanese heritage and traditional Australian tastes was always in a hurry to make money. His first full-time job was as a dishwasher at a suburban nightclub before he became a waiter. Later, he worked in security — a surprising choice for a man not much bigger than a football rover. But Mokbel was smooth. He found he could often persuade people to his point of view without overt violence.

Later, if he decided there was a need for bloodshed, he would employ others. Young and ambitious, he soon realised that to get the sort of money he wanted, he would have to be his own boss. It was in those early years, too, that Mokbel noticed that people who were partying often lost their inhibitions, and were prepared to pay for a good time.

In 1984, aged just nineteen, he bought his first business — a struggling Rosanna milk bar. For two years he and his young partner, Carmel — whom he would marry in 1989 and with her have two children — worked long hours seven days a week battling to make a living before finally selling out for their original investment price.

It would be the one and only time Mokbel didn't seem to make massive profits in his business ventures, despite an early police report saying he 'lacked financial acumen'.

In 1987, he bought an Italian restaurant in Boronia. In those days he was content to roll the dough — years later he was rolling in it. He steadily built the business, expanding when he bought the shop next door. He sold the restaurant as a going concern in 1994, but kept ownership of the building.

It would remain his long-term strategy — to invest in bricks and mortar, among many other things. It was a sound investment strategy, but it was also a simple way to transform fresh drug money into seemingly solid assets.

In 1996, he bought a bar and restaurant in Swanston Street, Carlton, but sold it a year later to a property developer for a substantial profit.

In 1997, he bought several adjoining properties in Sydney Road, Brunswick, and opened T Jays Restaurant. It was around this time he started being noticed as an ambitious developer with an appetite for consuming businesses. Police should also have been aware of the man on the make. T Jays was opposite Brunswick Police Station.

By 2000, the former struggling milk bar proprietor bragged to friends he owned or controlled 38 different companies. In the same year, he began his most ambitious development — an $18 million, ten-storey 'winged keel' apartment tower over Sydney Road. The plan was to build 120 apartments and townhouses, offices, restaurants, gym with pool and a four-storey car park on the old Whelan the Wrecker site. No-one seemed to wonder how he could generate that sort of money. Much later, police financial experts would find that he needed at least $2 million from drug money every year to fund the so-called 'legitimate' arm of his business.

Moreland development services manager Michael Smit was quoted as saying of the Mokbel monolith: 'It has the potential to be a strong landmark in the sense of buildings like the Eiffel Tower and Arc de Triomphe — which the architects have used as inspiration — and change people's perceptions of Sydney Road.'

Perhaps Mr Smit should get out more.

At the same time as Mokbel was planning to turn Sydney Road into a tourist attraction for visiting architects, he was also developing ten units in Templestowe that he intended to sell for $300,000 each. In 2000, he owned the Brunswick market site and claimed to make $500,000 a year in rent money.

His business portfolio was as wide as it was impressive, with interests in shops, cafes, fashions, fragrances, restaurants, hotels, nightclubs and land in regional Victoria. He and his companies owned two white vans, two Commodores, a red Audi, a 2000 silver Mercedes, a Nissan Skyline and a red Ferrari Roadster that he bought in September 1999. He even managed to give his wife a pub in the town of Kilmore as part of the family businesses. Intriguingly, the pub was granted a gaming licence to run lucrative poker machines after the owners passed the highest probity checks — even though Tony Mokbel was a convicted criminal and prolific drug dealer.

One of his fashion houses was appropriately named LSD — ostensibly an abbreviation for Love of Style and Design. It was apparently the drug dealer's idea of a private joke. He also opened a café near his old school — Moreland High. He owned fourteen properties in Brunswick, three in Boronia, two at Kilmore and one each in Coburg, Pascoe Vale and Templestowe.

Just about everyone seemed to know that Tony was a big-time crook — that is, except some of the bankers from the top end of town.

The National Australia Bank loaned Mokbel nearly $6 million, apparently unaware their cashed-up client was a drug dealer. He had nineteen accounts and an A-Grade credit rating with the NAB between 1985 and 2001. Clearly, credit officers were not prepared to ask too many questions of the 'property developer' with the flash clothes and the big dreams.

Mokbel was the drug dealer from central casting. He bought a top-of-the-range jet ski and was a regular at marquees at the Grand Prix. He once managed to get not one but two personally signed Ferrari caps from champion driver Michael Schumacher. The speed producer loved fast cars, fast horses and life in the fast lane.

He left his wife and in late 2000 began an affair with Danielle McGuire, who ran a Mokbel-owned South Yarra beauty shop. But she was not the only woman in his life — he apparently believed monogamy was a board game for bored people.

He'd been living with McGuire when he was found to have disappeared on 20 March 2006 — days before his cocaine trial was due to finish. Oddly, McGuire was unable to assist police in their enquiries about the whereabouts of her once-constant companion. But in the last days before he flew the coop, the love-birds were not living in sin. Mokbel's divorce from Carmel had finally come through. His long-suffering ex-wife was either extraordinarily naïve or born with no sense of curiosity. In court documents she swore she had no idea of her husband's prodigious criminal activity during their married life. In other words, Carmel claimed she was a Patsy.

McGuire was no stranger to police investigations — she was the ex-girlfriend of Mark Moran, the drug-dealing standover man murdered on 15 June 2000. She was truly unlucky in love. But with Mokbel she had the million-dollar lifestyle, living in a massive city apartment and dining at the best restaurants.

When Mokbel was arrested, he was living in a Port Melbourne bayside penthouse he rented for $1250 a week. He told friends he planned to buy the property. He would never have the chance. Not that his lifestyle suffered. He moved into the four-bedroom apartment in Southbank with panoramic views of Port Phillip Bay, which was a world away from his previous address — a one-bed cell in Port Phillip Prison.

But Tony, the former suburban pizza shop proprietor, never lost his common touch and loved nothing better than to snack on a Capricciosa.

He was a well-known customer and generous tipper at the city's up-market pizzeria — Sopranos, naturally.

Sopranos manager Frank Sarkis was quoted as saying: 'He came for breakfast, lunch and dinner and his favourite meal was medium-rare eye fillet steak topped with prawns and smoked salmon — about $50.'

When Tony wanted to snack in the privacy of his own home the restaurant would send over platters of pasta and pizza to the penthouse.

'My staff described it (Mokbel's penthouse) as something so beautiful they had only seen anything like it in movies,' the restaurant man said. 'And money was no object. He'd regularly spend $200 a night on pizza and pasta. The staff cried (when Mokbel absconded) — he was a big tipper, $100 bills.'

IT was not through drug dealing or shady business dealings that Mokbel first started to develop a questionable public profile, but through one of his other great passions — gambling. In later years, with nearly $20 million of his assets frozen, he took to describing himself as a professional punter, even though he was banned from racetracks and casinos as an undesirable person.

For years, Mokbel was the type of heavyweight punter who used inside information to tip the odds his way. He was the leader of the notorious 'tracksuit gang' — a group responsible for a series of suspicious late plunges on racetracks in Melbourne, Sydney and Brisbane.

His team once won $500,000 and demanded to be paid in green $100 bills, after lodging the bets with the older grey notes, in what was clearly a money-laundering exercise.

Some bookies refused to take credit bets for Mokbel because he was often forgetful on collection day. One claimed he lost more than $1 million from the non-payer.

Bookies soon learned it was best to write off the debts from the dealer with the long pockets and even longer memory.

In 1998, racing officials launched an investigation into the ownership of nine horses linked to Tony and Carmel Mokbel. The following year, the Victoria Racing Club banned them from racing horses.

But racing experts say Mokbel continued to own horses although they were officially under the names of friends and associates. He used the same strategy in 'legitimate' business, hiding his interests under the names of friends and family.

During the 2001 police investigation into Mokbel, police found the prolific drug dealer had strong links to seven jockeys and trainers. Phone taps picked up his regular conversations with three leading jockeys, but racing authorities were powerless to act, as the phone taps could not be released for a non-criminal investigation.

While under surveillance in the Flemington young members' enclosure on Derby Day 2000, Mokbel was seen to be unusually popular. Some of his 'friends' that day were household names — television identities and members of the 'A List' crowd endlessly photographed for the covers of glamour magazines and newspaper social columns. Police said he brazenly handed out small 'gifts' of cocaine to the partying punters.

Years later, he was still a regular at the races even though he was on $1 million bail for serious drug charges.

In 2004, despite having his assets frozen, Mokbel told friends he had won nearly $400,000 on the Melbourne Cup. He was also seen punting heavily at the Oaks two days later, backing three winners in a row, including the appropriately named Hollow Bullet.

The public display so angered senior police they moved with racing clubs to ban him from the Melbourne casino and Victorian racetracks.

He was also banned from entering licensed premises in the South Yarra and Prahran areas, meaning he could not walk into some nightspots he owned.

SO HOW did Tony Mokbel graduate from dishwasher to unknown amphetamine dealer and then to the Hollywood crime cliché of the millionaire, Ferrari-driving drug baron with the blonde girlfriend and the celebrity lifestyle?

It began modestly. In the early days, he was more bumbling crook than master criminal. In 1992, Mokbel was convicted of attempting to pervert the course of justice, after a clumsy bid two years earlier to bribe a County Court judge was undone in a police sting. He was trying to shop for a 'bent judge' who would give an associate a suspended sentence for drug trafficking. Typically, he wanted to pay the bribe in a mixture of cash and drugs.

Why he would imagine a judge would be interested in drugs is anybody's guess, although it was rumoured that he had provided some court staff with drugs in the hope they would be useful contacts some day. It was his version of networking.

Mokbel and two others were arrested as he handed over $2000 as the first payment of $53,000 that was supposed to have gone to the supposedly corrupt judge. Part of the 'agreed' payment was to be made in cocaine.

In 1998, he was convicted over amphetamine manufacturing but beat the charge on appeal. His lawyers successfully argued he should not have been charged with amphetamine trafficking when the drug he was handling was pseudoephedrine — a drug that could be used to make amphetamines.

People who had known him in prison remembered Mokbel as 'cunning and a fast learner'. The main lesson he learned was to ensure he insulated himself from hands-on drug dealing and use only middlemen he could trust.

Even in prison he craved the good life, bribing catering staff for extra food and a steady supply of alcohol. He also had access to smuggled mobile phones to maintain hands-on control of his business interests.

Police say he was one of the first of the major drug dealers to move into the designer pill industry, pressing tablets for the nightclub crowd.

According to the United Nations, Australia has the highest use of ecstasy per capita in the world and the second highest amphetamines use. Mokbel could cater for both markets, manufacturing speed in Australia and importing ecstasy from Europe. And for his top-shelf clients, he smuggled cocaine from Mexico.

He had pill presses hidden in Coburg and Brooklyn. A consummate networker, he developed his own team, which included an industrial chemist, rogue police, a locksmith, dock-workers, jockeys, trainers, a pill press repairer, distributors and cargo bonds officials. He had used two brothers as local speed lab cooks to make amphetamines, but also sourced drugs from Sydney.

His profits jumped from large to massive. Convinced he was born lucky, Mokbel started to spend $20,000 a week on Tattslotto. It was more than a Saturday night interest. First division wins and big plunges on the track helped launder drug money into punter's dividends. (Some of his laundering efforts were less successful. It was rumoured he left millions hidden in a large washing machine but that the cash mysteriously disappeared after an unwelcome late-night visit.)

No drug trafficker, no matter how powerful, can work alone and Mokbel was to develop an extensive underworld network, although his contact list has shrunk somewhat due to the gangland war. Among his associates were Nik Radev (killed in April 2003), Willie Thompson (July 2003), Michael Marshall (October 2003), Andrew Veniamin (March 2004), Lewis Moran (March 2004), and Mario Condello (February 2006).

He grew close to Veniamin after the sawn-off gunman took him to hospital after he was bashed in Carlton in November 2002. It was rumoured that Condello persuaded Mokbel to attend the crime conference that resulted in him being bashed on Radev's instructions.

When Veniamin was shot dead in a Carlton restaurant, Mokbel placed a death notice in the *Herald Sun* that read: 'To a friend I haven't known for very long, you were a true friend ... will be sadly missed.'

At the funeral, Mokbel was the first to kiss the body lying in an open coffin. Members of the Victoria Police Purana taskforce suspected Mokbel was involved in some of the killings, employing paid hit men to fire the bullets. While some say he was the puppet-master, police lacked evidence of his involvement, at least initially. As Mokbel's wealth and profile grew, so did the interest of drug squad detectives. Two police investigations into him failed, but a third, Operation Kayak, set up in 2000, began to track the activities of the massive drug dealer.

It would be a trusted insider who worked as a police informer who would destroy him. The informer, (who would flee the country only to be arrested, much later, in Amsterdam in late 2007) became an ethical standards department source and helped expose corruption within the drug squad.

The extremely persuasive informer was a born con man turned gifted double agent. He was a businessman who thought nothing of spending $5000 on a night out. A police profile showed he spent $80,000 in twelve months on hire cars, and $150,000 on air fares. He had 30 aliases, and was one of the biggest drug movers in Melbourne. After he was arrested with two kilograms of cocaine in August 2000, he agreed to turn informer and became an enthusiastic double agent.

The man knew most of Melbourne's major drug dealers but also had high-profile associates, including Channel 7's Naomi Robson, then the glamorous host of the *Today Tonight* current affairs program.

The informer bragged to police and crooks about his relationship with Robson, claiming she was his girlfriend, but at no time during the protracted investigation was she observed or recorded with the man and there were no suggestions she was involved in drugs.

Robson explained on air shortly after Mokbel fled Australia: 'I caught up with him (the informer), usually in the company of others on a handful of occasions over a couple of months and I decided I didn't want to take it any further.'

Once the informer took police inside the secret world of Tony Mokbel, they were able to establish the unprecedented size of the empire.

First there was his fake, or pseudo, ecstasy business. Using locally produced amphetamines mixed with other available drugs, he pressed millions of tablets. He told his friends he made them for $3 a pill and sold them for $12 to $14. You didn't need an MBA from Harvard to know that it was a massive profit margin while it lasted.

He imported hundreds of thousands of MDMA ecstasy tablets from Europe, paying $4 and selling for $17 in minimum 1000 lots. Still not satisfied at quadrupling his money, he would sometimes crush the pills and re-press them at half-strength to double his profits.

In late 2000, the informer said, Mokbel was part of a team importing 500,000 ecstasy tablets although he said his normal shipments were around 75,000 tablets. The load arrived in a container ship and cleared Melbourne docks just before Christmas.

Around the same time, Mokbel wanted to open a licensed restaurant under his own name but his criminal record was a slight problem. He tried to use high profile referees. For one of them, it was a ticking time bomb that would blow up seven years later.

In March 2007 Kelvin Thomson, the Labor Federal member for Wills, resigned as Shadow Attorney General after it was revealed he had given Mokbel a generous reference in 2000 — long after Tony had first been convicted of drug trafficking.

He said he was unaware of Mokbel's background when he gave him the reference for a liquor licence.

It read in part, 'Mr Mokbel is making a significant contribution to the community and employing a substantial number of people ... I urge you to take into account Mr Mokbel's last year of unblemished conduct, his commitment to family and his successful establishment as a local businessman in making your decision concerning his application.'

The application failed. Kelvin Thomson said he could not recall meeting Mokbel.

Another referee for the application was former drug squad detective Ray Dole, who was then the liquor licensing sergeant for Brunswick. Dole wrote that Mokbel was 'of reformed habits and is making a worthwhile contribution to society.' This must have come as a surprise to the drug squad, which was investigating Mokbel for trafficking.

After the application failed, Mokbel put his licensed premises and gaming facilities in other people's names and got back to concentrating on his core business. He planned a three million pill importation worth more than $50 million in March or April 2001. It is not known if it landed.

Always keen to explore new drug markets, Mokbel bought 80,000 LSD tablets for $5 a tablet, later being told by a colleague he had been ripped off.

Over an eight-month period in 2000, he made fifteen deposits in just one bank account, ranging from $10,200 to $125,000 for a total of $600,000.

For Mokbel, it was a glorified Christmas club account.

He would lend associates large sums of money knowing that he could call it back with no records ever being kept.

In August 2001, Mokbel was finally arrested over importing barrels of the chemical ephedrine to make an estimated 40 million amphetamine-based pseudo-ecstasy tablets. Police estimated the 550 kilograms of the chemical, once turned into pills, would have had a street value of $2 billion.

The battler from Moreland High had turned himself into the equal of a multi-national corporation.

But while Mokbel's arrest over the ephedrine importation made headlines, the charges didn't stick and were later dropped by lawyers from the Director of Public Prosecution's office. The case against Mokbel and several other major drug investigations, were compromised when a small group of drug squad detectives were found to be corrupt. The men whose word would have to be believed by juries were themselves facing charges or had already been convicted.

But in the Mokbel case it must have been a close decision. Mokbel spoke to an informer about the shipment, not only declaring when it arrived, but providing a sample that proved to be identical with the container load of chemicals. It was clearly a Mokbel-run operation. But the key witness — the high-flyer, who had flown overseas — would not be found to give evidence until much later.

While police lost their main case, separate charges of trafficking 5000 ecstasy tablets, and trafficking amphetamines and cocaine remained.

IT WAS the beginning of the end for Mokbel. His business assets were frozen after his arrest and were managed by the National Australia Bank, which had loaned him millions for his questionable property developments.

Without regular cash injections from his drug operations, the loans could not be serviced and his empire collapsed.

Federal police also charged Mokbel over importing three kilograms of cocaine from Mexico, an enterprise that Mokbel dismissed as 'just rent money'. Rent money or not, it was a compelling case. Even his lawyers advised him to plead guilty to get a reduced sentence.

But the punter was keen to back the long shot. Mokbel knew that many big drug cases had been delayed because some drug squad detectives had been charged with corruption. He pleaded not guilty and in 2002 was bailed after twelve months in jail. He was to report twice daily at a local police station, but at one stage had the conditions altered so he could take his children to Gold Coast theme parks. Naturally, he stayed at his own idea of an adventure playground, Jupiters Casino.

Two of the police involved in Operation Kayak, Stephen Paton and Malcolm Rosenes, were later jailed over drug trafficking charges. Rosenes bought some of his drugs, through an informer, from Tony Mokbel.

During the long court delays, Mokbel informally approached detectives offering a deal. He would plead guilty and guarantee two other drug dealers would also plead if they received only two years each. Then, he explained, all those nasty corruption allegations would disappear. It would be business as usual.

But there were no deals and one of the traffickers was sentenced to five years and the second to eleven.

During the trial, Mokbel remained relaxed — even to the point of appearing cocky — a puzzling performance considering his defence veered from ludicrous to laughable.

Certainly there were rumours that Mokbel had bought a juror, an allegation almost certainly put about by the accused man himself in a bid to abort the trial.

But just days before the jury was sent out to consider its verdict, the trial judge, Justice Bill Gillard, dismissed one of the jurors and told the remaining thirteen that their former colleague had done 'something today which compromised his position'. He told them he had also observed things weeks earlier 'which also caused this court a little bit of concern'.

But with the trial close to complete, Mokbel looked a beaten man. Either he knew his dream run was over or he had learned even more disturbing news: Tony Mokbel, the hands-off drug dealer, was under investigation for murder by the Purana gangland taskforce. Mokbel was given copies of statements that confirmed he was a main target of the Purana taskforce over his role in underworld killings.

The statements were not from a bit player who could easily be discredited, they were from a hit man who claimed Mokbel was the eye of the underworld storm.

The hit man known as The Runner worked for Carl Williams but he also told police he was employed by Mokbel.

These words, taken from The Runner's secret statements and passed to Mokbel, were the ones that convinced Tony his time in Australia was up.

The Runner was the career armed robber Williams had recruited when they were both in Port Phillip Prison's high security Swallow Unit in 2001–2002. This is what he revealed:

'Tony Mokbel came into the unit when he was on remand for drug charges. I hadn't had any dealing(s) with Tony before he came into the unit. After a period of time Tony became part of our crew; we used to eat together and occasionally drink alcohol. I was working in the kitchen at the time and used to smuggle food out for Tony as he loved his food.'

Over this time Tony and I became friends. I helped Tony with a dispute he had with another prisoner. I also managed to smuggle in a mobile phone for him whilst he was in Penhyine Unit. The mobile was later found by guards outside Penhyine unit near one of the cell windows. Tony told me later that he had thrown the phone out the window as he heard the guards were doing a search.'

Later, when Williams, Mokbel and The Runner were out of jail, they continued to associate. But it was no wine and cheese club. 'Although a lot of the meetings were social in nature they also involved conversations about business,' The Runner said.

He gave information that showed how Mokbel tried to pull stings without getting his hands dirty. 'Tony would also provide Carl with information on the movements of Jason Moran.'

The Runner told police that shortly after the murder of drug dealer Willie Thompson (gunned down as he sat in his car in Chadstone on 23 July 2003) he met Williams, Carl's father George, the gang's Lieutenant, Mokbel and others at the Red Rooster store in Moreland Road, Brunswick. 'Tony was upset and angry about Thompson's death, he mentioned that he went to school with him and was a very close friend. He made clear that he wanted to exact revenge on whoever was responsible.'

According to The Runner, Mokbel was obviously unaware there had been a treacherous double-cross: 'I was surprised because I knew that Carl was behind Thompson's murder but it appeared that Tony had no idea of that. That is why I didn't ask any questions. I was surprised that Tony didn't know what had really happened.'

And clearly Carl Williams was not about to fill him in over a chicken and chips snack-pack.

A few weeks later, according to The Runner's confessions, they met again at the same Red Rooster store and Mokbel was ready to put his money where his mouth was.

'At this meeting Tony confirmed that he believed Michael Marshall was responsible for Willie's death and he wanted him dead. Tony offered Carl and I $300,000 to kill Marshall. When I shook hands with Tony he passed a piece of paper to me, which had the details of Marshall's address.'

The agreement was that The Runner was to be paid $200,000 and Williams $100,000. But The Runner was understandably wary. After all, for the Moran murder, despite Williams' assurances, he had still only paid $2500. This time he wanted a serious down payment. According to the statement, Williams gave him $50,000 in a manila envelope outside a South Melbourne coffee shop saying, 'Here, this is from Tony.'

Most of the blood money disappeared at the casino and the TAB. It wasn't only Tony who backed the wrong horse.

The statements against Mokbel were part of the brief of evidence against Williams and were, quite properly, handed to his defence team.

Police would later claim in court the statements were then, quite improperly, handed to Mokbel by one of his many lawyers, the glamorous Zarah Garde-Wilson.

'Mokbel has been named by a Victoria Police informant as having paid for a contract murder and provided the firearms to commit the murder,' a federal police statement lodged at the Supreme Court alleged.

'A statement had been provided to this effect and is suspected to have been made available to Mokbel by his former solicitor and current girlfriend, Zarah Garde-Wilson.'

Justice Gillard said, 'Australian Federal Police were told on Friday 17 March 2006, that Victorian police proposed to arrest the prisoner and charge him with being involved in the murder.' In another unrelated hearing, Detective Sergeant Andrew Stamper, of the Purana taskforce, claimed in evidence, 'I understand that Ms Garde-Wilson is involved in an on-off sexual relationship with Mr Mokbel and is living in a house that belongs to him.'

The puppet-master who pulled the strings was no longer looking at a long but manageable jail term for drug trafficking. If charged and convicted of a gangland murder, he was facing life with no minimum.

During the Crown's final address, federal police took the unusual step of asking for Mokbel's bail to be revoked. But they did not tell Justice Gillard that the accused had just learnt he had become a Purana target and was facing imminent murder charges. If they had, perhaps the judge would have placed him in custody. As it was he would have revoked bail when he began his charge to the jury early the following week.

But if police suspected he was about to flee, they did not have hard evidence. If they had, they would have told Justice Gillard or, at the very least, put Mokbel under surveillance. They did neither.

There has been much implied criticism of Justice Gillard for not revoking bail, but in reality he was given no reason to take that step.

Mokbel must have sat in court on that Friday, knowing that if his bail was cancelled, it may have been his last moment as a free man. Facing inevitable conviction on the drug charges, he would have been out of the way as Purana investigators worked on their murder case against him. Then he would have been charged again and again and would have faced jail for the rest of his life.

But the Crown did not back up its claim — police were nowhere near ready to charge Mokbel with murder and had no evidence he planned to flee. At the end of the court day, he was free to go. So he went ... as far as he possibly could. There was only a small window of opportunity and Fat Tony slipped through it.

He was confident that those left behind would continue his drug business and he could take on the role of absentee landlord. Over the previous few years he had secretly moved money overseas and was ready to go.

On 20 March 2006, he did not report to South Melbourne Police Station, as dictated by his bail conditions. He left his three mobile phones, his regular girlfriend, his frozen assets, his city apartment and his high public profile and vanished.

Without a client, his legal team, led by Con Heliotis, withdrew. But as all evidence had already been led, Justice Gillard allowed the case to run. Mokbel was found guilty of drug trafficking and sentenced in his absence to a minimum of nine years jail.

'I think he has had an exit strategy in place for some time,' said a policeman who has worked on him for years. 'Tony never liked to back losers.'

FOR years Tony Mokbel survived because his underlings gave him unquestioned loyalty. They went to jail knowing they would be rewarded when they were released and their families would be cared for while they were inside.

But the Purana gangland taskforce started to work on some of the players, reminding them that this time there would be no reward on release because they might stay in jail until they came out in a cheap coffin or were ready for a nursing home. Professional hit men were likely to be sentenced to life with no minimum. 'Hop on the bus or risk being run over' was the blunt message they got.

Faced with the so-called underworld code of silence, police and prosecutors began playing a deadly game of Let's Make A Deal. And, for the first time, prosecutors were prepared to cut deals with trigger men.

The Runner was one Williams' hit man who took a seat on the bus, but there was another who jumped on board, too, and that was more bad news for Mokbel.

The first official sign that the underworld code had been smashed came in May 2006, when Supreme Court Justice Bernie Teague sentenced a career criminal we shall call, 'The Journeyman', to a minimum of nineteen years for two contract killings.

The Journeyman was the equivalent of a washed-up boxer who refused to retire. He was the product of a third-generation criminal family and connected with at least six killings. He once shot an unarmed policeman during a bank robbery and was a key figure in a vicious war inside Pentridge prison. Violent, manipulative and an underworld tactician, he presented during the gangland underworld war as an expert who was quoted in the media as a retired practitioner turned crime historian. But behind the scenes he could not bear the thought of being left behind. A contemporary said: 'He forgot that an underworld war is a young man's game. He wanted to be a part of it and jumped in. He was always a fool and now he's just an old fool.'

The Journeyman was a gunman who became the loose cannon, prepared to do jobs for both sides, and one-off hits on a freelance basis.

There is little chance he will ever reform. Put simply, he is no good. That is, except to the Purana taskforce.

In November 2005 The Journeyman was found guilty of shooting and dumping fellow gunman Lewis Caine in Brunswick on 8 May 2004. But after fighting the first case, he had a change of heart and pleaded guilty to the murder of Lewis Moran, shot dead in the Brunswick Club in Sydney Road on 31 March 2004.

The Journeyman usually persuaded someone close to him to take the fall. He repeatedly managed to paint himself as an unfortunate who just happened to be in the wrong place at the wrong time when shots were fired. But this time he knew he was trapped. In sentencing him to a minimum term of nineteen years, rather than life with no minimum, Justice Teague opened himself to critics claiming the sentence was under the odds.

Surely a career killer who was prepared to murder for cash should be jailed for the rest of his life? But ultimately, police and prosecutors concluded — and Teague agreed — the old hit man could be of more value in a witness box than spending a lifetime in a prison cell.

The Journeyman, then 53, was an old-style gangster who would not have survived a lifetime of crime without being able to sniff the wind. For instance, once when he had been suspected for a murder committed during a robbery, he was left a short message by a homicide squad detective. The message was: Come to the homicide squad to be interviewed or risk having the armed robbery squad shoot you in bed for resisting arrest. The next day at 9am, he was at the St Kilda Road crime department complex, freshly showered and well-dressed, ready to be interviewed. He felt safer there. Soon, four men were charged over the armed robbery and murder. According to police, The Journeyman used his own form of plea bargaining. He gave one of his co-accused a simple choice: plead guilty or die. The man pleaded guilty.

The other three were then able to blame the guilty man for the murder and The Journeyman was sentenced to thirteen years for the armed robbery, but was not convicted of murder. Until now.

Earlier in 2006, he asked Purana detectives to visit him in jail. He was ready to talk. This does not mean he suddenly found morality and remorse that had evaded him all his life; he just knew that if he remained silent, they would throw away the key.

By cutting a deal with the prosecution to give evidence against long-time associates in gangland murder trials — and providing new leads on others yet to be charged — he gave himself a chance of walking out of jail an old, but free, man.

With time served, he could be 71 when released. More importantly, he would not have to do his jail time in 23-hour solitary confinement.

For police, the idea of allowing The Journeyman to dodge the rest of his life in jail must have been repugnant. He had once shot a policeman and had lied and cheated to save himself for years.

But the move to deal with him showed that police and prosecutors were prepared to deal with the hands-on killers to gather sworn evidence against those who pull the strings.

It was a move that brought an unexpected dividend. After he was sentenced, The Journeyman confessed to a senior Purana detective that he had carried out another gangland murder — calmly dropping the bombshell that police were allegedly directly linked to an organised crime hit. His allegations were serious enough for a special taskforce to be set up to investigate his claims, which ultimately led to the explosive public hearings by the Office of Police Integrity in November 2007 that resulted in the disgrace of an assistant commissioner and a senior public servant, and internal divisions in the powerful police union. But that was later.

The Journeyman came to the negotiating table with another powerful bargaining chip. He was prepared to talk of Tony Mokbel's alleged direct connection to one of the murders.

According to The Journeyman, his hit team was to be paid $150,000 by Carl Williams and Mokbel to kill Lewis Moran. A few days after the killing, he was paid $140,000. He planned to get the remaining $10,000 later. It is now unlikely he will ever collect his debt.

In sentencing him, Teague said Moran's murder, 'was a callous, planned, premeditated execution for money. To some people, life is not as sacred as it should be. To some people, life is cheap'.

Police were confident they could make a case against Mokbel for murder. But they had to find him first.

Teague said: 'In your case, the indications are that the benefit from the co-operation will be extremely high.'

The Journeyman was reminded that if he tried to renege on the deal, he could be re-sentenced less sympathetically.

Others have also turned. At last count, eight underworld witnesses have been hidden away from the public glare to give evidence at a later date.

One Melbourne gang built on unquestioned loyalty and drug money has been destroyed. One of their hit men is dead, three have been jailed and other key figures are believed to be co-operating with police.

There can be no doubt that underworld solidarity has ruptured. Purana detectives and homicide investigators claim they have laid charges or have made inroads in seventeen recent underworld killings.

They say that in seven cases, the gunmen responsible were later themselves killed in the underworld feud.

Detective Superintendent Richard Grant, the head of police tasked operations, said, 'Our aim is to destroy the code of silence so the crooks can't trust each other.' So far, so good.

WITH The Runner, The Journeyman, The Cook, The Driver, The Lieutenant and many others lining up to tell tales on him, Mokbel was under siege. His asset base was frozen, his brothers jailed, he was under investigation for murder and he had a nine-year jail sentence waiting for him. And he was losing his hair.

But he had another powerful enemy — a man he had never met. A Melbourne figure with close connections to a famous northern suburban football club had been watching the underworld war develop in the streets of the city where his family lived and he wasn't happy. And this Melbourne man controlled one of the most feared gangs in Australia.

His name was Peter Costello, then the Treasurer of Australia and ultimate overseer of the tax department.

ALMOST twenty years earlier, when the tax department completed a secret investigation into a drug dealer who had evaded police for years, they hit him with a bill for $1,348,048.60. But instead of jail and certain financial ruin, the dealer was able to cut a deal.

The Australian Taxation Office ultimately negotiated a settlement of $440,000 as full payment for the period 1984—87. To the drug dealer, it was loose change. To the tax department, it was money in the bank.

The drug trafficker has long moved out of crime and is now a semi-retired — and semi-respectable — property developer in the moneyed area of Melbourne's north-west.

For decades, police have complained that the tax department has seemed happy to accept tainted money from crooks instead of using their powers to drain the gangsters' finances.

Many police considered tax officials to be revenue raisers rather than law enforcement officers, more interested in money than morality. With a few notable exceptions, it seemed, the pen pushers were reluctant to take on the drug pushers. Complex laws, which at times protected wealthy criminals who could afford to pay experts to conceal their wealth, did not help.

The tax office has traditionally pursued professional groups, the self-employed and small businesses, often choosing to ignore those who make their money through more nefarious means. On purely financial terms it makes sense. It is harder, and sometimes more risky, to track the assets of serious criminals than those of doctors, plumbers or schoolteachers.

The director of the Australian School of Taxation at the University of NSW, Professor Chris Evans, says the tax office concentrates on areas of evasion that generate large amounts of black money: 'They make decisions where they can get the biggest bang for their buck.'

He says gangsters who hide their assets and deal in cash are not considered cost-effective targets compared with businesses that keep ordered records.

'By the time their assets are identified they may be dead or have done a runner. I think sometimes they may be put in the too-hard basket,' he says.

But, in 2004, Treasurer Costello began to show obvious frustration at the underworld war that had broken out in his hometown. In a pointed message during a speech at Melbourne's Scots Church, he said: 'I pledge that if federal tax authorities can assist in tracking and taxing the flow of money that sustains the lifestyles of these drug barons, then everything that can be done will be done. We stand ready, anxious to assist.'

Weeks earlier, he had said he was worried that many of Melbourne's underworld figures had become celebrities and were being glamorised by the media.

Costello told the authors soon after Mokbel fled that investigators and police would work together to nail gangsters. 'These drug barons can expect to be hit harder under the Tax Act. Let us hope that they are hit even harder under the criminal law.'

Clearly, Costello was flagging the possibility of the tactics used by US federal authorities in the early 1930s to snare the mobster Al Capone, who had seemed immune from prosecution for his many criminal activities for years.

Back in the Prohibition era, the US Treasury Department charged Al Capone and other mobsters with tax evasion. Capone was convicted in 1931 and sentenced to eleven years, fined $50,000, hit with a back tax bill of $215,000 and charged $7692 in court costs. He was released from jail after serving seven years, six months and fifteen days, a broken and sick man. Syphilis can do that — even to seemingly tough guy gangsters. It would seem Al had needed a condom more than a bullet proof vest. He did not return to Chicago and died a 'vegetable'.

Many criminals see jail as an occupational hazard. They view it the way a farmer sees drought — nasty, but at times unavoidable. The main aim is never to lose the farm. It is the police's aim, now, to seize the farm. While arrests bring headlines, it is the methodical finding, freezing and seizing of assets that permanently damages organised crime groups.

'Cut the assets and you destroy their power bases,' is the philosophy of Detective Superintendent Richard Grant, who was assigned to modernise police investigations into organised crime.

While the Victorian Government introduced tough new asset seizure laws, financial and legal advisers urged their gangster clients to put their investments in the names of trusted family members.

Police say they will work with the Tax Office to chase the money that in some cases has been hidden for years. One senior policeman once complained that he had personally told the tax department of at least $10 million in a criminal's hidden assets but still couldn't claim the suit he wore to work as a tax deduction.

The difference is that police are now employing specialists to identify the hidden assets of organised crime figures so that the tax office will receive detailed information on people that were previously undetected.

Up to 32 lawyers, forensic accountants, analysts and administrators have joined specialist units and the Victoria Police criminal proceeds squad to track the finances of organised crime suspects and police have pledged to set up three Purana-like taskforces.

If police can't get them, they will pass the information to the tax man. Evans says the tax office can assess an individual's lifestyle and likely income and then lodge a statement to that effect. It is then up to the target to prove that the statement's assessment is not accurate. Individuals found to have cheated the tax department can be charged under the Crimes (Taxation Offences) Act and face a maximum of ten years' jail and a $100,000 fine. In addition, they can be ordered to pay back taxes, be hit with punitive double taxes and face a punishing interest bill.

All of which was bad news for the likes of Tony Mokbel, top of the list of drug baron tax evaders. Just months before he disappeared he was hit with a $4 million bill for back taxes.

Police say Mokbel's power base was always purely financial. Take the money and the trinkets and he would just be a former milk bar owner with a wig.

The underworld war has shown the sort of money some of Melbourne's unemployed gangsters have been able to acquire — wealth that is often kept in the names of family, friends and 'front' businesses. It can take the form of hidden cash, jewellery and luxury cars, as well as real estate.

Yet Mokbel tried to cry poor. He launched a failed court appeal to try to free assets frozen by police, saying he did not have enough money to support his lifestyle and to pay his lawyers.

But 'poverty' is relative. When he was arrested (again) in 2005, he was carrying nearly $40,000 in cash and six mobile phones. Later that year, he was still trying to buy businesses, including a men's fashion label, on the understanding that others would front the companies.

The family's preference for cash again surfaced in 2006, when police seized $116,255 after they arrested Tony's brother Milad Mokbel on drug charges. Milad's home was put up as surety for Tony before he jumped bail.

Peter Costello has made it clear that Mokbel is not the only crook in the tax department's sights.

A study of some of the victims of Melbourne's underworld war shows that Mokbel was not the only gangster to revel in the lifestyle of the rich and infamous drug traffickers.

Michael Marshall sold hot dogs for a living. When he was shot dead in October 2003, he had a property portfolio worth around $1.5 million, including a double-storey house in South Yarra bought from a Melbourne surgeon in 1991. Marshall was only 26 when he bought the house yet was able to pay it off within three years. Title documents show it had taken the surgeon many years to do the same thing. Saving lives does not pay nearly as well as ruining them.

Willie Thompson supposedly sold lollipops to nightclubs until he was shot dead in his expensive Honda sports car in Chadstone in July 2003. The former kickboxer and part-time actor listed his occupation as 'company director' and he had $245,000 in a Greek bank account.

Jason Moran had no known occupation other than career gangster when he was shot dead in Essendon North in June 2003. He had a life insurance policy worth $16,000 and $413,211.81 in the Stevedoring Employees Retirement Fund. But his wife Trish, who listed her occupation as home duties, had built an excellent property portfolio valued at $1.845 million — although some of the units were mortgaged through Moran Investments Pty Ltd.

Jason's half-brother Mark was shot dead outside his $1.3 million home in Aberfeldie in June 2000, when houses worth more than a million dollars were still scarce. He was an unemployed pastry chef at the time.

Frank Benvenuto was shot dead outside his Beaumaris house in May 2000. In the boot of his car was said to be $64,000. He owned property and was able to spend $5000 on his sport of choice — pigeon racing.

Nik Radev was a drug dealer who didn't pay tax for years. When he was shot dead in April 2003 he was standing next to his $100,000 Mercedes. He was wearing a Versace outfit and a $20,000 watch and had recently spent $50,000 to have his teeth fixed. He was buried in a gold-plated casket valued at $30,000.

Police say that no matter how well business is going, many gangsters hate paying tax and will try to take on the system.

In a celebrated case that changed tax law, a convicted heroin dealer successfully claimed a deduction for money he claimed was stolen during a raid.

Perth drug dealer Francesco Dominico La Rosa argued he should be allowed to claim $224,793 stolen from him in 1995 after the Tax Office had assessed his income in that financial year as $446,954.

La Rosa — who was sentenced to twelve years jail for dealing heroin and amphetamines — was quoted after he won his court battle saying: 'As drug dealers or business people, we should have the same rights as any taxpayer.'

The Federal Government changed the law so convicted criminals could not claim as deductions money spent or lost during unlawful activities. It is also illegal to claim bribes as a business expense.

But Evans says it is still technically possible for a non-convicted criminal to make claims. For example, a hit man who was paid to kill could theoretically claim guns, bullets and disguises as legitimate business expenses.

WHILE photos of Mokbel at the races or leaving court have filled newspapers for years, police artists have drawn a cartoon image that portrays the career criminal in a classic 'Where's Wally?' pose, complete with the Crime Stoppers number branded across his chest.

It shows Australia's most wanted man ready to flee Australia either by plane or ship, carrying suitcases of money and a plastic surgery kit. The satirical image suggests that Mokbel, who described himself as a professional punter, would leave his favourite track, Flemington — from which he was banned — for Dubai, where he could punt on the camel races, among other events.

Police were joking about the whereabouts of Australia's number one fugitive but it would take them more than a year to find, not for the first time in the gangland war, that truth can be stranger than fiction.

3

THE FUGITIVE

'It's like you sending me
to Hitler.'

WHEN Mokbel did a runner there was no shortage of theories
about what had happened.

He was said to have jumped on a ship using the same connections he used to import drugs from overseas: after all, if you can
import container loads of chemicals, surely you can export one
little Lebanese drug dealer?

Others had him driving north to be picked up by a luxury
yacht. The more imaginative speculated that a high flyer like
Tony would have escaped in a private jet. Bizarrely, it was claimed
he had flying lessons at Essendon Airport while on bail.

One thing was certain: his passport had been surrendered
when he was granted bail so there was no way he could have left
through usual channels under his own name.

The job of finding out the facts fell to the Federal Police but under international law they could only request assistance from overseas police.

Mokbel's name and photograph were lodged with Interpol. It sounded impressive but meant little as the international agency is nothing more than a bureaucratic clearing-house, not a global man-hunting outfit. For Interpol, the greatest risk of danger comes from a nasty paper cut while filing documents.

Mokbel was just one more name among thousands of drug dealers, bail jumpers, armed robbers and murderers scattered around the world. Foreign police are more interested in catching a local burglar than trying to find someone else's crook. It was only much later, when a million-dollar reward was offered, that Victoria Police were contacted by former European secret police and asked, 'Is that dead or alive?'

But, in the days weeks and months after Mokbel disappeared, the Federal Police needed a lead before anyone could help them. There was a lot of disinformation around.

At one point police were told he was dead and had been buried in country Victoria. Then police looked for him at the Dubai races, convinced he could not resist the glamour of the international event. A popular theory, possibly spread by Mokbel's family, was that he could have been hiding with relatives in Lebanon, but there were others: he could be back in his native Kuwait, sharing a cottage by the sea with Lord Lucan, or doing a warm-up act for Elvis in Brussels as far as police knew.

Some sections of the media breathlessly reported he had used an old escape route pioneered by the Moran clan, which came as a surprise to the surviving Morans, who had no idea of such a route.

He was then said to have been involved in a shootout in Lebanon but was saved by his own heavily-armed guards, which would have come as an even bigger surprise to Mokbel, who was not in Lebanon and didn't have guards.

In truth, police didn't know where he was but they were convinced he had planned his escape long before slipping out of the country.

But they were wrong.

It would now appear that Mokbel decided to run just days before he jumped bail. He had planned to see out his drug trial and was prepared to do several years jail, believing his syndicate would continue to prosper under the guidance of loyal family and friends. He would then emerge a slimmer, fitter multi-millionaire with his enemies in the underworld dead or jailed and his enemies in the police force retired or promoted to desk jobs. His enemies in the media would probably be in rehab.

For a career drug dealer, jail time is like splinters to carpenters and drunks to barmen: an annoying occupational hazard.

But when he learned just days before his trial was to end that he was in the frame for murder, the plan changed. It was time to go, ready or not: he would just have to wing it before he could wing it.

While police were calling on Interpol to scour the world and detectives and reporters were speculating on increasingly exotic escape theories, no one thought to have a good look closer to home.

No one, it seemed, thought to use the most basic police method of hunting an escapee: knock on his mates' doors.

While everyone was assuming that Mokbel was an international man of mystery, he was shacked up less than 160 kilometres from Melbourne in a modest farmhouse at Bonnie Doon owned by a subordinate and alleged syndicate drug courier.

From March until October the closest Mokbel got to Monte Carlo was when he snacked on a biscuit of the same name with his evening mug of Milo.

Mokbel lived the serene country life while his courier host was kept busy with company business. Bonnie Doon locals say they believed a relative had been staying on the property in a caravan next to the main house. It must have seemed a world away from his Melbourne penthouse but it was a much better alternative than the cell that was waiting for him in Port Phillip Prison.

In July 2006, Mokbel's mistress, Danielle McGuire, loudly proclaimed her love for the missing drug dealer and said she was delighted he had escaped. She closed her Mokbel financed hairdressing salon and announced she was moving overseas 'indefinitely'.

It was an elaborate ruse: the hairdresser was acting as Tony's hare. She was to distract the dogs with her very public flight from Melbourne. Police tracked her through Dubai, France and Italy and, for a woman suspected of being on her way to meet Australia's most notorious fugitive, she seemed remarkably relaxed. She visited resorts, tourist spots and went shopping with her ten-year-old daughter.

McGuire didn't need Mokbel to teach her about anti- surveillance and how to pick police on her tail. Years earlier, she had worked at a major Melbourne department chain as a store detective and one of the fellow part-time workers was a policeman — a drug-squad detective who would later be jailed for corruption. The detective showed his fellow workers — including McGuire — the latest surveillance methods. Much later, and before he was exposed as a crook, the investigator would work on the Moran and Mokbel drug syndicates, proving that it is indeed a very small (drug) world.

McGuire continued to play tourist, fully aware that international police had been alerted to follow her. She made no effort to conceal her identity and withdrew money electronically, allowing police to follow her movements. She even waved cheekily to international surveillance police tailing her.

Then, at what appeared to be a designated time, she slipped the net, easily dodging trailing police in Italy.

It was around the time that Mokbel left his Bonnie Doon hideout, slipped out of Australia to Asia on a ship and then flew to Europe on a false passport.

Round one to Tony.

AFTER Mokbel jumped bail, there was one group of police who didn't bother looking for him — the Purana taskforce.

While it was publicly embarrassing to mislay such a high-profile suspect, it actually worked in the taskforce's favour. Deputy Commissioner Simon Overland confidently predicted that Mokbel would surface eventually: 'You can spend five years on the run. That's fine. We will find you eventually, and we will bring you back to face justice.' Taskforce detectives knew Mokbel's ego would not allow him to hide under a Lebanese olive tree for long. He always craved the spotlight and would never retire gracefully from the drug world.

But his absence meant he could not control his network from the ground up. The head of Purana, Detective Inspector Jim O'Brien, (the fourth appointed boss since its inception), used the same methods that had brought Carl Williams down: he would destroy the syndicate from the ground up.

He knew that Mokbel's power was based on his money. Tony demanded loyalty and was prepared to pay handsomely for it. Stop the flow of money and drugs and, O'Brien predicted, the hired help would jump ship. But police had to work out the extent of the empire before they could bring it down.

When Mokbel was arrested as the master mind behind a massive drug chemical importation in 2001, police seized $6 million in assets. Later they estimated his wealth at $20 million.

The Purana taskforce was staffed with dedicated investigators, committed analysts and support staff. But because of a special grant from the state government it was also able to employ lawyers and forensic accountants. The man who led the asset identification team was Detective Sergeant Jim Coghlan, who had worked on Mokbel for more than four years.

Their findings were staggering. They estimated Mokbel had turned over $400 million through his criminal enterprises while other senior members had grossed $350 million.

The task of following the money trail was made all the more difficult because there rarely was one. They found that Mokbel spent $10,000 a week just as pocket money. The rest was punted, invested, laundered or ploughed back into the drug business.

Tony Mokbel ran his vast enterprises through the carrot and stick approach, exploiting greed and fear. There was no great paper trail — no contracts and no agreements — just a river of black cash. Mokbel would use drug money to set up companies and then put in an associate as the front man. Mokbel would tell his puppet he would be expected to hand over the company when instructed, and in return he could share in the profits along the way.

There wasn't much risk the front man would refuse to hand over the asset when he received the order. The subordinate would be paid well but when Tony wanted it sold it was immediately liquidated — or else the 'front' risked the same fate.

One of the first places Purana went to examine Mokbel's incomings and outgoings was the race track. They found that despite being banned from owning horses since 1999 and being banned from the Crown Casino and racecourses after his arrest, Mokbel had spent $80 million in gambling.

With the help of the Australian Crime Commission, Purana detectives examined his links to major racing identities.

Years earlier, Mokbel had led the notorious 'Tracksuit Gang' that regularly plunged money at race meetings up and down the east coast. With the benefit of hindsight it is obvious that Mokbel's minions were laundering millions with massive cash bets.

In the days of mobile phones and electronic money transfers, big punters rarely lay large cash bets. But it would appear that Tony was a leopard that wouldn't change his spots.

One Melbourne bookie started to become embarrassed when one serious punter kept displaying the $5000 cash he was about to wager.

The bookie eventually quietly advised the punter to discreetly place the cash in a bag before handing it over so track regulars who pass on gossip and tips with equal relish would not observe the transactions. If the bookie ever doubted who was behind the bets, he soon learned when the front man handed over the cash and whispered, 'Tony wants to do this.'

Few people achieve such fame or infamy that they are instantly recognized by their first name. Mokbel was one of the few.

He was one of the few punters, leaving aside the late Kerry Packer, bookies knew could lose millions and still come back for more (or less).

No wonder they were happy to receive fat envelopes of cash from Mokbel's runners. For some of them, Fat Tony was the closest thing to Santa they would ever find.

As part of the Purana/Australian Crime Commission investigation, two jockeys, two trainers and three bookmakers were subpoenaed to appear at secret hearings.

Purana used the commission because it can compel witnesses to answer questions under oath and demand financial and legal documents connected with investigations into organised crime.

Those given an offer too good to refuse by the crime commission included bookmakers Alan Eskander, Frank Hudson and Simon Beasley, jockeys Danny Nikolic and Jim Cassidy and trainers Jim Conlan and Brendan McCarthy. They were not suspects, but investigators wanted them to provide an insight into Australia's most wanted man.

The inquiry established that Mokbel set up betting accounts under the names of front men so he could place massive bets he hoped would never be discovered.

At least one bookmaker told the commission he knowingly accepted large bets from Mokbel more than a year after he was charged with importing $2 billion worth of drug chemicals and importing two kilograms of cocaine.

One bookie admitted opening a 'ghost' betting account to enable Mokbel to punt under another man's name. In just one week during the 2002 spring racing carnival, records show the account turned over $445,000. To Tony it was just pocket money. The bets were made just weeks after Mokbel was finally granted $1 million bail on the serious drugs charges.

The name on the ghost betting account was Emido Navarolli, a close friend of Mokbel's. But the bookie has admitted it was Mokbel and one of his associates who placed the bets and never the mysterious Navarolli.

Just two weeks after the drug trafficker disappeared, Navarolli returned a $500,000 Mercedes once used by Mokbel to a car yard, as it was surplus to requirements.

On 17 August 2005, Mokbel gave evidence before the Australian Crime Commission that his gambling winnings were paid into a bank account at the South Yarra branch of the ANZ bank under Navarolli's name.

Two days later, the Office of Public Prosecutions took out a restraining order to freeze the funds under assets-of-crime laws.

Mokbel liked to give the impression he had inside information but his betting was wildly erratic. One rails bookmaker claims to have won nearly $6 million from the drug dealer over several years.

Another said Mokbel once invited him to a Port Melbourne coffee shop, within walking distance of the drug dealer's bayside penthouse, to collect $80,000. He recalled they walked to Mokbel's car, where the trafficker opened the glove box. 'There was at least $300,000 there,' said the bookmaker, who is used to judging the worth of large bundles of cash. Mokbel handed over the required notes to square the ledger.

The big punter did not mind the occasional big loss. He was trying to launder drug money into semi-respectable gambling revenue that could not be seized as assets of crime.

While Mokbel appeared to have almost unlimited funds to bet, some bookmakers were not prepared to allow him credit. One claims Mokbel refused to pay a $1.8 million debt run up on credit bets. Another was owed $60,000 — Mokbel rang and declared he had placed a $10,000 winning bet on a six-to-one shot on the last race in Adelaide. The bet was non-existent but the bookie realised it was pointless to argue. He wrote off the debt rather than risk being written off himself.

But the man who liked to describe himself as a professional punter did have strong ties with some of the biggest names in the business — who either didn't know or didn't care where their rich friend made his millions.

In the months before Mokbel's arrest in August 2001, police telephone taps showed the drug dealer had regular conversations with key players in the racing world. Up to seven racing identities, including three top jockeys, were recorded talking to Mokbel on the police tapes.

In 2006, shortly after Mokbel disappeared, top jockey Jim Cassidy said he considered him a friend. 'I've got nothing but respect for him,' he told the *Herald Sun* in a frank moment.

Not everyone was as charitable as Gentleman Jim.

In 1998, racing officials started an inquiry into the Mokbel family's ownership of horses. They found Tony and his then wife, Carmel, owned a string of gallopers. They also found the Mokbels tried to 'give' a horse to the wife of a leading jockey.

In the same year, racing officials gave police a confidential report suggesting the Mokbels were dangerous, corrupt and out of control. One senior official was shocked when he was confronted by one of the Mokbel family and threatened just weeks after the information was passed to police. The official still believes the information had been leaked to the drug dealer.

It was part of a pattern where Mokbel seemed to know about investigations into him only days after they had begun.

In 1999, the Mokbels were banned from owning racehorses. It wasn't worth the paper it was written on. Tony still had a string of horses — he just kept them under the names of subordinates and associates. Sort of Trojan racehorses.

Again it was his standard business practice. Place your assets under your mates' names and collect later. Even after Tony's eventual arrest in Greece in 2007, his brother, Horty, was named in a public controversy over the ownership of three-quarters of a brilliant young galloper called Pillar of Hercules, which was banned from racing then auctioned by order of the stewards as a way of guaranteeing it was not controlled by a silent partner in the Mokbel camp.

The colt, which had cost $475,000 as a yearling, was auctioned for $1.8 million just days before the 2007 Melbourne Cup carnival. This was a lucky break for one Irene Meletsis, a woman reputedly with little knowledge of racing, whose name had appeared in the racebook as three-quarter owner of the colt. In an embarrassing twist for the trainer, Peter Moody, police had taped telephone conversations of him discussing the purchase and naming of the colt with Horty Mokbel. It wasn't really Moody's business who paid the bills, as he pointed out.

In 2004, Tony Mokbel bragged he won nearly $400,000 on the Melbourne Cup and was seen punting heavily on Oaks Day two days later.

The public display infuriated senior police and racing officials to the extent that laws were changed to ban suspected crime figures from Crown Casino and Victorian racetracks. Mokbel was one of the first to be blacklisted.

The ACC investigation was not the first time racing figures were questioned over their alleged links to major crime figures.

Cassidy and fellow jockeys, Gavin Eades and Kevin Moses, were suspended in Sydney in 1995 for race tipping, after their conversations were recorded during a major Australian Federal Police drug investigation code-named Caribou.

And in 1981, several racing identities, including jockeys and callers, were recorded on illegal NSW police tapes giving inside information to notorious drug dealer, Robert 'Aussie Bob' Trimbole.

They don't call them colourful racing identities for nothing.

WHILE the crime commission was busy on the racing side, Jim O'Brien continued the dual strategy of attacking Mokbel's resource base while turning trusted insiders into prosecution witnesses.

If Tony had been in Australia, even in jail, he may have been able to control his team but, with him overseas, the fabric began to fray.

Police began to target Mokbel's closest family and friends. They discovered the syndicate, code named 'The Company', had set up seemingly legitimate industrial businesses to buy massive amounts of chemicals used to make perfume. They then redirected the precursor chemicals to be used in the production of amphetamines and ecstasy. While it was inconceivable that the massive amount of chemicals they bought could be used for a small perfume production run, no one within the industry queried the purchases. For the Mokbels it was a licence to print money.

But slowly Purana put their hooks into the company.

In September 2006, they (literally) unearthed $350,000 in cash, eighteen watches, 61 items of jewellery and 33 jewellery boxes concealed in PVC pipes hidden on behalf of the Mokbel family in a Parkdale backyard.

They jailed Renate Mokbel, Tony's sister-in-law, after she failed to honour a $1 million surety she offered as part of Mokbel's bail conditions.

The Brunswick property used as surety was seized. It was the place Mokbel had run a speed lab in 1997 and, after a fire, had been rebuilt. Some close to Mokbel became disillusioned that he remained free when Renate was jailed.

His brothers were also arrested and charged. Milad Mokbel was charged after police discovered an alleged drug factory near a primary school in a shop that was supposedly being fitted out as a juice bar. Horse-loving brother Horty was also arrested on drug-related charges. Sister-in-Law Zaharoula Mokbel was charged over an alleged $2.3 million fraud.

A Mokbel financial adviser was arrested and his luxury car seized. When he saw reporters, the adviser loudly advised that they should get 'real jobs.' He may have had many assets but a sense of irony was not one of them.

Police needed the time that Mokbel was in hiding to build their case. Nearly one year after Mokbel had jumped bail, O'Brien was confident they now had enough information to charge him with two murders, Lewis Moran at the Brunswick Club and Michael Marshall in South Yarra. He was convinced they could finally charge Mokbel over being the head of a massive drug syndicate — although a jury will ultimately make that decision. Police had statements from two hit men, his alleged amphetamines cook and others close to the camp.

In February 2007 Mokbel was charged in his absence with Lewis Moran's murder. It was a strategy to show his followers he was now facing life in prison and so not a man to slavishly follow.

Having stripped Mokbel of his key advisers, police started phase two — Operation Magnum — the identification of Mokbel's hideaway and his ultimate arrest.

In April they announced a million-dollar reward for his capture. Mokbel had always used money to control his underlings and now police were using the same incentive to get them to betray him.

Deputy Commissioner Simon Overland intensified the pressure when he said: 'We've got no doubt there are people out there who know where he is, who are probably in regular contact with him. Every time he now contacts those individuals, there are going to be huge seeds of doubt in his mind: is this the person who's going to sell me out?'

It would be no coincidence that in the same month an insider code-numbered 3030 approached police, saying he could provide information on Mokbel and four of his top men. The informer was a trusted insider but his own brother had died of a drug overdose and he saw this as the moment he could exact the maximum in revenge.

While police were ready for the long haul the breakthrough came within weeks. By following the electronic transfer of about $400,000 to Athens they deduced that Tony was in Greece. But where exactly?

By using 3030 and introducing two police undercover agents they managed to get close.

The informer was the one who had been assigned to provide a passport and mobile phones for Mokbel. At least one of those phones was bugged by police before it was provided for the number one target.

The passport was later altered for Mokbel to the alias of a supposed Sydney businessman, 'Stephen Papas'. Why use that name?

It was rumoured that when a local football team supported by Mokbel used a ring-in player they always used the one alias — Stephen Papas. Dishonest habits die hard.

Thanks to the bugged phone, police could soon hear that Mokbel was still running his business, long distance. He would advise his staff when there was a problem with drug production and organise chemical deliveries.

And they continued to send him money — if not truckloads — at least bootloads.

On 5 May police watched as a Mokbel courier collected $440,000 hidden in Collingwood storage facility and then was given another $60,000 by a trusted insider.

But if detectives grabbed the cash courier it would alert Mokbel that Purana was getting close. Instead they used uniformed police to intercept the man — making it look as though they had accidentally discovered the money during a routine car check.

A marked unit slipped in behind the courier's car near Box Hill. The courier became nervous when he saw the police car and kept checking his mirror, which is why he didn't see the red light he ran on the Maroondah Highway. It gave police the perfect opportunity to pull him over and search the car. They found the package of $499,950 in cash. At the man's home they seized a further $8950.

One of the team rang Mokbel to tell him the cash instalment was gone. Tony, sunning himself in Athens, told the subordinate not to worry. He would ensure the same amount would be in his hands within six days. Put it down to a business expense, he said. He might not have been so casual had he known the truth: the police net was closing.

On 15 May the investigators narrowed the location to the prestigious Athens suburb of Glyfada, where Mokbel rented an upmarket home. They also found he was living with Danielle McGuire and their six-month-old girl, Renate. It is not known whether his sister-in-law, Renate, left in jail when he jumped bail, was chuffed that the baby was named after her.

According to Jim O'Brien: 'He was living in a double-storey apartment there with a rental of EUR2000 ($A3237) a month, living fairly high with a lavish lifestyle.'

In late May, Purana Detective Senior Sergeant Jim Coghlan, who had spent years unravelling the Mokbel empire and had previously holidayed in the area, flew to Athens with a federal investigator to work with Greek police to find the fugitive.

Mokbel spoke on the bugged phone of having 'coffee at Starbucks' — there were only two of the chain in the area. They were close, but not there yet.

In early June they thought they were. Danielle McGuire had given birth to Tony's baby and the doting dad was always there during infant swimming lessons. Police arrived at the pool just minutes after the family had left.

Three days later they were tipped off he would visit a small seaside restaurant for a financial meeting and would be carrying a folder with paperwork. They arrived at the crowded restaurant but could not spot the balding head of the fugitive. The local police then carried out what was to appear to be a routine identity check. When a well-tanned man with long dark hair opened a folder to produce a passport with the name Stephen Papas, Coghlan realised it was Mokbel in a wig.

At first Mokbel appeared relaxed, thinking he would be able to bribe his way out of any minor passport offence. But his face dropped when he saw the Purana detective. He had the good grace to say, 'I don't know how you did it but you've done a brilliant job.' He later lost his sense of fair play, telling the police he had 'evil dreams about what I was going to do to you and your families.'

Perhaps he should have checked his stars for that day, which read, 'Leos tend to feel they're entitled to more freedom and independence ... others might not agree today.'

On word of the arrest, more than 120 police in Victoria raided 22 properties (including the Bonnie Doon farmhouse where Mokbel had hidden) and arrested fourteen suspects. Later, eight people appeared in the Melbourne Magistrates Court charged with drug-related offences. Police also seized almost $800,000 in cash, drugs, eight vehicles, two power-skis, a Taser stun gun, mace spray, a pistol, a shotgun and a rifle.

It was also, by pure coincidence, Jim O'Brien's birthday.

Round two to the police.

TONY Mokbel was never going to come quietly. From day one he made it clear he was going to fight any extradition attempts.

Back in Melbourne authorities faced a race against time. They had to present the charges to a Greek court in Greek within 45 days. Under international law a suspect can only be tried on the charges approved under extradition treaties. Eventually Mokbel was charged with the Lewis Moran and Michael Marshall murders and drug trafficking offences. This meant he was facing life in jail — and he already owed a minimum of nine years for his cocaine conviction in 2006.

Despite the odds against him, Mokbel remained remarkably chatty. In the back of the court he spoke to *The Age's* European correspondent, James Button, declaring: 'I would be on a plane tomorrow if the Australian Government would agree to sort out the truth from the crap.'

He said he was not involved in the murder of Lewis Moran. 'Mate, I deny full stop all this.'

He claimed he had jumped bail because he knew he was facing more charges and would not have been able to defend himself from jail. 'Eventually, I do want to go back to Australia,' Mokbel said. 'All I'm asking is that the Australian Government sit down with me and talk and nut out the crap from the truth and I am hoping to go back.

'If they came and they talked to me and we came to an agreement I'm more than happy to get on a plane tomorrow.'

It was typical Mokbel bluster. He seemed to believe he had such political clout that he could deal directly with the government. His delusions were such that he had once been recorded saying that when 'Paul gets back from leave, Con will have a chat and sort it all out.'

'Paul' was the then Director of Public Prosecutions, Paul Coghlan, and Con was his barrister Con Heliotis QC. Mokbel was kidding himself. There would be no deals.

Mokbel went from delusion to denial and eventually to anger.

He said Purana was picking on him.

'If I were going to jail for things that I did that would be OK,' but Purana was 'hungry to convict whoever they would like, not for the right reasons'.

He said the underworld war had been a tragedy. 'We were all friends and it (the gangland killings) was the saddest thing happening, it was just sad.'

In a later hearing he was less relaxed, claiming that being sent back to Australia was like facing trial in Nazi Germany.

'It would be impossible for me to get a fair trial,' Mokbel told a Greek court. 'It's like you sending me to Hitler.'

The churlish may have pointed out that Mokbel was familiar with the concept of summary execution without trial.

Eventually a panel of three Greek judges granted the extradition. His local lawyer, Yannis Vlachos, said Mokbel would appeal.

'It is an uphill struggle, but we will fight it and remain optimistic,' Vlachos said.

The process was further delayed when he was sentenced to a year in a Greek jail on false passport charges. He was moved to the maximum-security Korydallos prison complex, fifteen kilometres from the city. Built for 640 inmates, it houses nearly 2000 and was described by Amnesty International as one of the worst jails in Europe.

So it was a surprise when the phone rang in the Purana office and the voice at the other end belonged to Mokbel, who had apparently bribed prison officials for access to several mobile phones.

Angling for a deal, he wanted the murder charges dropped if he was to return. He said he was prepared to talk about police corruption or anything else. He said to O'Brien, 'I'm a drug dealer, not a killer.' Hardly the best admission for your CV.

The House of Mokbel had fallen. Now he was trying to salvage something from the wreckage.

It meant the police could claim a massive victory against organised crime. But the win came twelve years after their failure to act had set the scene for gangster to turn on gangster in what became the underworld war.

4

OUT OF HIS LEAGUE

```
Al had got away with murder.
But, a few years later,
it would be his turn.
```

IN 30 years in the underworld, Gregory John Workman earned a name as a man who didn't dodge danger.

Like most of his breed, he had a lengthy police 'docket'. It had begun when he was a teenager, back in 1966 when Sir Robert Menzies was Prime Minister and imperial currency was being replaced with dollars and cents.

Workman's record included convictions for assault, theft, burglary, malicious wounding, abduction, illegal possession of a firearm, armed robbery and escape.

He began to build a reputation as a tough teenager in a tough place — the working-class Melbourne suburb of Preston. It was an area and an era in which many teenagers joined gangs — either the Mods or the Sharpies. Most moved on, but Workman used street violence as work experience in his chosen field. He was a diligent delinquent and eventually graduated from gang member to gangster. His reputation grew and, like many others, the young standover man turned to dealing drugs as he moved into middle age.

But when he was young he was just a big, good-looking kid from Preston East State School with a ready smile and an eye for the girls.

One of his first girlfriends remembered: 'All the girls had a crush on him. He had nice parents. I don't really know what went wrong for him.'

He once grabbed the author, then a tiny, but rather gifted, primary school boy, and threw him on his shoulders in what he considered to be a humorous street abduction.

At that moment in Wood Street, Preston, the budding author thought no good would come of Gregory John Workman. Neither knew their paths would cross again in tragic circumstances 30 years on.

The Workmans lived in a Housing Commission house in busy Albert Street — a few houses from a policeman who would one day become the head of the Australian Bureau of Criminal Intelligence and one of the country's few real experts on organised crime.

Even then, there were rumours around the teenage Workman that an older relative was dabbling in marijuana — a drug virtually unheard of in the suburbs in those days. Years later, there was no doubt Workman was into crime full-time.

'He was one of the better crooks in the area,' a policeman who locked him up more than once would recall much later.

'He would stay in the background and wouldn't do stupid things to bring police attention on himself. He had an air of confidence and a touch of class.

'He was rumoured to be behind some good stick-ups in the area, but he wasn't convicted over them.'

He was a good crook but he wasn't always a good bloke. Just ask his family. One of his close relatives became a manager at a successful Melbourne clothing business. Police later found a car boot full of clothes stolen from the factory. Workman was said to have stood over his relative to make him the inside man in a stolen clothing racket. The relative lost his legitimate job and gained a criminal record: a case of from rag trade to scallywag trade. It would have been an interesting Christmas Day at the Workmans' that year.

Workman was successful by his own lights but in underworld terms he was a middleweight and was finally caught fighting out of his division. It would not be the police who would stop him, but fellow criminals. One in particular.

On 6 February 1995, Workman and a crew of heavy criminals, including Alphonse John Gangitano, met for a wake at a Richmond hotel before heading to a party to celebrate the release of Mark Aisbett, who had been bailed on armed robbery charges earlier that day.

The party was already in full swing in a flat in Wando Grove, St Kilda, when the team from Richmond arrived around 1am.

After another three hours of drinking, the mood turned ugly. Gangitano was seen arguing with one of his old mates, Martin Felix Paul. According to a confidential police report: 'Gangitano was identified by an independent person as being in possession of a pistol and arguing with another male. It was apparent that Gangitano was being restrained by another person and was highly agitated.'

One of Australia's most experienced investigators into gangland murders, Detective Senior Sergeant Gavan Ryan, was later to tell the coroner that someone at the party overheard a conversation between Workman and another man, in which the issue of Workman's gambling debts was raised.

Ryan would not know that he was to spend most of the next decade investigating gangland murders and eventually would run the Purana Taskforce.

The witness later told another man at the party that Workman was about to be 'bumped' over the debt.

The witness left the party with the man and while in a taxi alerted the driver that he feared there was about to be a murder. The driver must have been convinced because he drove to the St Kilda police station to pass on his passenger's fears.

The argument was loud enough for neighbours to call the police. Several said they heard the name 'Harry' being used — a nickname for Alphonse used by his closest friends.

Police arrived to the noisy party, unaware that a Who's Who of the underworld had gathered. They were told that the two men who had been arguing in the driveway had left and they were assured there would be no further problems.

It was an overly optimistic call.

When Workman walked out the front door onto the porch he was shot eight times.

The woman who lived in the flat and had organised the party drove Workman to hospital, but he died without regaining consciousness. Eight .32 calibre slugs will do that.

If Gangitano had planned to kill Workman over a debt, he picked a stupid time and place to do it. In hindsight, it was a sign that Al was spinning out of control and would one day be seen as expendable himself.

A woman later told police she saw Gangitano standing near the body holding a small silver pistol before being led away by another man.

Coroner Wendy Wilmoth later found that a witness 'stated that she heard gunshots, went to the porch and saw Gangitano and Martin Paul standing almost at the feet of the deceased. She heard someone say, "Get him out of here" and saw Martin Paul lead Gangitano away.'

Ms Wilmoth said another witness, 'saw Gangitano run from the porch holding a gun in the air, soon after she came out of the front door, and saw the deceased collapse, injured, on the porch'.

It should have been an open and shut case. But it wasn't.

Two sisters who saw the shooting were whisked into a witness protection program to keep them away from the gangsters.

It seemed a huge breakthrough. The man who had become the public face of organised crime in Victoria was in deep trouble. His lawyer contacted homicide squad detectives and said his client was prepared to be interviewed.

Police said they were in no hurry. He may have fired the shots but now detectives were calling them.

But they made the mistake of not protecting what they had. They took their star witnesses for granted.

The sisters made statements implicating Gangitano and were then put under police protection and sent beyond Gangitano's influence — or so the theory went.

But it was not like the movies. Almost immediately, the sisters began to have doubts.

One was not allowed to visit her doctor for arthritis medication. They spent days in Carlton and were driven down Lygon Street several times, despite it being the area where Gangitano and his henchmen spent most of their time.

The witnesses were not allowed to collect clothes on layby at a department store and were forced to live on takeaway food. One of them told a detective they were 'made to feel like we're the criminals, not him'.

They were shunted into a cabin in a Warrnambool caravan park in western Victoria with a promise that their protectors were only a phone call away.

But when they tried to contact their police protectors three times the supposed 24-hour number rang out.

Increasingly anxious and annoyed, the women felt they had been left for dead — not a comforting thought when you were about to help police jail a ruthless gunman. 'The witnesses formed an opinion that their safety was no longer a priority of the Victoria Police and that the police were not in a position to adequately protect them,' according to a confidential police report.

Isolated, alone and frightened, they rang one of Gangitano's closest associates, Jason Moran, who arranged to meet them in Melbourne the next day. It was exactly two months after the murder.

Moran was a negotiator. His opening gambit, according to police, was to advise one of the women that if she gave evidence she and her family would be killed. He then took the sisters to his solicitor, Andrew Fraser, and to another lawyer's office where the witnesses made an audio tape recanting their original police statements.

Gangitano paid for them to fly out of Australia on 20 May to England and the United States. The murder case collapsed. Eventually, Gangitano's lawyer billed police for $69,975.35 over the failed prosecution.

But Coroner Wendy Wilmoth was able to investigate the case at Workman's inquest, even though the key witnesses had 'flipped'.

'It is beyond doubt that Gangitano was at the premises where the shooting occurred, at the relevant time, that he was in possession of a gun and that he was in an agitated state of mind. The retraction of their statements by the (sisters) can be explained by their extreme fear of Gangitano,' she said.

'Having considered this evidence, and taking into account the required standard of proof, I find that Alphonse Gangitano contributed to the death of the deceased by shooting him.'

In other words, Al had got away with murder. But, a few years later, it would be his turn. Another example of the truth of the saying, 'What goes around, comes around', a fitting epitaph for most standover men.

THE FIRST DOMINO

In a business where attention
can be fatal, Gangitano was
a publicity magnet.

IT was just after midnight when the two men in the green hire car cruised over the empty Westgate Bridge, heading away from Melbourne's city skyline.

The driver took little notice as his passenger casually picked up a McDonald's paper bag, apparently containing the remnants of their late-night snack, and threw it out the window.

It was only later that the driver would wonder why the bag wasn't sucked behind the fast moving car and, instead of fluttering onto the roadway, flew straight over the railing into the mouth of the Yarra River, 54 metres below.

And it would be months before police would conclude that the weight in the bag thrown from the bridge equalled that of a .32 calibre handgun — the one used to kill one of Australia's most notorious gangsters less than an hour earlier.

Alphonse John Gangitano was still lying dead in the laundry of his home with two bullet wounds in his head and one in the back when the two men crossed the bridge, but it would take four years before the events of that night were exposed.

GANGITANO was not Melbourne's best gangster, but he was the best known and certainly one of the best dressed. Glamorous, charming and violent, he played the role of an underworld identity as if he had learned it from a Hollywood script. Which, to some extent, he had. He watched a lot of films. Too many, maybe.

The sycophants would call him the Robert De Niro of Lygon Street. His critics — and there were many — called him the 'Plastic Godfather'.

In a business where attention can be fatal, Gangitano was a publicity magnet, first as a boxing manager, photographed with world champions such as Lester Ellis, and then as a crime figure whose court appearances were routinely followed by an increasingly fixated media.

He posed for photos and loved the crime boss image. He craved the centre stage and shunned the shadows. The only time he became outraged was when one of the authors said on radio, 'Alphonse Gangitano has the brains of a flea and the genitalia to match.' It is not known which part of the barb he found most offensive. He sued using his favourite lawyer, George Defteros, but when Al died, so did the legal action.

Some gangsters are born into the underworld, driven there by a cycle of poverty, lack of legitimate opportunities and family values that embrace violence and dishonesty. But that was not Gangitano's background. He came from a hard-working, successful family. His father had run a profitable travel agency and invested astutely in real estate.

Young Alphonse was given a private school education — at De La Salle, Marcellin and Taylor's College — but struggled to justify his parents' investment. He was remembered as a big kid with attitude, but not much ability and no application.

He was quick with his fists but not with his wits, though he was cunning enough to fight on his terms, usually king-hitting his opponents. He was charged with offensive behaviour when he was nineteen and, over the next five years, he graduated from street crimes to serious violence. Along the way he started to gather a group, which for two decades was known as the Carlton Crew.

Most young men eventually grow out of being fascinated with violence. Gangitano didn't. He was 24 when police first found him with a gun.

A confidential police report warned of Gangitano and his team: 'They approach (police) members and assault them for no apparent reason. They are all extremely anti-police and are known to be ex-boxers. They often frequent in a group numbering approximately fifteen. They single out up to three off-duty police and assault them, generally by punching and kicking them. On most occasions in the past, members have been hospitalised due to injuries received from these persons.' Gangitano was described as 'extremely violent and dangerous.'

In the early 1980s, Gangitano worked as a low-level standover man using an old tactic. He would walk into a club with a small group and tell the owners that he expected protection money or he would begin bashing patrons. Many quickly paid — others were slow learners. He was making more than $1000 a week. Not huge money, but enough for a young man on the make.

He was charged with hindering police, assault by kicking, assaulting police, resisting arrest, and other crimes of violence. Each time, the charges were thrown out. The fact he was able to beat charges helped build his reputation. Some suggested he had influence inside the police force.

Before long, he started to take on the trappings of a crime boss — wearing expensive clothes, reading biographies on Al Capone as if they were DIY manuals and watching videos such as *The Godfather*. He didn't seem to grasp that in Hollywood, the good guys almost always win and the bad guys end up behind bars. Or dead.

BEFORE poker machines and government-sanctioned casinos creamed off the easy money, the illegal gaming business was the underworld's most consistent money-maker. Gangitano might have been bored at school, but he was a quick learner on the street. He bought into a profitable baccarat school in Lygon Street and, some say, either part-owned or ran protection on Victoria's then lucrative two-up school.

Police intelligence reports listed him as a big punter and suggested he was a race-fixer in Victoria and Western Australia. He allegedly sold guns at an old Brunswick nightclub.

In the early 1990s, many police were confused about Gangitano. They were not sure if he was just another try-hard bash artist or a man building a serious criminal network. Their informer network reported he was a big underworld player yet several investigations found he was more style than substance.

If the aim of crime was to make big money, Gangitano was still an apprentice. But still the rumours continued that he was on the way to being 'The Godfather' of Melbourne.

He was seen with experienced and respected criminals. One of his new friends was Australia's best safebreaker, Graham Kinniburgh — who should have known better. It would be a disaster for Kinniburgh, who was sucked back into the limelight and, fatally, into the gangland war that was about to erupt. Alphonse also grew close to three brothers who controlled much of Lygon Street.

It perplexed police. Why did the big names of crime tolerate the dangerous and unpredictable new boy?

Gangitano brought publicity and the headlines made senior police demand reports from their organised crime experts. It was not good for business. In the underworld, fame rarely brings fortune.

Most major crooks need a semi-legitimate veneer. Like the American gangsters he mimicked, Gangitano chose boxing and aligned himself with the Lester Ellis camp. But Gangitano could not grasp the fundamentals of lawful business — even if it was only a front. He bashed and bit the well-known boxer Barry Michael, a professional rival to Ellis, in a city nightclub in 1987. More headlines followed.

Around the same time, Gangitano went into partnership to build a casino in Fitzroy with a well-known Lygon Street identity, investing $300,000 in the project. Unfortunately for the entrepreneurs, police raided and closed the club two days after it opened.

It was a classic police sting. Watching from a secret surveillance post in a building across the road, they allowed him to pour his money into the project before they shut it down.

Gangitano was handsome, smooth and liked to think he was well-read. He could quote Oscar Wilde, John F. Kennedy and Adolf Hitler. Or, at least, he got away with it. In his crowd, no one would check if the quotes were accurate. And even if they did, they would be too tactful to mention it.

On one occasion an off-duty detective was dining in Lygon Street with a woman other than his wife. He heard a group of men at a table behind him swearing and laughing. He turned and curtly told them to improve their manners — before he realised the head of the table was Gangitano. The policeman expected trouble. Instead, the group finished their meal and filed out. The waiter came to the detective's table with an expensive bottle of wine and an apology from Gangitano.

Yet he could also be short-tempered, irrationally violent and tactically naive. He often needed associates or his expensive team of lawyers to help clean up the messes he made.

A group of criminals, headed by Mark Brandon 'Chopper' Read, once planned to use land mines to kill Gangitano at his eastern suburbs house, but scrapped the plot because of the likelihood of others being killed.

Shortly before Read was released from prison in 1991, an associate of Gangitano went to Pentridge with a peace offer. But police say Gangitano had a back-up plan. He had placed a $30,000 contract on Read's head.

When Read was released, Gangitano produced yet another plan ... he took his family to Italy and did not return until January 1993, when Read was back in custody on another shooting charge.

Gangitano should have learned from Read's carelessness with pointing guns. It was little more than two years later that he had his own problems, when he killed Greg Workman.

It was lucky for Big Al that the two sisters who had witnessed the shooting later changed their stories because they felt abandoned in the police witness protection. But his good fortune cost him a small fortune when he picked up the bill for their extended overseas trip. He was, of course, compensated for legal costs of $69,975.35 over the failed prosecution. In the end, it might not have been worth humiliating the police.

Incensed that they had to drop the charges, police then decided on a campaign of death by a thousand cuts. Gangitano's Eaglemont house was raided. Police said he resisted arrest and so suffered nasty head injuries.

Within a few months, he was charged with assault, refusing a breath test and possession of firearms. He spent time in jail and was bailed on a night curfew. The myth that he was untouchable began to fade.

When reporting for bail, Gangitano saw an unflattering police Polaroid picture on his file. He paid for a professional portrait shot and took it to the station to replace the Polaroid mugshot. In September 1997, a crime report on radio 3AW stated Gangitano had fallen out with old friends and would be murdered. Gangitano scoffed at the suggestion — but police found a transcript of the report in his home the day after he was killed.

A television reporter contacted Mark 'Chopper' Read in late 1997 when the standover man was about to be released from jail. She wanted to organise an interview with Gangitano and Read.

'Not possible, darling,' Read said. 'He'll be dead before I'm out, I'm afraid.'

IN many ways Graham Allan Kinniburgh and Gangitano were the odd couple of the underworld.

Kinniburgh was wealthy, but tried to hide it — Gangitano was struggling but deliberately cultivated an image of affluence.

Kinniburgh was an old-fashioned Anglo-Celtic 'Aussie' who kept a low profile, preferring to conduct his business in private. Gangitano was the son of Italian migrants and loved the head-lines, even if it meant he was always the target of police investiga-tions.

Kinniburgh's apparently slight criminal record understates his influence on the Melbourne underworld. It lists crimes of dis-honesty, bribery, possession of firearms, escape, resisting arrest and assaulting police. But criminal records list only an offender's arrest history — his failures. Successful criminals learn from their mistakes and don't get caught.

Police became convinced that Kinniburgh — known as 'The Munster' — was close to the infamous 'magnetic drill gang', responsible for many of Australia's biggest safe breakings.

Right up until the day he was killed, Kinniburgh lived in a double-storey house in the affluent Melbourne suburb of Kew. Now a well-known media personality lives in the same street. Cynics say both made handsome livings from very little work. One difference was that Kinniburgh always carried plenty of cash.

The Munster's occupation seemed to be a mystery. Interviewed by police after Gangitano's murder, he struggled to remember how he paid the bills. When asked by the astute Detective Sergeant Gavan Ryan of the homicide squad what he did for a job, Kinniburgh eventually suggested he might be 'a rigger'.

But while regular employment was not at the top of his priorities, life had been kind to 'The Munster'. When police searched him outside the scene of Gangitano's murder he was carrying some change, keys, cigarettes and just over $3000 in $100 notes.

While Kinniburgh could afford imported suits, he preferred the casual clothes of an off-duty dock worker, but in middle age he had acquired expensive tastes and was a regular at the budget-blowing Flower Drum restaurant in Chinatown. He unofficially holds the record for spending more money on fried rice than any other human on the planet.

But the master criminal planner made a big mistake. He ignored the fact that Gangitano was a magnet for publicity and trouble.

ALPHONSE Gangitano didn't look like a worried man as he stood on the steps of the Melbourne Magistrates' Court after round one of his committal hearing.

Despite facing serious assault charges over a brawl in a King Street bar, he told friends he was confident he would eventually be acquitted.

He bragged that he was not concerned about the police case and his legal team would 'blow them away'.

But one of two co-accused, Jason Matthew Patrick Moran, was not so confident. After the assault on 19 December 1995, which had left thirteen people injured, Moran was recorded on a police listening device saying he had to 'shower to wash the blood off' and 'to cut a long story short, I started it'.

Gangitano's declaration that he would win the case was typical Al bravado. He was apprehended at the scene still swinging a pool cue and chasing yet another victim. Gangitano had done what police investigators could not — bring an open and shut case to conclusion. He was going to jail for a long time.

But Jason had got away from the scene. Perhaps he later wished he hadn't because when he was finally arrested, enthusiastic police fractured his skull.

Moran and Gangitano were long-time associates but their relationship was starting to fray. Moran was secretly taped saying of Big Al: 'He's a fucking lulu ... if you smash five pool cues and an iron bar over someone's head, you're fucking lulu.'

The case against Jason was strong, but not as strong as the one against Alphonse. If they stood in the same dock together Jason would sink with the weight of evidence against his mate and if Alphonse pleaded guilty it would add to the resolve of wavering witnesses to give evidence against Moran.

But Jason was brought up in the old school. It seems unlikely he would off a mate on the off chance he would get off. That would be off.

There must have been more to it. Even Jason's enemies acknowledge he was tough and he soon recovered from his police-inflicted fractured skull. The injury and the pain-killers did not help him see the light.

In 1996 Moran was again charged with assault-related offences after another attack in a nightclub. He was always close to losing control, but his family tried to keep him on track.

But Gangitano had no support network. Increasingly isolated, he was seen as a loose cannon that made problems for everyone. He was expendable. Those close to the Morans noticed there appeared to be growing tension between Jason and Alphonse.

But on the morning of 16 January 1998, as they left court together, they seemed as staunch as ever. They shook hands before moving off with a group, including four defence lawyers, for coffee at the Four Courts Cafe in William Street.

Later, Gangitano and his solicitor, Dean Cole, walked to George's Cafe in Lonsdale Street for a light lunch before going to a small TAB for two hours of punting. Gangitano placed bets on seven races before he was picked up and taken back to his Templestowe home by his regular driver, Santo.

Soon after arriving home in Glen Orchard Close, Templestowe, Gangitano rang Cole to say he was tired and would have a nap. It was 4.45pm. He promised to ring back later but didn't.

Gangitano was alone in his 30-square double-storey house. His de facto wife and their two children were visiting a relative in St Kilda.

Gangitano removed the expensive, imported grey suit he had worn in court and placed it on the banister before heading upstairs for a four-hour sleep.

Gangitano had bought the house four months earlier for $264,000, but still had a mortgage of $200,000. The house was large, comfortable and suited his purposes.

It was in a dead-end road. From the upstairs windows Gangitano could see any friends, enemies — or both — as they entered the street. The sloping block meant the ground floor was not visible from the road, making police surveillance difficult. A four-camera security system was used when Gangitano was not at home.

The crime boss was not so much concerned about other criminals; he wanted the video system to deter police — the secret 'tech' branch — from breaking in and hiding listening devices in his home.

For a self-made crime headline, Gangitano valued his privacy. He tried to protect his family from his working life. Many of his closest crime contacts had never been to his home.

Those who had been there found themselves in the back garden. Gangitano's fear of listening devices meant he didn't like to talk business inside the house.

He did not tell his wife about his work and she did not ask. Her job was to care for the children. His was to pay the bills. He had a full-time mistress who might have been more aware of his work, but she was just as coy when asked questions at his murder inquest years later. She said she thought he might have been some sort of a property developer.

Alphonse seemed to attract women who weren't curious.

GANGITANO rose from his sleep just after 9pm on 16 January 1998. Years of working as a night-time gangster left him with a nocturnal body clock. As part of his bail conditions, Gangitano had to be home after 9pm, although he did not always stick to the letter of the law.

While he liked to be seen after dark in Lygon Street, the bail restrictions meant his nationwide network of criminal associates knew where to find him.

Gangitano's unlisted number had found its way into the contact books of established and would-be criminals around Australia. In the hours before he died, Gangitano made — and received — many calls.

One was from his wife, telling him she was at her sister's house and would be home before midnight. An inmate from Fulham Prison rang, wanting a chat and some racing tips. A friend in Brunswick called, and a colourful West Australian personality, John Kizon, also rang.

Kizon was to Perth what Gangitano was to Melbourne. Big, handsome, charismatic and seemingly bulletproof, both men protested that they were not crime bosses, yet seemed to enjoy their public notoriety. They even shared the same lawyer — Croxton Park Hotel bouncer-turned-courtroom-fighter, George Defteros.

Kizon was a convicted heroin trafficker, nightclub owner and entertainment promoter. Like Gangitano, he claimed to be misunderstood. His range of associates included Rose Hancock (he once dated her daughter, Joanna, before she was mysteriously bashed and fled to England), jailed businessman the late Laurie Connell, and Andrew Petrelis, a man who went into witness protection before being found dead in bizarre circumstances in Queensland.

Police believed Kizon had been involved in trafficking large amounts of cannabis from Western Australia to the eastern states.

It was just before 11pm Melbourne time when Kizon rang Gangitano from a Chinese restaurant in Perth. They talked about how the court proceedings had gone that day. Gangitano chatted easily and sounded confident. He had a visitor who took the phone for a brief conversation. It was his long-time friend Graham 'The Munster' Kinniburgh.

The phone call lasted less than ten minutes. Kizon said he would ring back. He didn't get the chance.

Earlier that evening, Kinniburgh had had a drink with Carlton identity Lou Cozzo at the Laurel Hotel in Ascot Vale. Around 10.30pm, he drove his red Ford across town to visit Gangitano.

'The Munster' was one of the few men in Melbourne who could drop in on Gangitano without an invitation. According to Kinniburgh, the big man was on the phone when he arrived and told him to clear off for about 30 minutes as he was waiting for another visitor to arrive for a meeting. But those who knew them say the younger man would never be so dismissive of 'The Munster'.

Kinniburgh gave that version to write himself out of the house at the time of the murder. It didn't work.

So what really happened?

Gangitano was sitting downstairs at a round kitchen table. From this spot he could see down the hallway to the wooden front door, which was open to let in the cool night breeze. Through the mesh of the second security door he could see out but no one could see in.

It was eighteen degrees at 11pm and Gangitano hadn't bothered to change from his pyjama top and blue underpants. Judging from the time of Kizon's phone call, Kinniburgh was already in the house.

When Gangitano opened the door for a second visitor he didn't bother to put on clothes. It was a casual meeting with a man he knew well — his old mate and partner-in-crime, Jason Moran.

What was said in those few minutes will never be known as the three men present have now all been shot dead. But forensic evidence suggests Moran was standing in the kitchen to his victim's left and Gangitano ran towards the laundry to his right as shots were fired from close range. He was shot in the back, nose and head, before collapsing.

Kinniburgh said he had slipped away to a Quix convenience store in Blackburn Road to buy a packet of Benson & Hedges cigarettes. He was recorded on the store's security camera at 11.45pm and left a minute later.

Coincidently, Gangitano's wife stopped at the same shop eight minutes earlier to buy the children ice-creams and drinks on the way home. Kinniburgh said he was gone for 30 minutes. He has not yet explained what he did for the other 25 before he returned to his friend's home.

When he pulled up at the house, Gangitano's wife was already inside. She had found the body and dialled 000. The emergency tape recorded her call as she desperately tried to keep her children from seeing their dead father. Kinniburgh attempted to help, rolling the body over and trying to administer first aid, but Gangitano had already bled to death.

Kinniburgh must have known the big man was already gone. Did he go through the masquerade of trying to revive him to strengthen his alibi, or was it to ensure there was a logical reason for his DNA to be found on the body?

Those who knew the Munster say he placed himself back at the crime scene because he would not want the dead man's family to have to deal with the horrendous scene alone.

Police believe Moran and Gangitano argued, then Jason pulled a gun and shot his best friend three times. They think Kinniburgh was shocked, ran to the closed front security door and tried to burst through, cutting his hand on the strong mesh.

But the Munster didn't become a great underworld survivor by panicking. Even though he was in a mess not of his making, he coolly weighed up what to do. Police deduced that he immediately slipped upstairs to check the security video system, which would explain why blood matching his was found on the upstairs banister.

Gangitano was slack when it came to his security system. He sporadically used it when he was out to see if police had broken in to fit listening devices or telephone taps. He would leave one tape in the machine and re-record over it. But when police checked, the machine was off and the tape was gone and was nowhere in the house. They believe the Munster grabbed the evidence before he left.

RUSSELL Warren Smith was a dangerous man until the drugs beat him. In 1988, when he was more than half way through a ten-year term for killing a man, he noticed a tough youngster who turned up in Geelong jail.

The new kid was Jason Moran, born into a crime family and brought up with gangsters. When gunman Brian Kane was shot in the bar of a Brunswick hotel in 1982, the teenage Jason placed a respectful death notice in the paper to his 'Uncle Brian' from 'Your Little Mate'.

In prison, there are few loners. You team up with a gang, known as a crew, or you can be picked off.

'When Jason came into the jail he joined up with the crew I was running with,' Smith would later tell police.

'I found him to be a good bloke, but he was wild. He was always big-noting himself and I remember his big line, "Do you know who the f... I am?"

Jason was only a young kid and nobody in jail had heard of him (but he) could look after himself. Jail is a very violent place and Jason had to fight to protect himself.

Jason would always be threatening people, it was his nature.'

They lost contact when they left jail, but six years later they met again, through mutual friend Lou Cozzo, son of Melbourne furniture identity Frank.

In 1995, the three had been drinking in the Depot Hotel in Richmond. Cozzo and Smith were on day leave from the Odyssey House drug clinic and were not worried that a bellyful of beer would be a problem on their return — 'we always found it easy to get through the tests they would give'.

It was just after 11pm on a Saturday when Moran generously offered to drive them back to the clinic to beat the midnight curfew.

Like his long-time associate, Gangitano, Moran was a hothead who would act first and think later. Consequences were for others to worry about.

Another driver cut in front of Moran without using his indicator. The lights turned red and so did Moran. At one of Melbourne's busiest and best-lit intersections, the corner of Bridge and Punt Road, Moran grabbed a wheel brace, smashed the other motorist's windscreen, dragged him from the car and beat him severely. No one stopped to help.

Jason got back in the car and was laughing,' Smith said later.

'Lou and Jason were part of the Lygon Street crew and that is where I met Alphonse Gangitano. Alphonse would have been the leader of this crowd, some people called him the Lygon Street Godfather. All that crowd wanted to be known as gangsters. They all cultivated tough reputations. I don't know why they did this. It was just in their nature.' Smith said that Gangitano 'always seemed to keep his family separate from the Lygon Street crowd.'

On 16 January 1998, Smith was drinking at a hotel in Campbellfield and watching the lunchtime strip show when he saw Moran. The two talked and smoked some marijuana.

They went back to Smith's Preston flat to smoke some more. Moran promised to return that night to pay $500 for a marijuana debt.

He returned at 9.45pm. They smoked, talked and then Moran suggested a drive. Moran threw him the keys of his late-model green Commodore sedan.

Moran was no longer the new kid on the block and Smith was no longer the more experienced man. The pecking order had changed. When Moran suggested something, it was done.

The car had a no-smoking sticker on the glove box. Smith believed it was a hire car.

'I didn't know where we were going and I didn't ask.'

It was about 10pm when they left Preston and Moran told Smith where to drive — Jason was talking and seemed calm.'

They pulled up in Templestowe. One of the first things Smith the career criminal noticed was that 'most of the houses had alarms or sensor lights on them'.

Moran opened the passenger door and said, 'You can't come in. Just wait here and I'll be back in five or 10 minutes.'

But Moran didn't walk in to the double-storey house next to where they had parked but behind the car and down the street. Smith knew too much curiosity could be fatal, so he 'lost interest'.

After about fifteen minutes, Moran jumped back into the car and told Smith to drive. They went to a 24-hour McDonald's drive-through in South Melbourne.

Moran told him to drive to Williamstown. As they crossed the Westgate Bridge in the left-hand lane Moran picked up the McDonald's bag and threw it out the passenger window. Smith saw it clear the railing and fall towards the water far below. It was only later, he said, that he wondered how a paper bag didn't flutter behind a car travelling at more than 80kmh and instead went almost straight over the railing.

And it was only much later that he thought that Moran may have slipped his gun into the bag and thrown it into the river. Or so he was to say.

'I knew Jason always carried a gun. I don't know why he carried them, but he seemed to like guns.'

More than three months later, police divers spent a week trying to find the gun. Police threw paper bags with weights about the size of a .32 handgun off the bridge.

Detectives offered a bottle of malt whisky to the diver who could find the murder weapon. But tidal currents and the Yarra's permanent silt made it impossible.

A well-known underworld gun dealer lives in the Williamstown area. Police believe Moran made the trip to pick up a new gun after he threw the one used to kill Gangitano into the river.

Next morning, Smith was woken by radio reports that a 'gangland figure' had been murdered in Templestowe. 'I started to get nervous. I didn't know if Jason had anything to do with it but I started to think he may have.' When he found out the victim was Gangitano he become increasingly worried. 'To say I was shocked was an understatement.'

Two days later, Moran turned up at Smith's flat at 7am. Despite the hour they shared a bong and, according to Smith, Moran said, 'Alphonse has been put off ... don't talk to any of the crew, especially Lou (Cozzo) and don't tell anyone you were driving me the other night.'

A few days later Cozzo rang and asked him if he knew anything about the murder and asked 'if Jason was involved'.

Police arrested Smith for stealing cars more than three months after Gangitano's murder.

He then decided to tell them what he knew because he wanted a fresh start and was 'sick of always looking over my shoulder for Jason Moran'.

His evidence may well have been compelling in any future murder trial but Smith committed suicide by hanging himself in jail — eight months to the day after Gangitano's death.

WITHIN 48 hours of the murder, a freshly-showered Moran arrived with his long-time lawyer, Andrew Fraser, to be interviewed by homicide squad detectives in their St Kilda Road office.

Some might expect a murder victim's friend to be visibly upset and keen to help detectives. But Moran feigned indifference and refused to answer questions.

Kinniburgh was also interviewed and while he also refused to answer questions the old head was unfailingly polite. When police said they were about to get a warrant to search his house, he quietly pointed out that his money and house keys had been seized by police at the scene. If there was gunshot residue on the money then it may have come from contamination from the crime scene and if there was any evidence of a crime at his house then it could have been planted.

He was clever, but not clever enough to avoid a bullet.

More than two years after Gangitano's murder, Jason's half-brother, Mark Moran, was murdered in the driveway of his luxury home near Essendon. Police say Carl Williams was the shooter but the charges against him were dropped when he agreed to plead guilty to three other hits. Mark Moran was a victim but no innocent one.

Some in the underworld believe that Jason was not the only Moran in Gangitano's home that night. They say Kinniburgh tried to organise a peace meeting between the Morans and Gangitano, assuring Big Al there would be no weapons.

The theory goes that one of the Morans produced a gun and killed Gangitano in an ambush that shocked Kinniburgh — hence his reaction to the murder.

There were two witnesses who were in the street that night having an argument in a car. One saw a man walk down the road into Gangitano's house and leave a short time later. The description fitted Jason, but the witness insisted he had tattoos and Jason didn't. The witnesses identified a ute in the street — a car similar to the one driven by Mark, who did have impressive tattoos.

Jason Moran was eventually sentenced to jail for the King Street brawl where Gangitano was a co-accused. In September

2001, Moran was granted parole and released from prison. In an unusual move, the National Parole Board allowed him to leave Australia with his family because of fears for his life. But he was too stubborn and arrogant to stay away. Despite advice from his own family he returned to Melbourne on 20 November.

On 21 June 2003, he was shot dead with his friend, Pasquale Barbaro, while they watched an Auskick junior football session in Essendon North.

On 13 December 2003, the man who wanted a low profile, Graham Kinniburgh, made headlines when he was murdered outside his Kew home.

Criminal lawyer Andrew Fraser knew many secrets. His clients believed they could tell him anything and their conversations would remain confidential.

A ready talker himself, Fraser knew the value of silence. His first advice to his many clients was that if questioned by police, refuse to talk. He would tell them to provide their name, age and address, but to respond to every further question with a standard 'no comment'.

Private school-educated, Fraser prided himself on his ability to talk to his clients using the language of the underworld.

In September 1988, his private language became public knowledge when a conversation with a murder suspect was recorded in a city watch-house cell.

He was representing Anthony Farrell, one of four men charged with, and ultimately acquitted of, the Walsh Street ambush murders of young police constables Steven Tynan and Damian Eyre.

Fraser said to Farrell: 'All you've got to do is fucking keep your trap shut. So say fucking nothing. And don't consent to anything.

'So just keep your trap shut, mate. This is the rest of your life here, because, don't worry, if you go down on this you're going to get a fucking monster, and we all know that, right?'

Fraser's tough-guy talk and his 24-hour-a-day availability made him popular with some of Victoria's best-known crime families. Drug dealer and killer Dennis Allen always used Fraser and the Moran family swore by him.

But by the late 1990s Fraser was battling his own drug demons. He ignored his own advice to keep silent and by 1999 he was reduced to cocaine-fuelled rambles in his city office. In December 2001, Fraser was sentenced to a minimum of five years' jail for his part in a cocaine smuggling scheme.

A key piece of evidence was a conversation secretly recorded in his office by police on 16 August 1999, when he discussed with his usual supplier a plot to import cocaine valued at almost $3 million. But five days earlier, drug squad police from Operation Regent recorded another fascinating conversation.

Fraser told a colleague that one of his clients, Jason Moran, was 'crazy'.

The colleague asked the lawyer entrusted with many of the criminal secrets of Melbourne, who had killed Gangitano.

Fraser responded with one word: Jason.'

THE fact and fantasies of Gangitano's life and death will never be separated.

He gave the impression of wealth, but he had serious debts; he appeared unworried by constant police investigations and court appearances, yet his autopsy showed traces of the prescribed anti-anxiety drug — Diazapam.

He owed his lawyer George Defteros $100,000 and had about $2000 in a bank account. He was a paper millionaire, with assets valued at just over $1.1 million, but with debts of more than $300,000. Most of his wealth was in his late parents' property in Lygon Street that he and his sister had inherited. Most crooks use dirty money to invest in legitimate business. He used good money to try and build a crime empire.

There were more than 200 death notices for Gangitano. As has become an underworld tradition, hundreds packed St Mary's Star of the Sea church for the funeral. It made the headlines and led the television news. He would have liked that.

Gangitano referred to himself as a property developer, although the occupation listed in his will was 'gentleman'.

But the myth did not die with his murder and he proved to be more famous dead than alive.

The theatre continued at his inquest, four years later. Deputy Coroner Iain West heard that a musician had composed a song to Gangitano and the crime boss wanted Hollywood star Andy Garcia to play his role in a proposed movie. He would have been chuffed with the choice of local star Vince Colosimo in Channel Nine's $10 million series *Underbelly*.

Kinniburgh and Moran attended the inquest but both chose not to give evidence on the grounds of self-incrimination. Kinniburgh wore casual clothes befitting a man who didn't want to be noticed. Moran wore an expensive pinstripe suit and a flash diamond ring.

Observers noticed a large scar running down the side of his head, legacy of having his skull broken by police when he was arrested a few years earlier — an action which the trial judge said was 'remarkably heavy handed.'

Coroner West found that both Kinniburgh and Moran were in Gangitano's house and 'implicated in the death' but he did not have sufficient evidence to conclude who fired the gun.

Now Kinniburgh and Moran are also dead. The case is closed — dead men tell no tales.

THE MOURNING AFTER

'I hope a war doesn't go
on over this.'

OUTSIDE, the Mercedes and BMW coupes circle in the afternoon sun like sharks, cruising for parking spots among shoals of lesser vehicles jamming the usually quiet streets in West Melbourne. They're late models in dark colours, mostly black or midnight blue, and run to sharp personal number plates and mobile phone aerials tilted rakishly, like dorsal fins on sharks.

The whiff of menace and money — fat rolls of cash — wafts from the drivers, their hard faces blank as they join the silent crowd at the church door next to a big, black Cadillac hearse parked near a pile of wreaths banked against the bluestone wall.

Not everyone here is a big shot and many mourners are clearly not from Melbourne's underworld, but they dress the part. There's a generic quality about the gathering that strikes a watcher. There are men old enough to be grandfathers who move confidently through the crowd, escorted by leggy young blonde women who are not their grand-daughters.

116

There are young men, with their hair cropped short, tied back in tight pony-tails or slicked back, hard and shiny. They mostly wear dark suits, gold jewellery, lightweight slip-on shoes and sunglasses. Many are heavily muscled, with the bulk that comes from weight-lifting, and perhaps steroids. They tend to favour permanent scowls, and would look at home on nightclub doors, as some no doubt do. If they don't smoke, they chew gum. The clever ones manage to do both at once.

One hardboiled character dragging on a borrowed Winfield has on the compulsory dark suit, but with fawn slip-on suede loafers. He wears no socks, but it doesn't matter much. His ankles are tattooed almost solid blue and green.

Across the street, marooned on a traffic island, the cameras of the media contingent are trained on the crowd. Those who hold the equipment keep their distance, perhaps remembering the ugly scenes at the funeral of Robert 'Aussie Bob' Trimbole in Sydney in the 1980s, when angry mourners attacked cameramen and journalists.

This is the scene at St Mary's Star of the Sea Catholic church around 1.15pm on Friday 23 January 1998, as the minutes crawl towards the start of a funeral service for a man who died a week earlier the way he had lived: violently and fast.

His name is, or was, Alphonse John Gangitano, one of the few criminals in Australian history to be known — even by people he'd never met — simply by his first name. Like Squizzy. Like Chopper. Like Neddy. And, later, like Tony and Carl.

Alphonse, also known as Al, was shot several times at his Templestowe home by an assassin officially unknown, though his identity is no secret, who must have been well known to his victim.

An assassin trusted enough, it would appear, that he was let into the house unchallenged before he produced a weapon and squeezed the trigger at close range.

Some details of the shooting are a mystery. So is the question of how a boastful schoolyard bully, who left school with nothing more useful than a bad reputation, managed to support himself and his family in relative comfort most of his adult life.

Gangitano often claimed he was a 'property developer', but that was probably just another example of the mischievous sense of humour his friends and supporters claim for him, exemplified by the fulsome praise heaped on him by one of his more unusual friends, bail justice, Rowena Allsop, who addressed the packed church at the funeral.

Allsop, who was criticised for her close association with Gangitano, was asked to speak by the dead man's family.

She delivered a ringing tribute in which she compared his wit with Oscar Wilde's, gushed about his silk ties, cashmere overcoats and 'the lingering scent' of his Dolce & Gabbana aftershave, and noted his consuming interest in John F. Kennedy and Napoleon.

She said her friend had been 'like a king commanding a court, with his friends laughing at his old jokes'. She said she was touched by him turning up at Melbourne's Royal Children's Hospital last Christmas with a bag of toys for the children in the cancer ward.

Others, however, detected a darker side to Gangitano's gregarious character.

He might well have developed properties, they say. And no doubt he sometimes arranged for holes to be dug — but not always to pour foundations.

If the man in the coffin wasn't a gangster, he acted like one. And he was certainly buried like one.

A fitting exit, some might say, for the Black Prince of Lygon Street.

MELBOURNE is Australia's Chicago, but with a touch of London's old East End 'manor' tradition about it. A tradition of almost feudal loyalty to local 'crime lords' going back to the solidarity of the old working class inner suburbs in John Wren's and Squizzy Taylor's day.

Unlike the criminal subculture in other cities, Melbourne's underworld has a tradition of big occasion funerals, preceded by an avalanche of newspaper death notices. Many of these are effusive and ostentatiously long, implying that money is no object. Some are 'crocodile tears'.

A few are downright tongue-in-cheek, and contain coded jokes and messages. Police searching for clues to gangland slayings are known to comb the death notices carefully. Indeed, some are rumoured to write the occasional contribution themselves.

Gangitano wasn't the only one with a mischievous sense of humour. One notice read: 'The impression you left on me will stay eternally in my heart. Jim Pinarkos.' Pinarkos's headless body was found at Rye beach in July 1989. He died from an arrow through his heart. The murder was never solved.

Whatever the reasons, Gangitano's farewell was one of the biggest underworld funerals in Melbourne since the murder of master bank robber Raymond (Chuck) Bennett in the magistrate's court in 1979 and of Bennett's arch enemy, the notorious gunman Brian Kane, in a Brunswick hotel some time later.

The ritual ran over a week, starting with 22 death notices for Gangitano in the underworld's favourite newspaper, the *Herald Sun*, on the Monday after the murder.

The number of notices more than doubled to 48 on Tuesday, led by a joint tribute from Gangitano's widow and their daughters, and his sister, Nuccia, and including several from prominent underworld figures.

It peaked on Wednesday, with 68 notices, including one from Charlie Wootton, a reclusive but well-known and much-respected gaming identity whose past links him with the blood-spattered history of the painters and dockers union.

It's a well-worn legend that as a teenager in the 1950s, Wootton reputedly disposed of the empty shotgun shells left when an 'unknown' gunman shot Freddy 'The Frog' Harrison on the wharves.

Dozens of men saw 'The Frog' get croaked, the legend goes, but it was never officially solved. Like the others, young Charlie Wootton developed amnesia, a condition that still affects police investigations.

While some of Wootton's peers were dragged back into the spotlight during the underworld war he wisely remained in the background. Wootton survived — many didn't.

In the seven days before the burial the 209 death notices for Gangitano were a bonanza for Rupert Murdoch's classified advertising coffers — and a measure of the generous underworld protocol that makes a hero of a man dismissed by some as a thug who didn't have the brains to be a 'Mr Big'.

Criminal groupies who hardly knew the dead man put notices in the paper as though they were great friends. But columns of newsprint aren't the only measure of Gangitano's posthumous popularity. At least 800 people, and possibly 1000, turned up to the funeral, filling the church and spilling outside.

So why the big deal?

One reason could be that Gangitano was, in his own way, a 'crossover' criminal. He was from a respectable Italian family — not one, according to police sources, that automatically connected him with organised crime from birth, as with some inbred Calabrian and Sicilian peasant clans for whom kidnapping, extortion and violence are facts of life in the old country.

Gangitano went to school with other middle-class boys, and could just as easily have become a lawyer or an accountant if he'd studied, which he didn't. Schoolmates recall that he was always aggressive but that his father was outraged when he secretly tattooed his arms and forced him to have skin grafts to remove them.

When forced to leave Marcellin College, he did his last year of school at Taylors' College. Classmates there remember that even then, he was lazy, manipulative, on the make and constantly accompanied by the first member of what was to become his gang.

The picture that emerges is of an egotistical young bully whose nature made him gravitate towards a life of crime. His charm and his looks attracted attention. So did his vanity and appetite for extreme violence, especially when the odds were in his favour.

But whereas more traditional Italian organised crime figures kept largely to their own, the more urbane Gangitano slipped easily between the Calabrian and Sicilian crime syndicates, other ethnic crime groups, and mainstream Australian criminals connected with the painters and dockers union. In the end, this willingness to deal with all comers might have been what got him killed.

A former associate from the boxing world — who did not attend the funeral because of a violent disagreement many years ago — recalls being present when Gangitano spoke at length to the notorious Sydney standover man Tom Domican, with whom he evidently had a warm relationship.

Others describe Gangitano's links with one of Perth's heaviest criminals, the convicted heroin trafficker John Kizon, who has been named in connection with the late Laurie Connell, millionaire race-fixer and the most ruthless of the 'WA Inc' corporate robber barons.

Domican and Kizon were reportedly among several interstate criminals who flew to Melbourne to attend Gangitano's funeral. They were joined, rumour has it, by an Asian contact who counted Gangitano a close-enough friend to travel to Australia for the service.

In his private life, Gangitano was unlike the strictly-controlled members of the traditional Italian groups, where marriages are often arranged, often between distant relatives from the same region in Italy. He did not marry, but lived with his de facto wife, a private school girl who was not Italian. Her sister, a handsome and distinguished-looking woman, added a touch of class to the funeral proceedings by giving one of the readings during the service. And the sisters are school friends of a woman whose brother became a State Attorney General.

But, for all his wide-ranging contacts, Gangitano was best-known and — at least on the surface — most admired in Melbourne's little Italy, Lygon Street.

All of which has a bearing on the huge turn-up at his funeral. St Mary's Star of the Sea in West Melbourne, close to the Victoria Market, is the church of choice for Melbourne's mafia.

It was a case of history repeating itself. Hairstyles, hemlines and cars change, but among the older people in the congregation were some who have attended more than one big mafia funeral there.

When one of Victoria's earliest godfathers, Domenico 'the Pope' Italiano, died in 1962 he was buried from St Mary's. So were Vincenzo Muratore and Vincenzo Agillette, killed little more than a year later in the power struggle caused by Italiano's death.

They were all given elaborate funerals, early proof of the potency and loyalty of the Italian organised crime groups that had taken control of Melbourne's fruit and vegetable markets.

But none was more elaborate than Gangitano's. From the taped music to the singing of *Ave Maria* by his friend, Simon Pantano, it was a lavish production from start to end.

Of course, not everyone present was in mourning. Apart from a core of family and close friends, the crowd comprised mostly those who felt obliged to be there, and hangers-on attracted by the publicity.

One reason for the big crowd, joked a well-known criminal lawyer afterwards, was the number of undercover police there to execute outstanding warrants on elusive criminals drawn from cover for the occasion. Another, he said, was the number of lawyers trying to collect overdue fees for court appearances for some of the colourful identities in the congregation.

A former detective, who first ran against the young Gangitano in nightclubs in the early 1980s, and was respected by him, injects a sombre note.

'I hope a war doesn't go on over this, because the biggest losers are their kids,' he says. 'I have seen the toughest men, but all their lives consist of are a series of battles with the law and with their criminal counterparts. No kid deserves to have their father taken away like this.

'But it's happened to Alphonse's kids, and now there's probably someone out there scheming to kill some other kids' father.'

He couldn't have known how right he would be.

7

MAD, BAD, THEN SAD

One shot missed, but Charlie
had nowhere to run. He was shot
four times in the head.

'MAD' Charlie Hegyalji was always security conscious — those in the illegal amphetamine industry usually are.

He filled books with the registration numbers of the vehicles he believed might be following him, was always discreet on the telephone and chose a house that he believed offered him the greatest protection.

His comfortable brick home in Caulfield South was shielded from the traffic noise of busy Bambra Road by ten mature cypress trees forming a six-metre high hedge so thick it has been cut back to allow pedestrians access to the footpath.

The tall horizontal plank timber fence acted as another buffer to noise and, more importantly for Hegyalji, as a screen to stop possible police surveillance.

Near the front door a small white surveillance camera was trained down the six-metre garden path. From inside the house anyone entering or leaving the property could be safely observed on a video screen.

'Mad' Charlie lived in the house relatively secure in the knowledge he had done all he could to protect himself and his business from the untimely interruption of police or possible competitors. But, in the end, it wasn't enough.

Charlie was killed by a lone gunman who used the criminal's own security fetish against him. The killer crouched under the first tree inside the fence line, confident he could not be seen from the street, and waited until Hegyalji came home.

It was just before 1am on 23 November 1998, and it had been a long night for Charlie. A business associate had picked him up about 6pm and they visited the London Tavern, in Caulfield, the Grosvenor Hotel, in Balaclava and the Newmarket Hotel, in St Kilda. They met up with two other men for their night of drinking.

To an outsider it would seem like an old fashioned pub-crawl, but people like Hegyalji are always on the move, conducting business in pubs and clubs, avoiding set routines that would make him easy to track.

He drank beer and brandy and cokes with his friends. But he wasn't happy with just a night on the grog.

At one point he disappeared with a man and when he returned, his friends thought drugs affected him. They were right. An autopsy would later show he had used cannabis and amphetamines.

While in one of the hotels, he made a call from a pay phone. Police traced the number and found he had rung Dino Dibra, a violent drug dealing try-hard listed by police as a suspected hit man.

As with most of the underworld hits, those who were likely to have important information refused to talk and Dibra would not share with police the contents of the phone call.

Detectives put Dibra on a shortlist of suspects, but it is now a moot point because Dibra himself was murdered in 2000.

Another suspect is a former policeman turned gangster well known in the area and well known to Charlie. The ex-detective can best be described as colourful, particularly in relation to his eclectic sex life.

Charlie and one of the men went back to a unit off Inkerman Street, St Kilda, just after midnight. He called a Yellow Cab from his friend's unit to take the short trip home around 12.40am.

When the driver rang the doorbell, Charlie got up to go, leaving half a stubby of beer.

Instead of being dropped off outside his house, he ordered the taxi to stop about a block away from home. It was another security habit he had developed. The theory was that if someone were waiting for him, he could sneak up unheard. It was 12.50am.

Hegyalji opened the wooden gate and took two steps along the stone path inside when the killer, armed with a handgun, opened fire. One shot missed, but Charlie had nowhere to run. He was shot four times in the head.

A bullet wound was also found on his left hand — a defensive wound that was sustained as he tried to protect his head from the gunfire.

Neighbours heard the shots and called police, but Charlie's obsession with privacy, in the form of the hedge and the fence, concealed his body from the police torches. The patrol car drove off.

Not that it made any difference. He had died instantly and the killer was gone in seconds, running past nearby Freeman Street. About seven hours later, Hegyalji's de facto wife, Ellie, was about to prepare breakfast for their two children when she glanced up at the security camera screen focused on the front path and saw his body.

The security camera remained operational and should have provided the biggest clue in the case. But, for all his security precautions, Charlie had grown lazy — there was no tape in it. The sensor light at the front of the house had also stopped working and Charlie had not bothered to get it fixed.

It is almost certain the killer knew he would not be filmed or illuminated. The odds are he had been a guest in the house or had been told by someone who had.

Either way, it was an inside job.

WHEN Hegyalji, then aged thirteen, arrived at Station Pier as a European refugee he asked his mother in Hungarian: 'Where is the Statue of Liberty?' He eventually got over his disappointment at not being in New York, but never forgot the gangster dreams of his adolescence.

According to his long-time friend and underworld associate, Mark Brandon Read, Charlie always wanted to be a mobster. 'All he ever wanted to be was an American gangster in New York. Through his fantasies he ended up becoming everything he wanted to be, except it was in the wrong country,' Read said.

According to Read, Hegyalji once flew to New York and waited outside an old nightclub reputed to be a meeting place for members of the Gambino crime family. 'He stood in the snow for a week before he finally was able to say hello to Carlo Gambino. He pinched Charlie's cheek and said hello back. It was the best moment of his life.'

But he was to become more than just a tourist in the crime world. Hegyalji became a violent young standover man involved in rapes and robberies on massage parlours.

In the 1970s he began to call himself 'The Don' and modelled himself on the image of the US crime figures he revered. But by the 1980s he found there was more money to be made by being involved in the amphetamine trade than robbing fellow criminals.

In the 1980s a bright chemistry student, Paul Lester, quit university once he knew enough to produce the best amphetamines in Australia. He was a sought-after 'speed' cook more interested in tinkering with electronics as a hobby than making money from illegal drugs.

But Charlie was the sort who wouldn't take 'no' for an answer. He abducted Lester at gunpoint from a Rosebud street, and then drove him, blindfolded, to a Gippsland property where he forced him to produce amphetamines.

In another cook in Carlton, the process didn't work according to plan and Hegyalji poured the sludgy, volatile substance out on a tarpaulin, allowing the sun to evaporate the liquid and leaving the amphetamine powder. 'He called it "sun-dried speed",' Read said. In fashionable inner-suburban Carlton, it went with sun-dried tomatoes.

Police who dealt with Hegyalji said he was funny and, when it suited him, charming. 'He was always jovial but he was always trying to run you. He would ask more questions than he answered,' one said.

According to one detective, he bought a book on police informing from the US in the hope he would be able to keep the upper hand when being interviewed. 'He was prepared to inform, but only out of self-interest. He would give information to expose his enemies and to keep himself out of jail.'

There was no sign of him ever working and he saw no pressing need to collect unemployment benefits.

But if his quick wit failed, he had alternatives. When police raided a Narre Warren farmhouse in 1995 as part of an amphetamines investigation, they found a hidden armoury behind a false bedroom wall.

Inside they found almost twenty pistols, machine guns and shotguns, six cans of mace, false drivers' licences and silencers. They also found a computer printout from a national security firm that listed alarm systems used throughout Melbourne. A pink highlighter had been used to identify the systems used in police stations.

Hegyalji's fingerprints were found on the list.

Read said Hegyalji was called 'Mad' Charlie after he bit off the nose of an enemy when he was still a teenager, but when another criminal was given the nickname 'Machinegun Charlie' he became jealous and tried to persuade people to give him a more glamorous title.

'But to everyone he was still Mad Charlie,' Read said.

In the 1990s he was a semi-regular at the specialist Prahran bookstore Kill City, where he would pull copies of Read's books from the shelf and demand to know from the owner if the author had made 'a million dollars'. All the time one of Charlie's minders, a giant of a man, would stand in the doorway of the shop, silently watching his increasingly-eccentric boss make a nuisance of himself.

He once stood in a bar next to some of the biggest names in Australian television, poured a white powder on the bar, either cocaine or amphetamines, and snorted it.

'He just stuck his nose in it, then punched himself in the chest and started to shadow box. We decided it was time to leave,' one prominent television and radio identity said later.

He made a lot of money at times, but there was no gain without pain.

In 1989 Hegyalji was shot in the stomach outside a house in South Caulfield and he later shot a man in a St Kilda hotel carpark as a payback.

In 1997 he was involved in a gun battle with another criminal associate outside a panel beater's workshop in Prahran. Both men were unhurt.

Hegyalji was charged with attempted murder and kept in custody for just over a year until he was released in July 1998. The charges were dropped because, as in so many cases involving the underworld, witnesses refused to testify.

Charlie went back to his old patch of St Kilda and Caulfield, expecting business to return to normal but, according to police, others had filled his place. The people who had been left to run his business were not keen to relinquish control.

He had to flex his muscles and, when he was drinking, loved to wave his handgun around in hotels, playing up to his gangster image. But Hegyalji was forced to stop carrying his revolver with him at all times because, inconveniently, he was increasingly being stopped and searched by police.

In the drug business it can be as dangerous to be owed money as to be in debt.

Charlie was owed more than $100,000 when he was killed but the debt lapsed with his death. It is not a financial arrangement that can be listed on Probate documents.

Detective Senior Sergeant Rowland Legg, prone to the sort of understatement that comes from years of dealing with underworld murders, said: 'There was a little bit of business friction and there had been some ongoing discussions over the debt.'

In the world 'Mad' Charlie inhabited all his adult life, business deals were never committed to paper and some contracts could only be enforced with a gun.

Police do not like to use the term 'professional hit', believing it adds glamour to a gutter business, but Legg concedes: 'That someone was hired to kill him remains a possibility.'

Six days before his murder Hegyalji rang Read to wish the former standover man a happy birthday. 'I asked him how he got my number (it is unlisted) and he said, "You know me, Chopper. I've got everybody's number." '

What Charlie didn't know was that his own number was about to come up. He told Read he had a small problem with a mutual friend, but he said it was nothing he couldn't handle.

'He seemed anxious and I knew he had some sort of problem,' Read said.

Soon after Charlie's murder, Read found his then wife was expecting their first child. It was a son. He named him Charlie in honour of his murdered mate.

8

THE ITALIAN JOBS

Gerry may not have known until
the last second that his life
was about to end but someone
close to him did.

VINCENZO Mannella was nearly everyone's friend — he was outgoing, generous and funny — but some time during his life of wheeling and dealing, he managed to make at least one serious enemy. And Mannella moved on the fringes of a world in which it doesn't pay to rub the wrong people the wrong way.

His last night on earth started as a pleasant summer evening. It was 9 January 1999, with the sort of balmy weather that encourages socialising, and Vince didn't need many excuses to be out on the town.

He spent the evening with three friends in a coffee shop in Lygon Street, Carlton, and, later, at a restaurant in Sydney Road. Then, though it was almost midnight, the group decided to kick on to a wine bar in Nicholson Street.

Mannella, 48, and married with two children, drove his blue Ford Fairlane sedan back to his weatherboard house in Alister Street, North Fitzroy, from where he was to be picked up by one of the friends to go on to Elio's Wine Bar. He parked the car in the front driveway next to his wife's BMW and walked towards the front door. The sensor lit the front landing and a security camera pointed from the roof, but this would prove to be no help, as the camera had never been connected.

He carried a plastic bag filled with leather belts he had just bought, a packet of Peter Jackson cigarettes and his car keys. It was 11.45pm.

A gunman, who either waited outside the house or followed Mannella's car, walked up behind him and shot him repeatedly with a handgun.

Mannella fell forward, his head resting on the welcome mat at the front landing.

As with so many of the Melbourne hits, police found that Mannella's killer had carefully planned his escape route before doing the deed.

Police are confident that the killer ran about 800 metres along nearby Merri Creek and then up Albert Street to an agreed pick-up point. He obviously did not want any potential witnesses to connect his distinctive getaway car with the sound of gunshots.

MANNELLA was the sort of criminal who was big enough to make a good living, but small enough to avoid constant police attention.

Detectives who investigate organised crime knew of him, more because he associated with some of the biggest names in the underworld than as a result of his own activities.

According to police, he was an associate of crime figure Alphonse Gangitano, shot in his Templestowe house almost a year before. He also came to attention as a possible source of amphetamine chemicals during the drug squad operation, code-named Phalanx, into Australia's speed king, John William Higgs.

When Gangitano opened an up-market illegal casino above a restaurant in Carlton in 1987 he invited many of Melbourne's major crime figures for the launch. When police raided the place at 1.30am they found Mannella, Higgs and another major amphetamines dealer in the crowd. When asked by police why he was there Mannella said 'I come here to eat' while Higgs said he was, 'Having a feed'.

Police say Mannella was a middle-level crime entrepreneur who was always looking to turn a profit, and wasn't too bothered what product he had to move — or steal — in order to make one.

In late 1998, he became involved in a gang that specialised in stealing huge quantities of foodstuff. Police believe the gang hit two regional targets and Mannella was the man with the contacts to sell the produce.

Detectives have found he was a heavy gambler, and had owned or part-owned nightclubs and coffee shops.

While he was well-liked in his own circle and, for a man who didn't work or receive unemployment benefits, extremely generous, there was an element of violence in his nature.

He was arrested when he was 21 for carrying a dagger in his pocket and six years later was found carrying two pistols.

In 1981 he displayed a savage temper. It happened when the owner of a small coffee shop in Nicholson Street, North Fitzroy, told Mannella that he was no longer welcome to play cards there because he was 'acting tough, carried a loaded pistol and drove a Mercedes even though he didn't work'.

Mannella drove to the coffee shop on 20 February 1981, and three times called the owner outside to try and persuade him to change his mind. But the man wouldn't budge. Mannella then pulled out a pistol and, from a distance of less than a metre, opened fire. The wounded man ran down Nicholson Street while Mannella shot him a total of seven times. Miraculously, he survived, having told hospital staff in Italian that if they didn't save his life he would come back and haunt them.

Mannella was later sentenced to nine years, with a minimum of seven, over the shooting. Like 'Mad' Charlie Hegyalji, Mannella went back to what he knew when he was released from prison and, like Charlie, he was owed a six-figure amount when he was murdered.

One of the difficulties police face in an investigation into the murder of a man like Mannella is that 'friends' can be enemies and that business deals are never documented.

Arrangements are confirmed with a nod, plans are hatched in the back rooms of coffee shops and interested partners tell no-one of their schemes for fear they will be leaked to the police — or, worse, competing criminals.

Mannella was definitely owed money and may have, in turn, owed others big amounts. For a man who drifted in and out of the lives of some of Australia's most dangerous criminals, either situation could have cost him his life.

He was heavily connected with a team who had just stolen more than $400,000 worth of food, including imported cheese. He was known to be a major broker in the lucrative black market tobacco — or chop-chop business — and in that business smoking can be deadly.

'We are exploring possible motives including his criminal associations and debt matters, but nothing has been discounted,' says veteran homicide investigator Rowland Legg.

Mannella had $500 in his pocket when he was murdered. The killer didn't bother to take it. He would be paid much more by the person who ordered the hit.

VINCE Mannella's brother Gerardo would have known in the last few seconds of life the answers to questions homicide squad detectives are still trying to solve.

As he left the house of his brother, Sal, in inner-suburban Melbourne on 20 October 1999, Gerardo saw two men walking out of a lane fifteen metres away. Police say he immediately yelled 'No' and ran, dropping a power tool and mobile phone he was carrying. It was likely Mannella recognised the men or saw the guns and knew they had come to kill him.

He ran from the footpath out to the middle of the road, but they caught him, shooting him repeatedly in the head.

Mannella, 31, had been to work as a crane supervisor at the City Square project and to a union meeting before going to his brother's home in the middle of the afternoon. He had not been in trouble with the police for years and his last problem had been for carrying a pistol seven years earlier.

Police don't know if he was followed to the house or the killers had been tipped off, but they were waiting when he left to go to his Avondale Heights house about 8pm.

A third man, driving a dark Ford station wagon, picked up the killers moments after the hit.

As in the case of his brother's murder, the killers had done their homework. Mannella, the father of three, gave no indication when he left the house that he thought he was in danger, but one career criminal with a history of providing solid information said Gerardo had repeatedly said he intended to find and kill the men who shot his brother, Vince.

'It is most unwise to speak openly about these matters because if people take you seriously they will be forced to get in first.' Dead men can't hurt anybody.

Gerry may not have known until the last second that his life was about to end — but someone close to him did. The person had known for days — perhaps weeks — that he was about to die but kept silent. She still does.

Armed and dangerous ... action scene from *Underbelly* drama series.

Alphonse Gangitano ... accused killer and later a victim.

Vince Colosimo as Gangitano.

Jason Moran dresses up for the inquest ... it did him no good. He was still blamed for Al's murder.

Les Hill as Moran.

Andrew 'Benji' Veniamin: prime suspect in seven gangland murders before he was shot dead.

A blood-spattered Damian Walshe-Howling as Veniamin.

Mick Gatto invited 'Benji' to a Carlton restaurant and left Veniamin dead on the floor ... he claims self-defence.

Simon Westaway as Gatto.

Tony Mokbel: the drug-baron before he jumped bail.

Robert Mammone as Mokbel.

Judy Moran: lost two husbands and two sons to the gun.

Caroline Gilmer as the Moran matriarch.

Lewis Moran is greeted after being bailed in July, 2003.
Police said he was safer inside ... they were right.

Kevin Harrington as Lewis.

Danielle McGuire: flew overseas to muddy Mokbel's trail.

Robert Mammone's Mokbel with Madeleine West's McGuire.

RISING early was no problem to Joe Quadara — after all, he had been getting up before the sun for as long as he could remember.

Horse trainers, newsagents and people in the fruit and vegetable industry don't bother grumbling about early starts because they are a fact of life. And death, sometimes. Early risers do make tempting targets. For Quadara, his last trip to work would take only a few minutes on the empty streets from his unit in Toorak, one of Melbourne's most expensive suburbs, to the Safeway supermarket in nearby Malvern Road.

After more than 30 years in the fruit and vegetable industry, Quadara had gone from being a millionaire to a bankrupt. He had once owned a string of big fruit shops and was a popular and generous patron of the Collingwood and Frankston Football Clubs, but interest rates and an over-stretched line of credit brought him crashing down.

He had to sell his shops in Frankston and Mornington, his lavish Mt Eliza house and virtually everything he owned to try to pay off his debts, but there were still at least 60 creditors when he closed his doors.

He owed various creditors from $2000 to $50,000, although they would admit he hadn't run away from his debts and had battled to try to make good.

Even though his business reputation may have been in tatters, he was still acknowledged to be a perfectionist in fruit and vegetables, presenting only the best produce and providing the warm personality that makes customers want to come back.

While his customers loved him, some of his suppliers didn't, as he had a habit of sending produce back that didn't reach his exacting standard. And in that cut-throat industry there were some suppliers who would kill for their market share.

By then aged 57, he had become the produce manager at the Toorak supermarket and when it was taken over by Safeway he kept the job. He had worked at the wholesale market and in shops almost all his adult life and was known for his boundless energy and enthusiasm.

But recently he had not been feeling well and had yet another doctor's appointment for later that day. He had already been told he might need surgery for cancer. What he didn't know was that his problems were terminal.

At 3am on 28 May 1999, he drove his green Commodore into the rear car park and stopped behind the Crittenden's liquor shop. Two men, armed with handguns, ambushed him and shot him repeatedly before he could get out of the car. People heard screaming and yelling before the shots. A Safeway truck driver found the body about 90 minutes later.

It was seemingly a murder without motive and police are yet to find the answer to a series of basic questions such as:

- Why would two men execute a seemingly harmless fruiterer in a deserted Toorak car park?
- What was it about Joe Quadara that would drive other men to kill him?
- And why, at his funeral a few days later, did some of Melbourne's most notorious gangsters, including Jason Moran and Graham Kinniburgh, turn up to pay their last respects?
- Why was a stolen car connected to a market identity found burning near the murder scene just minutes after the killing?

Detectives were to find that many years earlier Joe had an affair with a woman who bore him a son. In a bizarre coincidence the woman is related to the Melbourne hit man known as 'The Journeyman' who would be a key figure in Melbourne's underworld war.

Police have now established the two killers were seen in the car park the previous day in a dark-coloured Toyota Camry station wagon. The trouble is, 32,000 cars fit that description.

It is possible the killers believed Quadara had the keys to the safe and that the yelling seconds before he was shot was part of a failed robbery bid.

But Joe Quadara wasn't even the purchasing officer at the supermarket, so he didn't carry company funds or have access to the safe.

Detectives said he was a good fighter when he was younger and had a strong survival sense developed from three decades in an industry with more than its share of seemingly unexplained murders.

'If someone had put the squeeze on him the pressure would have been put on gradually and he wouldn't have been parking in a dark carpark at work,' one detective said. If robbery was not the motive, then the killers were checking the scene the day before as part of their plan to execute Joe Quadara.

Police believe debt is the likely motive for the murder but in the murky world of the markets they cannot be sure.

There is another Joe Quadara, also aged in his mid-50s, also with connections in the fruit and vegetable industry — and with a more colourful past.

This man was named in an inquest as having prior knowledge of the murder of Alfonso Muratore, who was shot dead in 1992. He denied the allegations.

Muratore was the son-in-law of Liborio Benvenuto, the godfather of Melbourne who died in 1988.

Certainly one suspect named as the person who paid for the hit on Joe Quadara was Liborio Benvenuto's son, Frank, who was himself shot dead in remarkably similar circumstances a year later.

Frank Benvenuto had two different gunmen work for him at different times, One was the veteran Victor Peirce and the other was an ambitious youngster named Andrew Veniamin.

Police now believe the paid hit man who shot Quadara was Andrew 'Benji' Veniamin and that it was his first known hit. He is also the man police say killed Frank Benvenuto. He may have been a hard worker but he was not a loyal one.

9

ALAS MAD RICHARD

About two weeks before
Mad Richard was killed
he squared off against another
drug dealer on the make
Carl Williams.

THE Esquire Motel had about 40 rooms and most nights almost all were occupied by people wanting cheap accommodation close to Fitzroy Street in the busy heart of St Kilda.

The fashionable suburb, where millionaires and professionals now rub shoulders with street people, still has a few hangovers of its seedier past — and the Esquire is one of them. The 1970s building in Acland Street has packed a lot of low life into its three decades.

Drifters, backpackers, runaways, prostitutes and drug dealers could all get rooms. Some just stayed the night; others stayed for as long as they could afford the tariff, not having what it takes to look for something more permanent.

Late in 1999 a man moved in to room 18 and made himself at home. He showed no sign of wanting anything better. For him the location was perfect — and at $50 a night the price was right.

And it was positively roomy compared with the prison cell he had vacated only a month earlier. He was a drug dealer and he turned the room into a 24-hour-a-day business address. There was no need to advertise. Word-of-mouth in the street is all a pusher needs.

Local police say that for six months he worked 'red-hot' and built a strong customer base. The dealer had visitors at all times of day and night. One of them was Richard Mladenich, standover man and serial pest. The fact that it was 3.30am, that one man was asleep on the floor, a woman was asleep in a bed and a third person was also in bed, would not have fazed the man, who loved nothing better than an early morning chat.

When the door of room 18 swung open a little later to reveal an armed man, it was one of the few times in his life that Mladenich was caught short for words.

The assassin didn't need to break down the door — underworld murders are seldom that dramatic. The door was unlocked and all he had to do was turn the handle slowly enough not to forewarn the victim. Before he walked in, he yelled the name of the resident drug dealer — almost as a greeting — to show that he was no threat.

By the time Mladenich realised he was in danger, it was too late. When he stood to face the young man in the dark glasses and hood, he saw a small-calibre handgun pointing directly at him.

His experience of more than twenty years of violence would have told him that only luck could save him. It didn't. Before he could speak, the gun barked and the man holding it was gone, leaving Mladenich fighting a losing battle for life.

MLADENICH was a drug dealer, a standover man and a loudmouth. He was also funny, outrageous, a showman and a jailhouse poet with a sense of theatre. When the 37-year-old was hunted down by a hit man that night, on 16 May 2000, detectives had a big problem. It was not to find suspects who wanted him dead, but to eliminate potential enemies from a long list of possibilities.

If the killer had been trailing Mladenich then he did a professional job, as his quarry had visited several other rooms at the Esquire before he reached room 18 just before 3am.

But after an extensive investigation, police believed the killer knew Mladenich's movements because he was close to him. He was either someone who made money in the same business as Mladenich and decided to eliminate him or, more likely, he was working for somebody who wanted him out of the way. In the underworld it is almost always associates, rather than strangers, who finally pull the trigger. The rivals just provide the bullets.

There was more than one reason why Mladenich's days were numbered. As well as being a prolific drug dealer, he had another gig. The big man with the bigger mouth was a minder for drug dealer Mark Moran. Moran was murdered outside his luxury home in June 2000 — a month after Mad Richard.

About two weeks before Mad Richard was killed he squared off against another drug dealer on the make — Carl Williams. The two crooks with dreams of being major players had argued heatedly in the underworld's then nightclub of choice, Heat, at Crown Casino.

No guns were drawn but lines were crossed.

When the two had been in jail, the bigger and stronger Mladenich was an inmate to be feared and respected. Williams told him that when they were released he wanted them to work together — he planned to recruit Mad Richard as a bodyguard and possible hit man.

But on his release Mladenich sided with the Morans, dreaming of becoming a key figure in their established network. He told

Williams he didn't need him and abused his former prison mate in the process.

Mad Richard could not have known that Williams was already committed to destroying the Morans, starting with Mark. The confrontation convinced Williams he had to get rid of Mladenich before he moved on Mark Moran. Police believe Williams recruited a hit man from a small violent western suburbs crew that included Dino Dibra, also killed later that year.

One of Dibra's best mates was fellow gunman Rocco Arico. Police have been told that Arico accepted the contract to kill Mad Richard and Williams acted as the getaway driver.

Arico was later jailed for seven years after he shot a driver five times during a road rage attack in Taylors Lakes in 2000. The victim survived and gave evidence in court despite an attempt to buy him off.

Arico was with Dibra (who was driving the car at the time of the shooting) and when Arico was later arrested at Melbourne Airport he was with Williams. The car involved in the road rage shooting was later found at Carl's house.

Homicide detectives later failed in an application for a court order to remove Arico from jail to interview him over Mladenich's murder. But he won't be in jail forever.

It would seem that Mad Richard's short, brutal and wasted life ended simply because he backed the wrong side.

According to former standover man Mark 'Chopper' Read, Mladenich was 'a total comedy of errors' and 'without a doubt the loudest and most troublesome inmate in any jail in Australia'.

In 1988 Read and a then young Mladenich were both inmates in the maximum security H Division of Pentridge Prison during the so-called 'Overcoat War' between prisoner factions.

'Poor Richard fell over and hit his head on a garden spade, but he told the police nothing and dismissed as foul gossip and rumour suggestions that I had hit him with it.' Read was never charged with the attack, but Mladenich carried permanent reminders of it in the form of scars on his forehead.

Rumours that prison officers, who were tired of Mladenich's dangerous ways, stood by when Read allegedly attacked him were never substantiated.

But there is no doubt that he made enemies wherever he went. One night in jail Mladenich grabbed his plastic chair and banged it against his cell bars from 8.30pm until 4.20am — not as part of a jail protest, but simply because he thought it was funny.

'He was never short of a word,' Read explains. 'Once, he went to Joe the Boss's place and stood outside yelling threats. This was not wise and a short time later he was shot in the leg in what was an obvious misunderstanding. He kept yelling abuse before he limped off. He could be flogged to the ground and then he would say, "Now let that be a lesson to you".'

Mladenich was 14 when he was charged with stealing a car in Footscray. He was to end with a criminal record of more than nine pages and 24 aliases, including Richard Mantello and John Mancini.

But while he considered himself a smart criminal, his arrest record is filled with offences involving street violence. He was no master gangster.

His lengthy police file included a large number of warnings, including one that he had 'violent rages that can be triggered off at any time ... he will attempt to kill a (police) member or members'.

One entry read: 'According to prison officers with years of experience they stated (Mladenich) was one of the craziest and most violent offenders they have seen. (He) is a mountain of a man who has a very violent and unpredictable nature. He must be approached with caution and extreme care. A tough cookie.'

Read said Mladenich had a fierce heroin habit from the mid-1980s. 'He would come into jail looking like a wet greyhound and then he would pump iron and build up while inside.'

Read always predicted that Mladenich would die young. 'The drugs will kill Richard and it's sad to see.'

Read, now a best-selling author and artist, says many of his old friends and enemies were being murdered because they refused to accept they were too old to dominate the underworld.

'The barman has called last drinks, but these people won't go home and they just hang around to be killed. I have found that the writing of books is a far better way for your middle-aged crim to spend his winter nights, well away from excitable types with firearms.'

Former drug squad and St Kilda detective, Lachlan McCulloch, said Mladenich was one of the more bizarre criminal identities he had investigated in his years in the job.

McCulloch said that during a drug raid in Albert Park armed police were searching a house when there was an amazing scream. 'Mladenich jumped out into the lounge room pointing a gun at everyone and going, "Pow! Pow!". He had this toy laser gun and was running around shooting all of us with the flashing red light. The trouble was we all had real guns with real bullets. We could have blown his head off.'

McCulloch said that while Mladenich was eccentric and violent ('He was as crazy as they came') he lacked the planning skills to be successful in the underworld.

The former detective said Mladenich, who liked to be known as 'King Richard' but was also known by others as 'Spade Brain' and 'Mad Richard', had ambitions to run a protection racket. He stood over prostitutes and drug dealers, but wanted to broaden his horizons. 'He wore this black gangster's coat and a black hat and walked into a pub in South Melbourne. He said he wanted

$1000 a week for protection money and he would be back the next day.'

When he came back 24 hours later he didn't seem to notice a group of detectives sitting at a nearby table, sipping beers. He was arrested at his first attempt at a shakedown.

Read said one detective tired of dealing with Mladenich through the courts. He said the detective walked him at gunpoint to the end of the St Kilda Pier, made him jump in and swim back. 'Would have done him good, too,' Read said.

As a criminal he was a good poet, reciting his own verse to a judge who was about to jail him. He once was waiting in a Chinese restaurant for a takeaway meal when he started a friendly conversation with the man next to him, complimenting him on a ring he was wearing.

When the man left the restaurant, Mladenich was waiting outside to rob him of the ring. 'He nearly pulled the finger off with it,' a detective said.

He had a long and volatile relationship with many Melbourne barristers and judges. He was known to have stalked a prosecutor, Carolyn Douglas (later appointed a County Court Judge), to disrupt Supreme Court trials and to abuse lawyers who had appeared against him.

He once chested a respected barrister, Raymond Lopez, in the foyer of Owen Dixon Chambers. 'It is the only time I have felt under physical pressure in that way. I thought he was as high as a kite,' Lopez recalled. 'He calmed down but he struck me as the type who could turn quickly.'

He walked into the office of one of his former lawyers, locked the door and asked for money. At the same time he noticed the barrister's overcoat on the back of the door and started to go through the pockets. This was an outrageous breach of protocol — it is acknowledged in the legal fraternity that it is the barrister's job to fleece his clients, not the other way around.

One member of the underworld said many people would be happy that Mladenich was dead. 'He was a hoon, a pimp and lived off everyone else. He never did one good job, but he would come around looking for a chop out.'

But the death notices in the week after his death included some from many well-known criminals, including career armed robbers and an underworld financier dying of cancer.

It is believed that Mladenich had run up drug debts with at least two major dealers who were prepared to write off the money. Neither was likely to order his murder.

Richard's mother, Odinea, said society should take some responsibility for the criminal her son became. She said he was bullied by his step-father and was eventually sent to a state institution.

'They took my little boy and they gave me back a zombie. He was a victim of this rotten society.'

She said he was the second youngest inmate sent to the notorious top security Jika Jika section in Pentridge (later closed on humanitarian grounds). 'He had to become like he was to survive,' she said.

Mrs Mladenich said many children who went to boys' homes had their lives destroyed — and there is evidence to support her claim. Many of the worst names in crime can trace their criminal beginnings to what happened in boys' homes, some of which were deservedly notorious.

Mrs Mladenich said that the same families she saw at boys' homes 'I would see later at Pentridge.'

Elder brother Mark said: 'He was 16 when he was in the hardest division in an adult jail. He wasn't allowed to be soft. He had to be hard to survive.

'I know about his record, but when he was with his family he was different. He was good-hearted.'

Mladenich was released from prison only a month before his death and told friends and relatives he was determined to keep out of trouble. But as usual, Richard wasn't telling the whole truth.

Within weeks of his release he was trying to establish a protection racket by standing over restaurants in Fitzroy Street.

In May 2003, three years after the murder, Coroner Lewis Byrne concluded: 'Richard Mladenich lived at the margin. He had friends and acquaintances who lived outside the law. He had quite an extensive criminal history and had only shortly before his death been released from prison. I only include this aspect of Mr Mladenich's personality to make the point that some of his friends, associates and indeed enemies are part of a subculture where violence and death are not unknown. Although comprehensive investigation undertaken by the homicide squad has been unable to identify the killer of Mr Mladenich, the file remains open and should it be warranted, if further information comes to light, this inquest can be reopened.'

Don't hold your breath. Carl Williams and Rocco Arico aren't talking because they don't want to and Dino Dibra isn't because he can't.

10

BLACK MARK

Carl Williams was to be involved
in at least eight murders and
have knowledge of another four
but this would be the only time
he pulled the trigger.

THREE generations of Morans have knocked around in Melbourne criminal circles and their reputation was not built on pacifism.

But Mark Moran, 36, had seemed to be the white sheep of the family, the one who stayed in the background and kept a low profile. However, as stock breeders will tell you, blood in the end will tell. Mark Moran was bred for trouble and it was only a matter of time before it found him.

His mother, Judith Moran, was attracted to gunmen all her life. Mark's natural father was one of them. His name was Leslie John Cole and he was ambushed and shot dead outside his Sydney home on 10 November 1982.

History repeats itself. Mark went the same way as his dad when he was shot dead outside his million-dollar home in the Melbourne suburb of Aberfeldie on 15 June 2000. He was the latest victim in the underworld war that had then claimed up to nine lives in less than three years — and would rack up a death toll of more than 30.

Within 24 hours of the murder, the homicide squad's Detective Inspector Brian Rix said police were receiving little help from the Morans. The family might not have known then that they had been targeted and were to be hunted down by other crooks as if they were feral animals. They had built a reputation as criminal hard men but were to find out what it was like to be the intimidated.

But that was in the future. Back in June 2000 Rix would state the obvious when he said the Mark Moran murder had 'all the hallmarks of an underworld slaying'.

'The indications are that he was out of his car at the time of the shooting, which means that perhaps his killers laid in wait,' Rix said.

Sometimes you can guess more from what police don't say.

What Rix didn't mention was the reason why Moran had left his house for less than half an hour on the night he was killed.

He had gone to meet someone, but who?

Did the killer know Moran would go out and then come back that night?

It is fair to conclude that a killer would not sit outside a luxury house in an affluent street all night on the off chance the target would venture out. He had to have some inside knowledge.

In fact the killer only had to wait ten minutes for his target. That killer was Carl Williams — then a little-known drug dealer who would become one of the biggest names in the underworld. Williams would be involved in at least eight murders and have knowledge of another four — but this would be the only time he pulled the trigger.

Williams would also have known that his target was at his most vulnerable. Mark's half-brother, Jason, was behind bars and his minder, 'Mad Richard' Mladenich, had been shot dead in a seedy St Kilda hotel a month earlier. Carl had been close by during Mad Richard's shooting, but on that occasion a henchman had fired the gun.

So the real question became, who set up Mark Moran?

As Rix said, 'Mark fancied himself as a bit of a heavy. I would think the underworld will talk about this to somebody, and I'm sure that will get back to us in some way.'

He was right, they did talk but the talk remained a long way short of admissible evidence. No-one knew then that Mark Moran's death would be just one in the most savage underworld war in decades.

For Moran that day had been like many others. As a self-employed drug dealer he would mix daily chores with lucrative drug sales.

He had taken his children to school, shopped with his mother, and had lunch with his wife. He also picked up his high-powered white Holden ute from a local panel beater. The car had been registered in the name of one of the Moran clan's most trusted insiders. Mark would not live to learn that the man was a police informer.

That evening he went to the nearby Gladstone Park Shopping Centre to meet a local drug customer but the deal fell through. The reason remains in dispute. The customer told police he wanted to buy marijuana and ecstasy tablets from Moran and was 'surprised that Mark didn't have the smoke because when we make a meeting like this he usually had what I need.'

But police were also told that the customer did not have the money to pay and the deal was done on credit.

Either way, Moran arrived home around 7.45pm but told his wife he was going out for about 15 minutes shortly after 8pm.

Williams was waiting. But how did he know of the proposed meeting when Moran rarely left home at night?

Moran was a rarity amongst gangsters: he was no night-owl. Moran and his wife were normally in bed by 9pm and up at dawn for a daily exercise routine. Moran — who was a personal trainer before he found the drug business more lucrative — would do 100 sit-ups and then head to a local gym.

But this night he walked out the door and down the drive to where his car was parked outside in Combermere Street. He had become lazy and sloppy and hadn't bothered parking behind the house's heavy metal gates or inside the double garage.

As he went to step into the car, Williams emerged from the shadows and hit him with two shotgun blasts and at least one from a handgun.

The force knocked him into the car, killing him instantly. Police found amphetamines and cocaine on him, and wondered if he had been lured out on the promise of a last-minute sale?

It was no surprise when it became known that a Moran had been murdered. The surprise was that it was Mark and not his younger half-brother, Jason, then serving two years and six months over a nightclub assault in King Street.

While Jason Moran was seen as wild, violent and erratic, Mark was calmer and tried to keep a lower profile.

Jason was out of control, Mark was the brains,' said one policeman who has investigated the family.

But as Jason became increasingly restrained by court action and stints in jail, Mark began to take a higher profile. After Jason had shot Williams in the stomach in a nearby park in October the previous year it had been Mark who'd urged his brother to 'shoot him in the head.'

Whether he started to mimic Jason's behaviour or just learnt to play the role of the gun-toting tough guy, Mark developed that fatal gangster swagger.

About 18 months before his death, he took offence when an associate made a disparaging comment about a female relative.

'He went around to the guy's house, stuck a gun in his mouth, took him away and seriously flogged him,' a criminal source said.

In 1999, he was involved in the assault of a policeman at Flemington racecourse on Oaks Day — not a good business move. Neither was the Moran brothers' decision to shoot Williams in the guts.

The incident was a warning, not an attempt to kill. But sometimes it can be more dangerous to goad a snake, even a fat, slow one, than to leave it alone or kill it outright, as the Morans were to find out the hard way.

On 17 February 2000, police noticed Mark Moran driving a luxury car. When they opened the boot of the rented vehicle, they found a high-tech handgun equipped with a silencer and a laser sight.

They also found a heap of amphetamine pills that had been stamped in a pill press to appear as ecstasy tablets.

The day after Mark's murder, police raided an associate's home and seized another 5000 tablets similar to those found in the boot of the rental car.

Months before, Mark Moran had been ejected from the County Court after he tried to use a false name to get access to the plea hearing after his half-brother was found guilty over the King Street assault. AFL footballer Wayne Carey gave character evidence for Jason Moran, which was a case of history repeating itself.

A high-profile Carlton footballer of impeccable credentials once gave character evidence for Moran's maternal grandfather over a stolen-property charge.

Not surprisingly, the property had been stolen and hidden at the grandfather's place by the teenage Moran boys and the old man was obliged to shoulder the blame for his delinquent descendants. The star who gave character evidence for him was doing the right thing.

Police described Moran as one of a new breed of drug traffickers known as the 'Bollinger Dealers', who wore designer suits and associated with minor celebrities and the new rich.

MARK was a former professional chef and a 'gym rat' often seen at the Underworld Health and Fitness centre beside the Yarra in the central city. But like so many of his class, he had not worked regularly for years and police say his high-income lifestyle and expensive home could only have been supported through illegal activities. He refused to speak about business on telephones and rarely spoke with associates in his house because he feared police had the place bugged.

He was proud of his fitness and physique and was described as 'extremely narcissistic'. He liked to be well-dressed in a gangster-chic style. When he was shot, he was wearing a huge diamond stud in his left ear.

Mark Moran was young, good-looking, rich and fit. But in the months leading up to his murder, he was depressed and at one point was hospitalised when he told friends he was considering suicide. In the end, someone beat him to it.

The day before Moran's murder, police conducted a series of raids on a sophisticated amphetamines network and a number of criminals, including one known as 'The Penguin', were arrested.

In the beginning there were several theories as to why he was murdered — people like Moran make many violent enemies in their business.

But the homicide squad knew of Williams' hatred of the family and within 24 hours was interviewing the suspect.

Williams claimed he could not have committed the murder because he was picking up a hire car from Melbourne Airport at the time. But police say they have found a gap of nearly an hour in which Williams could have travelled to Aberfeldie for the killing.

Years later, one of Williams' key men we call 'The Driver' told police he drove Williams to a street near Moran's home and drove him away after the shooting.

Another witness, not connected with the underworld, has been able to corroborate much of The Driver's story. A second criminal source also made a statement against Williams.

The case against Williams was good, but not great. And that is why it was dropped when Williams agreed to plead guilty to the three other murders (Jason Moran, Lewis Moran and Mark Mallia, having already been found guilty of killing Michael Marshall).

Mark's mother, Judy Moran, has always maintained Williams should have been prosecuted over the murder.

Within days of the murder there were reports of shots fired near a North Fitzroy home connected to the Williams syndicate.

'It is not the right time to be taking sides,' a detective said after Mark's funeral. He was right, as the murders continued for years, with people who took sides getting killed.

In accordance with underworld union rules, the *Herald Sun* was filled with death notices to a 'lovely gentleman' after Mark Moran's death. There were many from former league footballers including one from a former Carlton captain who fondly remembered the Moran boys running a victory lap with the team after a premiership in the 1980s.

There was one notice falsely placed under the nickname of a drug squad detective. Police suspect it was placed to give the appearance Moran was talking to police when he was killed.

The funeral was the usual procession of real friends, hangers-on and crims in black suits who refused to remove their sunglasses, even though it was a cold winter's day.

Jason Moran was allowed day leave from prison to speak at the funeral. Mourners said the brother spoke with real emotion but his death notice worried police. It read: 'This is only the beginning, it will never be the end. REMEMBER, I WILL NEVER FORGET.'

It was an empty boast. Within three years Jason would join his brother as an underworld victim.

Because the funeral was going to choke local streets, a request was made for uniformed police to control traffic, but a senior policeman vetoed the plan. He didn't want media images of police holding up traffic for a mob of Melbourne gangsters.

While Mark Moran had a low public profile, he had a long and violent criminal history. Career criminal Raymond John Denning once told an inquest Moran was one of three men involved in an armed robbery in which a guard was shot dead.

He said the three men involved were Russell 'Mad Dog' Cox, Moran and Santo Mercuri. The robbery was on 11 July 1988, in Barkly Square, Brunswick. Two armed guards were leaving a Coles warehouse with a cash tin when they were held up at gunpoint. A struggle followed and one of the guards, Dominic Hefti, 31, was shot in the chest and the leg. He died two days later at the Royal Melbourne Hospital.

Denning said the three men planned to kill a woman whose car Mercuri had stolen for his getaway. Denning said: 'It was decided among the three of them that they try to find her home address and knock her because she was the only one that Sam believed had identified him.'

In a chilling postscript to the story, when the armed robbery squad later raided the Doncaster home of Russell Cox, they found that the page of the telephone book carrying the woman's name and address had been torn out.

Hefti's murder sparked another spate of killings. Police wrongly believed that armed robber Graeme Jensen was responsible and he was shot during an apparently clumsy attempt to arrest him on 11 October 1988.

The following day two young uniformed police, Constables Steven Tynan and Damian Eyre, were murdered in Walsh Street, South Yarra, as a payback.

LES Cole didn't think lightning could strike the same place twice. He was wrong. The former painter and docker was shot dead in the same garage in which a gunman had ambushed him and seriously wounded him just two months before.

That was on 10 November 1982, at Cole's heavily-fortified Kyle Bay home in Sydney. It was to prove eerily similar to the death of his biological son, Mark Moran, 18 years later. Each was shot dead as he returned home. Each was living well above his legitimate means at the time. And each almost certainly knew they were in danger.

Cole managed to live one year longer than his son would. He was shot at 37; Mark at 36.

It was the second attempt on Cole's life. He had been shot just two months before by a man he described as 'a bad loser.' But if the gunman was a bad loser then Cole was a fatally slow learner.

He was still recovering from the first attack, and was returning from a physiotherapy appointment for treatment for his injuries, when he was killed.

In the first shooting he had been wounded in the right foot, right knee, midriff, right shoulder and twice in the forearm.

But the second time the gunman left nothing to chance, shooting Cole twice in the chest and once behind the right ear.

When police interviewed him over the first shooting he said, 'I don't want to say anything. I will sort it out myself.'

Police said Cole knew the Kane brothers and the senior Moran brothers, Lewis and 'Tuppence', and had visited Melbourne the day before his death. 'He was not a bad little bloke, a bit of a knockabout,' one policeman recalled.

His widow, Jennifer Ann Cole, told the inquest into his death she had never bothered to ask her husband what he did for a living. 'He always said what I didn't know wouldn't hurt me.'

Cole was supposedly a security officer at Sydney's Sea Breeze Hotel, but he failed to sniff the winds of change. He didn't realise until too late that someone had a terminal grudge against him.

Like the Kanes, Cole was heavily into protection and debt collecting and moved to Sydney to advance his career. Police at one stage believed he was killed by a Melbourne hit man flown in for the job, but the whisper was that a Sydney gangster called Mick Sayers pulled the trigger. Sayers was later murdered.

Cole had installed state-of-the-art security. He had electronically operated doors, a video surveillance system, floodlights, steel bars over windows, steel mesh over the backyard and he kept two guard dogs.

But even though he had been shot once before, he became slack and left the garage door open, allowing the gunman the perfect position to hide. It wasn't the action of a prudent man — but if he were prudent he wouldn't have been a career criminal.

The fruit doesn't fall far from the tree. Years later, Cole's son Mark became slack, too, and didn't bother to drive his car behind the iron gates and into the secure double garage. If he had been a little more cautious then, perhaps Williams, who was inexperienced with firearms, wouldn't have been able to shoot him at point-blank range.

11

POP CULTURE

'Mate, I've just watched
Reservoir Dogs too many times.'

TO be a top gangster you need to be ruthless, dangerous and cunning — but most of all you need to be born with a survivor's instinct.

Dino Dibra found out the hard way that the first three without the fourth was a fatal combination.

Certainly Dibra was ruthless and dangerous. Take the case of when he and three of his gang kidnapped a man — punching, kicking and pistol-whipping him before throwing him into a car boot.

According to police reports, the team grabbed the man in the Melbourne western suburb of Ardeer, on 2 August 1999.

Dibra and his soldiers were seemingly unworried that successful abductions were usually carried out under cover of darkness. They chose to grab their man in broad daylight.

Despite his injuries, the kidnap victim wasn't cooperative. As they drove off he popped the boot, jumped out and ran. The gang simply chased him down and, in front of shocked witnesses, dragged him back into the boot. Even *The Sopranos* scriptwriters would think it was a bit rich.

They took him to what they believed was the privacy of Dibra's Taylors Lakes house. Sadly for the kidnappers, they might as well have taken him to the set of *Big Brother*.

Police technicians had been to the house much earlier to install listening devices and a small video camera because Dibra was the main suspect in an earlier shooting outside a popular nightclub.

The kidnap team demanded $20,000 from the victim's brother but, being practical men, were prepared to settle for $5000.

The listening device caught Dibra and his loyal deputy, Rocco Arico, discussing their negotiations.

Arico: 'Hey, if I'd have known he's only gonna get five grand, I would have put one in when he tried to jump out of the car.'

Dibra: 'You're an idiot. Listen to you.'

Arico: 'I would have just went fucking whack. Cop this slug for now. I would have slapped one in and I would have said "Hold on to that for a while, don't give it to anyone and jump in the coffin".'

The tape was damning but there was another key piece of evidence: the kidnap victim was still in the boot when police arrived.

There can also be no doubt that Dibra was dangerous.

On 15 July 2000, he and Arico were driving in separate cars on their way back from a nightclub when they cut off another motorist in Taylors Lakes. It was 7am.

The motorist spun his car 180 degrees at a roundabout and narrowly avoided a smash. Understandably enraged, he followed the two cars a few streets then, seeing three men, continued to drive on — but two of them, in one car, decided to chase him.

When they stopped, a discussion of road etiquette followed. Arico asked the motorist: 'So what do you want to do about it?'

He unwisely replied: 'Well, I wanted to put his head through the windscreen.'

Arico pulled an automatic pistol and fired six shots — five hit the driver — before the man could even unbuckle his seatbelt. He was struck on his forearms, abdomen, right elbow and shoulder but, against the odds, he survived.

Police arrested Arico in the company of Carl Williams two days later at Melbourne Airport as he was about to board a flight to Perth. He was alleged to have $100,000 of cocaine in his pocket at the time. He later claimed police planted the drugs.

He had a business class ticket and although he had no luggage he told police he was heading west for a three-week holiday.

Later the road rage victim and his family were offered hush money to say he had incorrectly identified Arico.

But the victim stuck to his testimony. The Arico family owned a pizza shop in the area and the victim recalled seeing young Rocco working there on the rare occasions when he was cutting pizzas rather than drugs.

Dibra would not have to worry about the subtleties of the legal system because he would be dead before the trial.

Dibra was well known at nightclubs and not because he liked to dance. He was a drug dealer who moved pills and powders, but he wanted more than money. He wanted respect and a reputation in the underworld.

Before he became well-known in the drug field, Dibra ran a lucrative stolen car racket and became an expert at car 're-birthing', buying damaged cars and 'repairing' them by stealing identical models and transferring identification details.

But if he needed wheels in a hurry, he would intimidate night clubbers into handing over their keys and then simply drive off in their car. Dino, full of steroids and bad manners, was not a man to reason with.

Dibra seemed to think he was above the law from a young age. As a teenager he would ride his unregistered motorcycle past police patrols, trying to goad them into a high-speed pursuit.

When he was jailed in 1996 for 18 months, and had his licence cancelled for five years in 1996, the presiding magistrate commented Dibra had 'one of the worst driving records I have seen'.

When his dog was impounded for biting a woman, Dibra organised an escape plot to get the dog out. When a policeman came to the door as a result of a complaint that the dog was dangerous Dibra told him to 'fuck off'.

Sometimes he did his own dirty work, but as he rose up the criminal pyramid he found others eager to please.

He stood by and watched as some of his team shot two bouncers outside the Dome nightclub in 1998.

He was also an associate of 'Mad Charlie' Hegyalji, who was shot dead outside his Caulfield South home on 23 November 1998.

Police had Dibra on the top of a very short list of suspects for Mad Charlie's murder. They found that hours before the death Mad Charlie contacted Dibra from a hotel pay phone. Dibra refused to tell police the content of their conversation, but it was unlikely to have been about stamp collecting.

He was also an associate of Mark Moran and several other gangsters who were murdered during the gangland war.

Dibra was living his fantasy. On the walls of his house were framed posters from Hollywood gangster films — *Pulp Fiction*, *Scarface* and *Goodfellas*.

In August 2000, he told a *Herald Sun* reporter outside the Melbourne Magistrates Court during one of the many days he had to attend court: 'Mate, I've just watched *Reservoir Dogs* too many times.'

He probably thought the title of Quentin Tarantino's ultra-violent signature film referred to the northern Melbourne suburb of Reservoir, near Preston, and that it involved pit bull terriers and police informers.

He would have been better off studying the classics. Then he might have learned the wisdom of the saying that 'he who lives by the sword dies by the sword'. For, just as the young gunman filled with steroids was getting the gangster reputation he craved, he got himself shot.

On Saturday 14 October 2000, Dibra, then 25, was shot dead outside a house in Krambruk Street, Sunshine.

And as would happen so often in the underworld war it was those close to the victim who would set up the killing. The western suburbs crew had been tight and a key member was Andrew 'Benji' Veniamin.

In Hollywood gangster style, Dibra was shot with two guns. The trigger men were fellow drug dealers, Paul Kallipolitis and Veniamin.

They would both later see the other end of an assassin's gun. But there was a third man present when Dino became DOA. He was another so-called friend and he is very much alive.

Detective Inspector Andrew Allen, of the Purana taskforce, said much later: 'The homicide investigators have established that three people are involved in this execution murder and someone out there holds the key to solving this violent crime.'

A $100,000 reward has been offered in connection with the murder. Dibra may have lived like a millionaire but court documents listed his only asset as a half share in a block of land. His estate was valued at $60,000.

Which made it official ... Dino Dibra was worth more dead than alive.

12

THE DEADLY CIRCLE

In police circles no name
is more detested than that of
Victor Peirce. Many openly
rejoiced when he was
finally shot.

SHE was the ace in the pack — the witness that could prove to a jury of strangers how a gang of Melbourne armed robbers became ruthless police killers.

Taskforce detectives had worked on her for months, chipping away, hoping they could turn her against the men they were convinced had ambushed and murdered two young police constables in Walsh Street, South Yarra.

But she knew the rules. To talk to police, let alone give evidence for them, was an unforgivable act of betrayal. In the vernacular of the underworld, to give evidence — to tell the truth — is to turn 'dog'. And she seemed set to be the biggest dog of all.

She was to be the 94th — and most important — witness, not only for what she was going to say under oath, but because of who she was.

Experienced defence barristers could easily discredit many of the witnesses in the case. These were criminals looking to curry favour, men trying to do deals with authorities over their own criminal activities, or those who could provide only small snippets to add to events that took years to build, hours to plan and minutes to execute.

But Wendy Peirce was no outsider looking in. She was the wife of the alleged ringleader and could provide the jury with the chilling details of how and why the gang chose two young policemen they didn't know to ambush and murder.

Wendy was no tourist passing through. Her adult life had been spent in the black and bloody world of Australia's most notorious crime cell — the Pettingill-Allen-Peirce clan, in which violence was seen as a solution and murder an attractive option.

Her husband, and the father of her children, was Victor George Peirce, the leader of a gang of armed robbers hitting targets around Melbourne.

Wendy Peirce was the reason police were confident they could convict the men charged with the murders of Steven Tynan and Damian Eyre, who were shot dead on 12 October 1988.

The prosecution case was that Peirce and his crew were driven by a pathological hatred of law enforcement after police killed two of their mates the previous year — Mark Militano in March and Frankie Valastro in June.

Detectives maintained that both men, who had long histories of violence, were shot when they refused to surrender and chose to threaten police with guns.

The gang was convinced members of the armed robbery squad had become trigger-happy and embarked on a policy of being judge, jury and executioner. They believed that when frustrated detectives couldn't find the evidence to convict suspects they would shoot them and later argue the killings were self-defence.

After Militano's death, detectives claimed Peirce and his team began to talk of fighting back. If more of their mates were killed by police they would respond by killing two police in return, the story went.

There were rumours and whispers of the revenge pact and there was talk that members of the squad could be ambushed in the driveways of their own homes.

At the same time detectives grabbed Victor Peirce, told him they knew he was committing armed robberies and advised him he should pull up while he could.

The stakes were raised and a confrontation of sorts was inevitable.

On 11 October 1988, Peirce's best friend and prolific armed robbery partner, Graeme Jensen, was shot dead by police in a botched arrest at Narre Warren after the suspect went to buy a spark plug for his mower.

It was now flashpoint.

On Wednesday 12 October, a Walsh Street resident reported to police that a white Holden Commodore was apparently abandoned in the street with the bonnet raised, the driver's side door open and the rear passenger side vent window smashed.

At 4.34 am a D24 operator assigned the job to a patrol car using the call sign Prahran 311.

The two young policemen on night patrol in Prahran 311 were too inexperienced to be bored with routine calls and responded immediately.

The driver, Steven Tynan, 22, had been a policeman for two years and nine months. His partner, Damian Eyre, 20, was from a police family and had been in the job for six months after graduating from the academy on 27 April 1988.

It took just seven minutes for the pair to reach the suspect sedan. They had no reason to suspect a trap.

Tynan parked the divisional van behind the Holden. Both vehicles were facing north. Eyre got out of the passenger side of the van and walked to the car.

He glanced at the registration sticker on the front window and jotted down the number and expiry date on a sheet of paper on his clipboard.

Meanwhile, his partner went to the open driver's door and slipped behind the wheel.

Eyre then walked around the car and squatted next to Tynan, who was still in the car.

They would have seen that the ignition lock was broken so that the car could be started without a key.

Tynan had started to get out of the car when the shotgun blast hit him. The deadly force threw him back into the car, where he collapsed, with his head between the front bucket seats. It was 4.48 am.

Eyre began to rise from the squatting position when he was shot across his back in the upper left shoulder, also with a shotgun.

It should have been enough to stop anyone dead, but Eyre somehow rose and turned to face his attacker. He grabbed the gunman and fought. Police believe the shotgun discharged twice more, one blast hitting the wall of a Walsh Street house.

Even though he was seriously, but not fatally, wounded, Eyre continued to fight until a second man slipped up next to him and grabbed the policeman's service .38 revolver from its holster, put it to the policeman's head and fired.

Eyre collapsed and was shot again in the back as he lay next to the rear driver's side wheel of the stolen car. He was already dying when the second revolver bullet hit him.

Both Tynan and Eyre died in hospital from massive gunshot wounds without regaining consciousness.

It didn't take detectives long to work out that this was a cold-blooded ambush.

The dumped car had been used as bait to lure police — any police — into the quiet street. At the top of a very short list of suspects were Victor Peirce and his team.

Within a day Victor's mother, Kath Pettingill, the matriarch of the notorious crime family, was quoted as saying she knew her children were the prime suspects but denied they were involved.

'It wasn't us,' she said. 'I hate coppers but those boys didn't do anything. Our family wouldn't do that. We were not involved.

'You don't kill two innocent coppers. If you want to get back you would kill the copper who killed Graeme.'

Police responded immediately, conducting a series of sometimes brutal raids. They were sending a clear message to the underworld: all business was off until the police killers were charged and in jail.

But one of the most defiant in the face of constant raids was Wendy Peirce.

Apparently blood loyal to her in-laws, after one heavy-handed police raid on her house she posed in the debris for the media with one of her children, looking every bit the innocent victims of police brutality.

Homicide squad detective Jim Conomy formally interviewed her on 9 November 1988.

Not only did she refuse to implicate her husband but she gave him an alibi. They were together all night in a Tullamarine motel and he did not leave, she said.

It was a lie.

On 30 December 1988, Victor Peirce was formally charged with two counts of murder over Walsh Street.

Three other men, Peirce's half-brother Trevor Pettingill, Anthony Farrell and Peter David McEvoy, were charged. Two other suspects, Jedd Houghton and Gary Abdallah, were shot dead by police in separate incidents. Peirce's young nephew, Jason Ryan, was also charged, although he became a protected witness for the prosecution.

With no witnesses, police built a complex case that relied heavily on forensic evidence linking a shotgun used in Walsh Street to an earlier armed robbery alleged to have been conducted by the suspects, and a series of witnesses who were prepared to swear on oath that the men charged were the killers.

Much of the testimony was tainted by the fact it was from career criminals who were never going to be seen as reliable.

Many had at first denied any knowledge or helped provide alibis for the suspects.

Then, after being subjected to sustained pressure from detectives, they finally agreed to testify.

Members of the Ty-Eyre taskforce set up to investigate the murders continued to visit Wendy Peirce. They didn't use tough-guy tactics but gently tried to persuade her that this would be the one chance she had to change her life — to leave the underworld and make a fresh start. They told her she had reached a fork in the road and had to choose which way she wanted to go.

In July 1989 — eight months after the murders — she would spend three days with Detective Inspector David Sprague and Senior Detective Colin McLaren of the Ty-Eyre taskforce, making an explosive 31-page statement.

On Sunday 16 July, she told the detectives she wished to go into the witness protection scheme. Two days later, in an interview room in homicide she repeated her statement on videotape — a confession that could have condemned her husband to life in prison.

Sporting bleached blonde hair and wearing heavy make-up, she appeared remarkably relaxed as she read her statement. Yes, she had been with her husband at the Tullamarine Motel on the night that Jensen had been killed but, 'Victor was absent from the motel most of the night until the morning.'

In other words, he had plenty of time to drive to Walsh Street and return.

She read her statement in a monotone, stumbling over some of the words. But the message was clear. 'He disliked police so much that he would often say to me, "I'd love to knock them dogs". His hatred of police was so vicious that at times I was scared to be with him.'

She said the whole family hated police, but Victor was the worst.

'On many occasions he would be holding on to a handgun and would say, "I would love to knock Jacks".'

Wendy said there was one armed robbery squad detective 'he wanted to put off'.

In February 1988, after police raided his family, Peirce 'was yelling and screaming and in such a rage from yelling that he started crying from temper,' she said.

Why then had she protected him with a false statement to police?

'I have been an alibi witness for Victor many times. I did so out of loyalty to him and also out of fear. I was well aware he would bash me if I didn't ... I was fearful that Victor would kill me if I didn't supply an alibi.'

In this version of events, she said that when Peirce first learned police had killed Jensen, he had said, 'Oh, Jesus', and had tears in his eyes.

She told police he then rang McEvoy and said, 'What can we do, mate? Graeme's dead, what can we do?'

She said he told her, 'I'm next. They'll shoot me now. They're dogs; they knocked Graeme for no good reason.'

What she then said could have blown a hole in Peirce's story that he spent the night with her.

She said they went to bed with his arm under her head. She heard him get up and get dressed. But she had learned over the previous thirteen years when it was best to mind her own business and she chose not to move or call out.

'I heard him leave the motel.' She dozed and when he came back to bed he was cold.

The taskforce was delighted. They had infiltrated the family that lived by the code of silence. Wendy Peirce continued to talk. Tape after tape was recorded that implicated Peirce in murders and unsolved armed robberies.

Police and prosecution lawyers were confident that once a jury heard her version of events they would convict the four men in the dock without hesitation.

After all, why would a woman lie to help convict the father of her children?

For more than a year Wendy Peirce lived in witness protection waiting for the day she would be called to help send her husband to jail.

The committal hearing at the Magistrates' Court proved to be the perfect dress rehearsal. She answered all questions and made it clear her husband was the key figure in the group that killed the two police as a random payback after their mate, Graeme Jensen, had been shot dead by police during an attempted arrest the previous day.

She answered all questions, implicating her husband as the driving force behind the Walsh Street killings. She was cross-examined ruthlessly but stood up to the examination. A court veteran, she had acted as an unofficial legal assistant during many of the family's battles with the law.

But there were warning signs. In November 1990, shortly after the committal hearing, Wendy Peirce's brother told taskforce joint leader Inspector John Noonan they were about to be ambushed — that she would not give evidence when it counted.

It worried Noonan enough to front Wendy Peirce, who said the claim was 'utter rubbish'.

But it wasn't.

The jury would never hear her testimony. In the pre-trial *voir dire* — closed hearing — at the Supreme Court, Wendy Peirce suddenly changed her story and so effectively sabotaged the police case.

After eighteen months in witness protection and after swearing to her husband's involvement at the Magistrate's committal hearings, Peirce betrayed her police minders and saved her husband, Victor, from conviction and a certain lifetime prison sentence.

Not only did she deny that her husband was involved, but she declared that she had never seen him with guns in their Richmond home.

Yet in her earlier police statement she said her husband was an expert at hiding guns and that when she saw him in their shed sawing off a shotgun barrel he said to her with the pride of a home handyman, 'This will be a beauty, Witch.' ('Witch' was her nickname).

She also knew first hand of her husband's interest in gunplay. She told police that once while sitting with Graeme Jensen, Victor became annoyed because they had run out of marijuana. 'He was playing with a revolver and said, "Get up and dance".' When she refused, 'he shot twice between my legs' — the bullets were left implanted in the skirting board.

In December 1992, Wendy Peirce was found guilty of perjury and sentenced to a minimum of nine months jail.

In sentencing her, Judge Ross said the perjury was premeditated and she had shown no signs of remorse.

Seventeen years later, Wendy Peirce finally admitted what police had always known and no jury would ever hear. Her husband did do it.

IT is an early spring afternoon in Port Melbourne where new money, empty nesters and old crooks exist together with feigned indifference towards each other.

Wendy Peirce sits at an outside table near Station Pier, ignoring the bite from the wind off the bay while leafing through a bestselling true crime book.

The other tables outside are empty.

In the next block is the penthouse Tony Mokbel had to abandon after he was arrested and bailed.

Inside, the café is warm and busy but outside no-one minds if you smoke — and you can chat without worrying about eavesdroppers.

She sees a picture of her husband in the book. A detective is leading him in handcuffs to court. The prisoner's right eye is puffy and closing.

'They bashed him with gun butts,' she says matter-of-factly. 'He needed a few stitches.' She speaks without anger or grief. To her it seems to be just an occupational hazard for a career criminal.

Parked just ten metres away is her husband's 1993 maroon Commodore sedan — the car he was sitting in when he was shot dead in Bay Street, Port Melbourne, on 1 May 2002.

When all the forensic checks were done and the police finally returned the car, Wendy Peirce immediately slid her fingers under the front ashtray with practised ease.

The grieving widow found what she was looking for — almost $400 in cash. She was pleased but not surprised at this small legacy. 'It was his favourite spot to stook (hide) money,' she shrugs.

Once police finished with the maroon sedan, Wendy had it detailed — which included patching a nasty bullet hole, replacing the shattered driver's side window and fitting seat covers.

Now it looks good as new.

She decided to keep it 'for sentimental reasons.' Victor, she explains, always had a soft spot for Commodores and they were his vehicle of choice to steal for getaway cars. It was also the type he left abandoned in Walsh Street to lure two young police to their deaths.

Wendy Peirce has spent nearly 30 years watching, committing and concealing serious crime. She talks of her history with no obvious signs of guilt or embarrassment. What is done is done.

But she has finally agreed to talk, she says, to set the record straight. 'I have been an idiot. If I could have me life back I wouldn't have done this. It has been a total waste.'

She is considering changing her name and trying to bury her past. She says her son, Victor junior, is burdened with carrying the name of the brutal gunman, drug dealer, police killer and gangland murder victim.

Her daughter is still filled with anguish at losing her father. Her youngest son goes to school near where his father was shot dead.

So why did she agree to give evidence for the police and then change her mind before the trial?

Peirce says she was never going to give evidence: that her decision to go into witness protection was part of a long-range family plan to sabotage the prosecution from the inside.

She now says that although Victor organised the murders, he felt there would never be enough evidence to justify his arrest. 'He covered his tracks and he didn't think he'd get pinched,' she says.

But when Victor Peirce's sister, Vicki Brooks, and her son, Jason Ryan, went into witness protection, the police case became stronger.

At first Wendy Peirce stayed staunch, following the underworld code of refusing to make admissions. 'My first statement was to Jim Conomy (on 9 November) stating that we had nothing to do with it. Noonan wanted to charge me with murder.'

Wendy Peirce claims she knew her alibi was worthless and no-one would believe her. She claims that Peter Allen — Victor's half-brother and the jailhouse lawyer of the family — was the one who decided Wendy would be more valuable if she appeared to change sides.

'He said, "If you give evidence for Victor he'll go down (be convicted). With your priors (convictions) the jury won't believe you".'

'He said that if I somersaulted them (changed sides) ... Peter said I would get no more than 18 months for perjury and he was spot on.'

She said she never intended to give evidence against Victor and that she stayed in contact with him, even when in witness protection.

'I would talk to mum and Kath (Pettingill, Victor's mother) was there to pass on messages to Victor. I was posting him letters and photos. I always loved Victor and I was never going to give evidence against him.'

Police claim the suggestion that Wendy was planted as a witness is a fantasy.

One member of the taskforce says she saw the chance to start a new life and grabbed it but had second thoughts when she realised that she would have to work rather than living off the proceeds of drugs and armed robberies.

Another said she was happy when she was duchessed by the taskforce but felt miffed when moved to Canberra and put in public housing by witness protection.

'She saw that even before the trial she was no longer special. She realised that after she had given evidence she would be left to fend for herself,' one policeman said.

One detective said she was besotted by one of her guards and decided to flip sides and return to the Peirce camp when the policeman was moved to other duties.

Inspector John Noonan, who was joint head of the taskforce, blames the legal system. It was simply too long from arrest to the trial to hold the unreliable Peirce.

He says he has no doubt if a jury had heard her evidence all four accused men would have been convicted.

'They (Victor Peirce and his family) kept at her. Getting messages to her that everything would be all right and if she changed her story back she would move back with Victor. She was getting messages from Peirce in prison through third parties that he understood the pressure she was under, but they belonged together.'

'They told her they could look after her better than the police.'

The treatment of Wendy Peirce split the taskforce when some members were banned from dealing with her for fear their confrontational style would push her out of the prosecution camp.

Joint-taskforce head, Commander David Sprague, said police lacked the professionalism in witness protection at the time to deal with someone like Wendy Peirce.

'She could not cope with witness protection. I think we had a real chance in the early days but as the case dragged on she changed sides again.'

He said she was difficult to control, continuing to shoplift and drive without a licence while under witness protection.

In the early months, she was protected by the taskforce and treated as a star. She stayed in hotels — some of them luxurious — and was constantly moved.

She was flattered, taken out for meals and her children entertained with outings that included sailing trips around Port Phillip Bay.

But as the months dragged on towards the trial, she was put into the much less glamorous witness protection program.

Many of her young guards had trouble concealing their contempt for the wife of a police killer. She had lost her friends and her extended dysfunctional family and the detectives who had persuaded her to become a prosecution witness were no longer there to fortify her weakening resolve.

Senior police say she had a glimpse of her future as a struggling single mother. And she didn't like it.

WENDY Peirce says her husband was a criminal with two great passions — his love of armed robberies and his hatred of police. 'Victor was the planner. He loved doing stick-ups. He was the one who would do all the planning and tell the others what to do.'

Police say the core members in the team, known as the Flemington Crew, were Jedd Houghton, Graeme Jensen, Peter David McEvoy, Paul Prideaux and Lindsay Rountree. The specialist car thief for the gang was Gary Abdallah.

Jedd Houghton would be shot dead by police in a Bendigo caravan park on 17 November 1988. Abdallah was shot dead by police in a Carlton flat in April 1989.

'He (Abdallah) was always good with Holdens. Victor would tell him to steal two and have one left at a certain spot.' The armed robbery team would do the job in one stolen Holden before swapping to the second a few kilometres away.

To Peirce it was a job. Nearly every work-day he would head off to observe possible targets and plan armed robberies. 'He was an absolute expert,' she says proudly.

But if it was a job, he certainly loved his work.

'He told me he often got an erection when he charged into a bank. He was just so excited. He planned the jobs and then they did the robberies. He loved doing banks — he just loved it. He got off on it.

'I always got him to ring me straight after a job to make sure he was okay. Then I'd tell him to get home with the money. I loved it.'

The most money she saw was $200,000 after Peirce robbed the ANZ bank in Ringwood in January 1988. 'He did heaps, he did over twenty armed robberies.'

The money, she now admits, was laundered through lawyer Tom Scriva, but none remains.

'We wasted it all. We wanted to buy a new house near Toolong (near Port Fairy). We had five acres picked out but we just spent all the money.'

Gaetano 'Tom' Scriva, 55, died of natural causes in July 2000 but by then much of the black money he was holding for his gangster clients had disappeared.

Scriva's father, Michele, was a Melbourne mafia figure connected with the wholesale fruit and vegetable market. In 1945, Scriva senior was acquitted of the murder of Giuseppe 'Fat Joe' Versace in what was probably Victoria's first mafia hit. Versace was stabbed 91 times.

Michele Scriva was later sentenced to hang for stabbing Frederick Duffy to death in North Melbourne, but the sentence was later commuted and he served 10 years.

Scriva was a trusted lieutenant to Godfather Liborio Benvenuto, who died of natural causes in 1988. Much later, Benvenuto's son, Frank, would become good friends with Peirce.

According to Wendy, her husband robbed banks in East Bentleigh, Ringwood and Knox City in 1988. He also hit security guards carrying cash boxes into banks and attacked couriers who were picking up large amounts of cash.

'He would knock them out and take the money,' she recalls.

She says that when armed robbery squad detectives came to interview him, he told her 'if he didn't come back they had loaded him (fabricated evidence to justify an arrest). He came home and said they told him to pull up on the banks or they would load him'.

She confirms the stick-up crew saw the armed robbery squad as its enemy and believed the detectives were methodically murdering criminals they could not convict.

The pact to kill two police for every armed robber? 'It was more Jedd and Macca (McEvoy) than the others.'

Jedd was the trigger man; he had the shotgun. Macca took the (Damian Eyre's) handgun. Victor was pissed off with him for that. Abdallah knocked (stole) the car. I don't think (Anthony) Farrell and Trevor (Pettingill) were even there.'

Wendy Peirce says Victor was convinced police were going to kill him. 'We went on the run, living in motels with the kids.

'It (Walsh Street) was spur of the moment. We were on the run. Victor was the organiser.'

But she says he showed no regrets over what he did. 'He just said, "They deserved their whack. It could have been me".'

According to Wendy, Jensen's violent death hit Peirce hard. 'Graeme was his best mate. He idolised him.'

But what Peirce didn't know at the time was that his best mate and his wife were having an affair. 'It just happened. Graeme would come over to see Victor to talk about jobs and he would wink at me. Then he came over and Victor wasn't there and it just happened.'

It was the relationship rather than the double murder that led Peirce to his only moment of remorse.

He told her, 'If I had known about the affair I wouldn't have done it (Walsh Street).'

IT has taken Wendy Peirce almost two years — since agents acting for the *Underbelly* conglomerate first approached her — to finally agree to tell her story.

She has been interviewed on the record and then later asked for her story to remain unpublished. Now she says she is ready to tell the truth.

Her private life is a disaster, her family is collapsing and she is heavily in debt.

She says she hopes her life can show others that there is no glamour in the underworld. She claims that the death of her husband has finally given her the victim's perspective of crime.

She was just a teenager from a law-abiding family when she met Victor Peirce and his mother, Kath Pettingill. She fell in love both with the criminal and his gangster lifestyle.

But in 1983, she says, Victor wanted to leave his criminal past and get a job.

He had just been released from Ararat prison after serving two years and they moved into a rented unit in Albert Park, suburbs away from the rest of his criminal family.

But Peirce's half-brother, the notorious Dennis Allen, offered to give them a house next to his, in Chestnut Street, Richmond.

'Once we moved in, that was the end. Victor was always helping out Dennis. If we hadn't moved there, then none of this would have happened — none of the murders, the armed robberies and the drugs. If we hadn't moved there, then Victor would be alive today and so would those two police (Tynan and Eyre).'

Allen was a prolific drug dealer in the early 1980s. 'I saw Victor with cash, sometimes $50,000, sometimes $100,000. I saw Dennis with $500,000.'

Allen had many bank accounts but also liked to bury cash so it could never be traced. Much of it was never recovered when he died of natural causes in 1987. 'When he got sick, he couldn't remember anything. It must all still be buried around Richmond.'

Police say Allen was responsible for up to 11 murders and Wendy says she learned from experience to read the signs when her brother-in-law 'was about to go off'.

One day in August 1984 she saw him turn and look coldly at small-time crook Wayne Stanhope, then turn up the volume of the stereo — not because he loved music but to drown the shots he was about to fire.

'I told him, "Not in my house".' Allen grudgingly agreed and took Stanhope next door to shoot him, but left the body in the boot of a car in the street for two days.

Wendy Peirce later took police to a bush area near Ballan where Stanhope was buried. Detectives found the burnt-out car but could not find the body although they remain convinced they were close.

Allen was blamed for the deaths of Victor Gouroff and Greg Pasche in 1983, Helga Wagnegg in 1984 and Anton Kenny in 1985.

'Dennis gave Helga Wagnegg pure heroin. They poured buckets of water from the Yarra River down her throat to try to make it look like she drowned.

'Anton did nothing wrong. There was no reason. Dennis didn't need a reason.

'Victor Gouroff killed Greg Pasche. Dennis killed Gouroff because he didn't get rid of the body properly.

'Pasche said something out of school and Gouroff stabbed him. He was in the kitchen saying, "Dennis, help me, help me". Dennis picked up a bayonet and stabbed him in the head. They dragged him into the backyard and wrapped him up. There was no need for any of this. It was madness.'

After the Walsh Street trial, many police expected Wendy Peirce to eventually be murdered by her husband or one of his criminal associates — but they remained together, when he was out of jail.

VICTOR Peirce got away with murder — and from the moment he was acquitted of killing two police he was a marked man.

When he was released from prison after serving his armed robbery sentence, the crime world had moved on. New security measures meant armed robberies were no longer lucrative. Old stick-up men like Peirce had to either go straight or find a new line of crime.

An honest living was never an option for Victor. He moved into the stand over business — trading on notoriety — and also into the drug game.

Peirce, a traditional Australian crook, began to hang out with Italian organized crime figures. The introduction probably came through his links to bent lawyer, Tom Scriva.

There was trouble at the wholesale fruit and vegetable market, a flashpoint for violence in Melbourne since the 1960s, and Frank Benvenuto employed Peirce as his minder.

The middle-aged gunnie was quick to make a point when he fired a machine gun in the market to show that he meant business.

But, unfortunately for him, someone else did as well.

On 8 May 2000 Peirce's best friend Frank Benvenuto was murdered by Andrew 'Benji' Veniamin — another gunman who had been employed down at the markets.

Some suggested Peirce had been offered a contract to betray Benvenuto but, if so, why didn't he warn his best mate?

Wendy believes Benvenuto was murdered because he had ordered the killing of another market identity in the 1990s.

When Benvenuto lay dying, he managed to ring Victor on his mobile phone. 'He just groaned.'

A few minutes later, the phone rang again. It was a major crime figure informing Peirce that Benvenuto was dead. How the man knew so quickly has never been explained. 'There was $64,000 in the boot of Frank's car and they didn't even take it,' she said.

'Benji wanted a meeting with Victor and they met in a Port Melbourne park. He wanted to know if Victor was going to back up for Frank. He was his best mate. Victor took a gun and Benji would have been armed.'

They agreed there would be no payback. Well, that's what Victor thought. History shows that Veniaimin went after anyone he suspected could come looking for him.

'Frank kept my family going for six years (While Victor was in jail). Frank was a lovely man.'

Peirce was not the man he once was. He began to take the pills he was selling and was losing his rat cunning. He took to dressing like a young gangster and believed his reputation made him bullet proof.

Police were told Peirce accepted a $200,000 contract to kill Jason Moran. The story goes that Peirce was paid $100,000 in advance but then refused to carry out the contract and warned Moran his life was in danger.

Perhaps tellingly, Jason Moran was a prominent mourner at Peirce's funeral although the two gunmen were never considered close. Moran could not know that his funeral would be held across town just over a year later.

Police suspect convicted murderer Mark Anthony Smith also accepted a contract he did not fulfill. But an attempt to kill Smith failed when he was shot in the neck in the driveway of his Keilor home on 28 December 2002. He recovered and fled to Queensland for several months.

With all underworld murders, police look to those close to the victim to find a link.

On the evening of Wednesday 1 May 2002, Peirce was relaxed and chirpy. Forensic tests later indicated his good mood was chemically induced. His autopsy revealed residues of ecstasy, Valium and amphetamines.

He had played football with his son, Vinnie, and then kissed Wendy and daughter Katie before saying 'he had to meet a bloke'.

'He told me to go home and put his coffee machine on for his short black,' Wendy says. 'The last thing he said to me was, "I love you, Darl".'

As he sat in his car, waiting for the meeting, two men in a stolen Commodore (hit men, like old armed robbers, prefer the home-grown Holden) pulled up. One was Veniamin, who walked over and shot Peirce twice from point blank range. A third shot missed, lodging in the pillar between the doors.

At the last second Peirce used his right arm to try to block the shots as he sat in the driver's seat. Both bullets travelled through his arm into his body, causing fatal wounds to his liver, diaphragm and lungs.

'They revived him twice there but he was unconscious and they couldn't save him,' Wendy says with little emotion.

He was taken to the Alfred Hospital — the same hospital where Steven Tynan and Damian Eyre were taken 14 years earlier.

Detectives found that Peirce, 43, was unarmed. He clearly was not expecting trouble and must have thought he was meeting a harmless friend.

They also found he had two mobile phones in the car — one rigged by a friendly technician from a telecommunications company so that it operated without charge. 'He had one for home and the free one was for business,' Wendy says.

So who was the 'bloke' Peirce was supposed to meet when he was ambushed?

It was Vince Benvenuto — Frank's brother.

Peirce was murdered one week short of the second anniversary of Benvenuto's murder.

GANGSTER. Drug dealer. Gunman. Cop killer. Victor Peirce was called all these things before he was shot dead in Port Melbourne.

But when he was buried eight days later he was just someone's father, someone's son. The grief of those who loved him was as real as anybody else's, a sobering thought for the most hardened observer.

There were plenty of those at St Peter and Paul's Catholic Church in South Melbourne, where mourners mingled with plainclothes police, reporters and at least one known gunman; a prime suspect in another, unsolved, gangland slaying.

It wasn't, however, a huge funeral by underworld standards.

Whereas almost 1000 people had jammed St Mary's by the Sea in West Melbourne to farewell Alphonse Gangitano four years earlier, perhaps a quarter of that many went to Victor's.

And whereas Gangitano — a 'celebrity' gangster known by his first name — cultivated a Hollywood image, Peirce lived and died on a smaller stage.

Gangitano was a middle-class private schoolboy who turned his back on respectability to become the black prince of Lygon Street.

Peirce, by contrast, wasn't so much working class as underclass, condemned from birth to a sordid life cycle of crime and violence. The wonder was not that he died violently, but that he survived as long as he did.

His mother, Kath Pettingill, once a notorious thief and brothel madam dubbed 'Granny Evil', had seven children by several men. With Victor's death, she has buried three of her children and must wonder how many more family funerals she will attend. She herself narrowly escaped death years ago, when a bullet blinded her in one eye.

The mourners gathered well before the service, under a sky the colour of lead. Most of them looked as sullen as the weather.

The men tended to mullets or close-cropped hair, the women were mostly bleached blondes, tattoos half-hidden under dark stockings. Sunglasses and cigarettes were compulsory for both sexes, chewing gum and earrings optional.

In the church, many shied away from the pews, preferring to stand together at the back of the church, as deadpan as the inmates of a prison exercise yard. Which many undoubtedly had been.

Father Bob Maguire, whose inner-city flock has included many a black sheep, conducted a service, as he called it, 'designed by the family'. Instead of hymns, popular songs were played. Instead of a formal eulogy, the dead man's children and friends read out personal tributes that were clapped, like speeches at a birthday party.

Katie Peirce said her father was a 'strong, kind, family man' who had hired a double-decker bus for her 16th birthday and taken her out to get her drunk as a treat. His pet name for her was 'Pooh Bum'.

His youngest son, Vinnie, named in honour of his honour Justice Frank Vincent after Peirce's acquittal in the Walsh Street murders, said he would miss his dad picking him up from school, buying him lollies and driving around.

'I remember when he used to go fast in the car with me,' he said.

The first line of the opening song (*Soldier Of Love*) began with the words 'Lay down your arms'. The song chosen for the exit music was *When I Die*, by the group No Mercy. It sounded like a portent of funerals to come. Outside, it had begun to rain. A guard of honour, of sorts, lined the street, blocking traffic. It stretched about twenty metres. At Steven Tynan's police funeral, more than thirteen years earlier, the honour guard stretched for kilometres.

But there was real sadness. As the hearse took the outlaw Victor Peirce for his last ride, hard faces softened briefly.

Under a tree in the churchyard, a homicide detective watched, wondering if the killer was in the crowd and how many more were destined to suffer the same fate.

WENDY Peirce was convinced that police would not try too hard to solve her husband's murder. After all, he had killed two of them.

In police circles no name is more detested than that of Victor Peirce. Many openly rejoiced when he was finally shot.

The investigation was handed to Purana and nearly five years after the ambush the head of the taskforce, Jim O'Brien, stood next to Wendy as he made a plea for new information.

Years earlier, O'Brien had been a member of the Ty-Eyre taskforce that had been betrayed by Wendy.

In 2007 the Purana Taskforce arrested a man accused of being the driver of the getaway car. They claim the hit was ordered by a senior gangland figure connected to an established Italian crime syndicate.

But Peirce was a man with many enemies. And Veniamin needed only half a reason to kill.

13

A HOLE IN THE IRON CURTAIN

*In each case they were set up,
not by an enemy but a friend.
It is the way of the drug world.
Loyalty is a commodity to be
bought and sold.*

NIKOLAI Radev, a young Bulgarian wrestler, arrived in Australia in 1980 without any assets, but was welcomed by his country-of-choice and granted refugee status. It would prove a fatal mistake.

In 1981 he married Sylvia, a teenage hairdressing apprentice in Melbourne.

He worked at a Doveton fish and chip shop owned by his in-laws and then opened a pizza shop nearby. But after about a year he decided there were better ways to make a crust than from pizzas.

From 1983, until his death twenty years later, Radev did not work or pay tax, yet maintained the lifestyle of a millionaire.

He was quick to collect debts but not so quick to repay them.

'His attitude to personal accounting has always been cavalier,' said Mark Brandon Read, a keen observer of local criminal matters and manners.

Soon after arriving in Australia, Radev made contact with-known members of Melbourne's flourishing Russian organised crime syndicates. His reputation had preceded him and he was already known as a ruthless young gangster from his early years in Bulgaria, yet Australian authorities were not aware of his record before granting him refugee status.

His former wife, Sylvia, says Radev always wanted to be a gangster. 'He had no fear and no shame. It was just a power thing for him. He wanted to be like Al Pacino in *Scarface*.'

When they were married he could be occasionally charming but more often brutal — and he would disappear for days. 'He would say he was going to the shop and then not come back.' She soon learned not to ask for an explanation.

'He told me later that he married me just to get Australian citizenship. He ended up just wasting his life. It was really sad.'

In 1985 he was first jailed in Victoria for drug trafficking. After experiencing prison in Bulgaria, Melbourne's jails were like weekend retreats for the hardened gangster. It was just another place to pump iron and plan his next standover campaign.

Radev's criminal record shows his life-long love of violence. His prior convictions include assaults, blackmail, threats to kill, extortion, firearm offences, armed robbery and serious drug charges.

A police report said: 'He is a dangerous and violent offender, well connected within the criminal underworld. He carries firearms and associates with people who carry firearms.'

In early 1998 Radev began a relationship with a Bulgarian woman twelve years his senior. She was financially comfortable, but that was not enough for Nik. Soon they were trafficking heroin in the St Kilda district.

When Radev was again jailed in 1999 the older woman sold drugs to try to pay his legal fees. She was caught and sentenced to prison. When he was released, Radev was, in crime terms, upwardly mobile and began to flaunt his wealth. From 2000 he found a rich vein of crime and, according to associates, 'went up in the world'.

Radev told associates that he was now a businessman and involved in property development, a job description that covers a lot of ground. He started to deal with other gangsters on the move such as Housam Zayat, Sedat Ceylan and Mark Mallia.

In 1998, Radev and Zayat were charged over a home invasion in which a 71-year-old man was bashed and his five-year-old granddaughter tied to a bed and threatened with a handgun. Radev's friendship with Ceylan was short lived — and so might Ceylan himself have been if Radev had got his way.

Ceylan falsely claimed to have bought electronic equipment worth about $10 million, resulting in a GST refund of almost $1 million.

Radev thought it was an excellent scheme, but expected his cut. He abducted and tortured Ceylan, demanding $100,000. The GST fraudster fled to Turkey with his money and is still wanted in Australia.

Certainly Radev loved violence. He once firebombed the car of rival drug dealer, Willie Thompson.

Willie must have been delighted when he heard of Radev's death, although his delight, like a lot of Radev's friendships, would have been short lived. Thompson was shot dead in Chadstone just months after Radev's murder in remarkably similar circumstances.

Strangely, after his car was firebombed, Thompson went out and bought a soft-top convertible. Go figure.

The Bulgarian even threatened police who had the temerity to arrest him. He intimidated one of the arresting officers, Ben Archbold, who eventually resigned because of the stress.

Archbold later gained some notoriety himself when he became a contestant in the television reality program, *Big Brother*. He was evicted, therefore failing to win the Archbold prize.

In 2001, Radev the standover man had become big enough to employ his own protection, using a professional kickboxer as muscle. He rented a home in Brighton and had no trouble finding the $530 weekly rent, paying promptly in cash.

He showered his de facto wife and their child with expensive gifts, but chose not to live with them. He paid the rent on their flat and their substantial expenses.

Just weeks before his death, he bought a 1999 Mercedes for $100,000. It was black, naturally.

For the one-time penniless refugee, Australia was the land of opportunity — even if nothing he did appeared legitimate.

He began to wear expensive clothes, preferring the exclusive Versace range. When he wanted his teeth fixed he paid a dentist $55,000 in cash for a set of top-of-the-range crowns.

Life was good for the wrestler-turned-gangster — so why was he shot dead?

Radev was well-known in the drug world and was an associate of Carl Williams and Tony Mokbel. He would sometimes buy drugs from the pair but, as always, the former wrestler wanted to be on top. He pestered Williams to be introduced to their drug cook — the man who made the pills and powders for the syndicate.

But Williams knew that the introduction would lead to an abduction — and a messy one.

He was told Radev would grab the cook, take him to an isolated farm and torture him to force him to work exclusively for the Bulgarian. Radev was said to have claimed he would have the speed chef 'cook 24 hours a day.'

It was time for the classic double cross.

Radev met a group of drug dealers for coffee at the Brighton Baths not far from his home. It is believed Tony Mokbel was present at the meeting. It was 15 April 2003.

As soon as Radev was told he could meet the drug cook across town in Coburg, the Bulgarian was keen to move.

Radev and some others at the meeting travelled in at least three cars to Coburg.

Radev left his car in Queen Street to talk to two men. He then turned and was walking back to his Mercedes when he was shot up to seven times in the head and body. He died next to the car he had bought with his hard-earned drug money.

Police found a witness who saw a small red sedan, possibly a Holden Vectra, in Queen Street, near the intersection with Reynard Street. The car left the scene moments before the shooting.

It was the same make, model and colour of a vehicle owned at the time by George Williams, Carl's father and fellow drug dealer.

Much later, the hit man known as The Runner told police that in 2003 he was introduced to Veniamin by a Williams' adviser in a Coburg hotel. Only a short time later, he said: 'I drove Veniamin to murder Nik Radev.'

After the Radev murder, Veniamin refused to help police with their inquiries. He was so uncooperative on principle that he even warned his own parents not to help the police if he were killed. He must have had a crystal ball. He knew he, too, was living dangerously and stood a big chance of being killed — he just couldn't tell when and where.

When Williams pleaded guilty to three murders in 2007 after being earlier found guilty of a fourth, he did so on the understanding that he (and his father) would not be charged over the Radev killing.

When Radev was shot, he was wearing a watch valued at $20,000 and a complete Versace outfit — including shoes.

His passing saddened not only friends and criminal associates. He owed one Versace outlet in Melbourne $8000 at the time, a debt that was never paid. One well-known legal identity also wrote off Radev's substantial unpaid legal fees. But at least the legal identity knows he will have a steady income on retirement, as he is now a respected judge with a healthy superannuation scheme.

Although Radev was known often to carry several thousand dollars in cash, his Commonwealth Bank accounts remained dormant for months at a time.

He flew overseas five times in four years and always travelled business class. His last trip was to Israel, the year before his murder.

He was a regular at some of Melbourne's best restaurants and often stayed in five-star hotels. After his death, police found receipts for $400 bottles of Cognac and $50 cigars among his possessions.

But what they didn't find was cash. They believe his friends went to his Brighton home and took at least $200,000, claiming it was their share of the profits.

But Radev was living, and later dead, proof that money can't buy class. Apart from having the word 'taxi' tattooed on his penis — the 'joke' was that 'it's always available and goes everywhere' — Radev loved his wealth so much he was buried with at least some of it. His casket was gold plated and said to be valued at $30,000.

Most of his associates lived the same way. They spent up big on bling and baubles and drove Porsches, Jaguars and an Audi coupe.

But like Radev, Gangitano and the Morans, they were to find too late that money doesn't buy protection. Eventually the hunter becomes the hunted.

Next to go was Mark Mallia, a close friend of Radev. Mallia, 30, was another standover man connected in the drug world.

Soon after Radev's death, Mallia went to Radev's home to collect certain valuables, including the prized $20,000 watch, claiming that as the Bulgarian's best friend he was entitled to the keepsake.

It was a cunning move by a greedy man but he wasn't smart enough to work out that for him, time was also running out.

His close links to Radev meant that Williams saw him as a threat and increasingly Williams took to killing anyone he felt may come after him.

In 2007, Williams pleaded guilty to the murder of Mallia but, as with most of Carl's killings, he did not act alone. This time he used several members of his gang to abduct and torture Radev's good friend.

Williams tried to organise a meeting with Mallia but he would not fall for the same trick as Radev. He knew that any meeting with Williams and Veniamin would end in tears — and blood. His.

On 7 August 2003, a police phone tap recorded Williams ringing Mallia to try and set up the meeting. Mallia initially refused saying the 'Safety issue is too much,' and, 'If I don't see anybody, nobody can hurt me and I can't hurt anybody.'

But eventually he was persuaded, on condition the meeting was held where there could be no ambush. It would be done in the underworld's version of neutral ground: Crown Casino, where security cameras would record any attempt at a double cross.

The meeting at a restaurant at the complex was to assure Mallia that Williams and his team were not responsible for Radev's murder. In fact, said Carl, he was furious with the hit and had the word out that he wanted to find who killed Nik so he could seek revenge.

But Veniamin was to play the bad cop against Williams' good cop.

Benji, it is claimed, lent across the table and accused Mallia of plotting to kill him and Williams. He said he had spotted two men outside his house and suggested they were there to set up the hit.

One of those at the table said Veniamin muttered in a low threatening voice that he would kill Mallia and his family if he didn't back off.

Mallia, understandably in tears, said he just wanted to find out who killed his mate, Nik. They parted, apparently with their differences sorted. For the moment.

Later Williams found that Mallia had four heavies sit off the meeting and was still plotting his death. It was enough for him to move.

Mallia would never agree to a second meeting so Williams knew the best way to lure his target to the ambush was to persuade someone close to the victim to change sides.

He is alleged to have met one of Mallia's closest friends at a pokie venue in Lalor and offered him $50,000 to swap allegiance. The deal was done and Mallia's death certificate was signed.

Now all it needed was to be dated.

He was allegedly driven by two friends to a Lalor house where he was taken to the aptly-named 'torture room'.

Mallia was beaten, allegedly burnt with a soldering iron and throttled with a rope. Police say there were five men present, with the chief torturer being the remarkably energetic Veniamin. When Williams turned up at the torture room with $50,000 cash in a plastic bag Mallia was bound, gagged and very much alive.

But not for long.

Why torture the victim? Police say Williams was convinced Mallia had hidden large amounts of cash from drug dealing and

Carl wanted the buried treasure before Mark was made to walk the plank.

Mallia's charred remains were found inside a wheelie bin in a drain near a reserve in West Sunshine on 18 August 2003.

With every hit, Williams became more powerful but as his profile grew so did his paranoia.

In the western suburbs, Paul Kallipolitis was the prince of drug dealers. 'PK' was a close friend of Dino Dibra and Andrew Veniamin. Such a network was no guarantee of longevity.

PK was not a drug dealer who ordered others to do his dirty work. When he had a dispute with another drug dealer, Mark Walker, they decided to sort it out with fists. But Walker brought a gun. It was a fatal mistake. A court was told that Kallipolitis wrestled the gun from him and shot Walker twice in the back of the head. He was convicted of manslaughter and served just four years, despite the wounds indicating that it was an execution.

While some drug dealers drove Ferraris, Kallipolitis, a qualified panel beater, preferred a rebuilt Holden Kingswood with the personalised number plates, 'CORRUPT.'

At least he wasn't shy.

Whether Williams decided to kill Kallipolitis because he feared PK would want a slice of his growing drug profits or whether he just wanted to rid himself of potential rivals is not clear.

What is clear is that the person who killed PK was a friend. That is why he was invited into Kallipolitis' fortress home in Sunshine, through the triple-locked front door.

PK was shot twice in the head. Just metres away — and just out of reach — was his own handgun. The victim felt relaxed enough in the company to remained unarmed until it was too late.

The man who pulled the trigger was his long-time trusted friend — Andrew Veniamin. It was October 2002. Two years earlier PK and Benji had shot dead their supposed friend Dino Dibra in a similar act of betrayal.

While senior police were in the last stages of planning to expand the Purana gangland taskforce, another case emerged.

This one was yet another associate of Radev. Housam 'Sam' Zayat, 32, of Fawkner, went to a late-night meeting at a paddock near the junction of Derrimut and Boundary Roads in Tarneit, west of Melbourne, on 9 September 2003. A man with a gun made sure he didn't return.

Zayat was facing drug-trafficking charges, but had been released on bail only a week before his murder. His co-accused included suspended and former police. His committal hearing was due to begin the week after his death.

A suspended articled clerk, Ali Aydin, who managed to escape the ambush, ran twelve kilometres to the safety of the Sunshine police station. He had allegedly driven Zayat to the meeting.

In 1994, Zayat was charged with the murder of his 50-year-old lover in a Footscray house and the attempted murder of her teenage son. He was later convicted on the attempted murder charge.

His brother, Mohammed Zayat, was found hanged in 1999 at Port Phillip Prison. Another brother also served time in jail.

A well-known criminal called Nicholas Ibrahim was charged with Zayat's murder. The key witness against him was to be Ali Aydin, who had told police he had seen Ibrahim chase Zayat before shooting him five times with a pump-action shotgun.

It was compelling evidence — or would have been had he repeated it in open court. But during the committal Aydin refused to co-operate and would not answer questions.

He said he would not acknowledge his statement to police and wanted it withdrawn, but later he agreed he had signed it as true and correct.

In 2005 Aydin was jailed for contempt for refusing to testify. Surprisingly, a former policeman had confidently predicted that

Aydin would never give evidence in the trial. Was it a case of an experienced deduction or inside information?

On 17 February 2006, Nicholas Ibrahim stood in the dock of the Victorian Supreme Court and appeared shattered when he heard the jury announce he was guilty of murder. In fact, it was all a mistake. The forewoman had pronounced the wrong verdict — she had meant to say guilty of manslaughter.

Ibraham was later sentenced to fifteen years in jail, with a non-parole period of thirteen years. It could have been worse.

On 6 February 2007, Sam Zayat's brother was also murdered. Haysam Zayat, 37, was found dead in his Noble Park home shortly before 7am. He had been stabbed to death. A man was later charged with his murder.

For men like Radev, Mallia, Kallipolitis and Dibra, the inexhaustible demand for amphetamines and ecstasy created a gold rush. Men too lazy to hold down a job on a factory floor found they could maintain the lifestyle of wealthy industrialists. But only for a while. Eventually, they screwed it up by killing each other.

In each case they were set up, not by an enemy but a friend. It is the way of the drug world. Loyalty is a commodity to be bought and sold by the bogan bandits of the urban badlands.

14

SITTING DUCK

The truth is that Moran
was born into a life
of violence and crime
and revelled in it.

EVERYONE in the underworld knew Jason Matthew Patrick Moran was a dead man walking.

Too erratic to be respected and too violent to be ignored, the drug dealer and suspected killer was always the popular tip to become a murder target in Melbourne's crime war.

At the funeral of Jason's half-brother, Mark Moran — murdered outside his Aberfeldie home on 15 June 2000 — a well-connected crime figure gave a friend a two-word warning that he should distance himself from the younger Moran. 'He's next,' he whispered.

Not that underworld identities and a select group of police were the only ones to suspect that Moran's name was on a death list. It was Australia's worst-kept crime secret.

Standover man turned author, artist and renowned after-dinner speaker, Mark Brandon Read, released his tenth book, *The Popcorn Gangster*, in November 2001. On the back cover Read stands in an old Tasmanian cemetery near three weathered grave-stones. The photograph has been digitally altered to show one headstone with the name, 'Mad Charlie' (a murdered gangster friend) and the date of death; on the second is, 'Big Al' (Alphonse Gangitano) with the date of his murder. On the third is simply, 'Jason' with a question mark. The message was clear. The fact that Moran was to be murdered was no longer an issue. It was simply a matter of time.

Less than two years later that date was filled in — 21 June 2003. And so it had come to pass: Chopper Read was not just making a crime-writing profit, he was a crime-writing prophet.

But there were no jokes about the way the murder was carried out. It was unusually brutal, and smacked of a South American drug-cartel killing in Miami or Colombia rather than the old painter and docker way of doing the business. For, while Moran's murder came as no surprise to police, criminals or true-crime devotees, the nature of the double execution shocked almost everyone — making him more famous in death than in life.

The details are now well-known: Moran was with a group of children after a game of junior football when he was gunned down with his friend, Pasquale Barbaro, at the Cross Keys Hotel car park in Essendon North.

Murdering two men in front of hundreds of people might seem reckless, but to the killer it made perfect sense.

Moran was no easy target. He had carried a gun since he was a teenager and was considered an expert in counter-surveillance. For added security he had repeatedly changed addresses in the previous year.

After selling his luxury home in Grosvenor Street, Moonee Ponds, he moved into his sister-in-law's, before relocating to the large house of a friendly hotel owner. He made sure he had a bodyguard with him when he did business at night.

Months earlier, there had been an incident where shots were exchanged near a pizza parlour. In James Bond style, Moran had flicked the boot of his car to act as a shield as he sped away.

Three weeks before being shot, Moran was again warned he was a target. Never short of guns, he made it known he wanted fresh stock and was prepared to pay $3500 per handgun — well over the going rate.

The killer would have found Moran's unpredictable movements hard to track. But Moran did have a habit he was reluctant to break: he loved football and regularly took his children to the local Auskick clinic.

On Saturday mornings he would park his pale blue Mitsubishi van at the Cross Keys Hotel overlooking the reserve.

To the killer, it was ideal. Moran was at his most vulnerable at the children's football: more like an average suburban dad than a gangster in survival mode, although associates say he always carried a gun, even there.

The gunman knew no-one would notice him in the crowd. A stranger in a quiet street sparks interest. A man in a busy car park is anonymous.

The spot also gave the killer a clear escape route — across a footbridge over the Moonee Ponds Creek to a waiting car. The killer had to be confident in his running ability — relying on his pace and the shock of the gun blasts — to be sure no one followed.

He pulled a balaclava over his face and blasted Moran through the closed driver's side window with a shotgun. He then used a handgun to shoot Moran's mate Barbaro, in the passenger seat.

At least five children, including Moran's twin girl and boy, aged six, and Mark's fatherless children, were in the Mitsubishi van when the gunman fired. Several other kids were playing near the vehicle. 'I have just seen my uncle shot,' one of the girls from the van told an Auskick umpire moments after the attack.

Barbaro, known as 'Little Pat', was a long-time friend and a low-level crook. His criminal history included nine convictions for possessing cannabis and one for trafficking and using heroin. A big drug syndicate once used him as a trusted courier.

West Australian organised crime squad detectives arrested him at Perth Airport on 11 May 1999 with a bag holding 367 grams of amphetamines.

His choice of lawyer said much about his criminal connections. Andrew Fraser, who later that year was arrested in Melbourne and charged with cocaine trafficking, defended him. Fraser was also the Moran clan's lawyer of choice.

Fraser told the court Barbaro was paid $3000 for carrying the drugs and was financially ruined after losing $100,000 at Crown Casino. He said his client was an alcoholic who drank Scotch and smoked marijuana as soon as he woke up in the morning.

When Judge Alan Fenbury sentenced Barbaro to six years' jail, he said the prison term 'might even save your life'. In reality it just postponed his death.

When 'Little Pat' was released in 2001, he returned to Melbourne and quickly re-established his links with Moran.

The killer selected his weapons with care. He used the shotgun to blast through the closed window. In the crime world, the shotgun is considered perfect for close-range work. You don't miss from a metre with a 12-gauge and don't provide much for ballistics experts to work with.

The killer then dropped the sawn-off gun next to the van and used the pistol to shoot Barbaro up to five times.

The same types of weapons, a shotgun and handgun, were used to kill Moran's half-brother, Mark, three years earlier.

It was no coincidence. The one man, Carl Williams, was behind both killings.

The 12-gauge shotgun used to kill Jason was a popular, and

cheap, Miura model Boito brand imported from Brazil in the early 1970s.

An inscription engraved on the metal breech of the shotgun reads: 'Mitch on your 21st ... from The Boy's' with the date '22-4-56', suggesting the gun had been originally bought in 1977.

One of the first on the scene that Saturday was, ironically, an ex-detective called Phil Glare, who was working at a scrap-metal merchant's across the road. He found Moran and Barbaro already dead in the van.

Glare, an old-style detective from the disbanded consorting squad, is no stranger to gangland wars and public executions. He was escorting Raymond Patrick Bennett to an armed robbery hearing when Bennett, also known as Chuck, was shot dead by an unknown gunman inside the old Melbourne Magistrates' Court building in November 1979. Bennett's murder remains unsolved.

The court hit was a payback. Bennett had been one of three men who had walked into the Wantirna unit of well-known gangster Les Kane and shot him in the bathroom, using modified automatic rifles fitted with silencers. Kane's body was never recovered.

Les had been married at least twice. His daughter from his first marriage, Trish, went on to marry a young Jason Moran. Police insist the bald facts are that Kane's brother, Brian, was the gunman in the City Court who killed Bennett. In November 1982, Brian Kane was shot dead in the Quarry Hotel, Brunswick.

Days later the young Jason Moran placed a death notice in *The Sun* to 'Uncle Brian' from 'Your Little Mate'.

But the Moran family connection to underworld murders does not stop there.

Jason and Mark Moran were half brothers. They had the same mother, Judy, but different fathers. Mark's father was a Sydney gunman called Les 'Johnny' Cole, originally a painter and docker from Melbourne who became a standover man for NSW gangster Frederick Charles 'Paddles' Anderson.

Cole was gunned down outside his luxury home at Kyle Bay in November 1982, in what was the first of eight murders in a Sydney underworld war.

Jason's father was Lewis Moran who, together with his brother 'Tuppence', was respected by Melbourne's underworld. Both were well-known figures at the racetrack.

But Tuppence's health had been failing for years and he had become less active than he once was. He indulged in breeding a few racehorses at a property near Melton, west of Melbourne. Tuppence was well-liked. So much so that he would be the only adult male Moran to survive the war.

Lewis had his own problems and was on remand over drug charges when Jason was shot. He was refused permission to attend his son's funeral on security grounds and declined to share his thoughts on the murders with homicide squad detectives.

Besides crime and punting, the Morans' great love was Carlton Football Club. Judy Moran's father, Leo Brooks, was the club's doorman and general assistant. Many star recruits, from rogues to Rhodes scholars, boarded with Brooks during the 1970s and '80s.

For some, the bonds remained for life. Premiership star Wayne Johnston told a reporter he met Mark and Jason through Brooks. 'In those days a lot of the players, myself included, used to come down from the country and stay with Leo and that's where I first met the boys. I used to babysit them.'

For one of the Moran funerals, the club lent the family one of its treasured Premiership flags. It took years to get it back. Judy Moran insisted it was a gift. Perhaps she was confused.

JASON Moran came from a family of career criminals, but had many chances to break free. In the end, he loved the idea of becoming a gangster too much.

The deaths of his wife's father and uncle, as well as the murder of his half-brother's father, didn't seem to show him that it was a career with clear limitations. In the underworld, fringe benefits can be tempting, but the redundancy package is distinctly unattractive. It is small, made of lead and arrives suddenly. You don't even see it coming.

Educated at a solid middle-class private school, Moran excelled at sport but was not interested in taking advantage of academic opportunities or tertiary studies. Why be a lawyer when you could buy one?

Never too concerned about blood, he worked at the City Abattoir near the Newmarket saleyards for three years before the business closed. He then worked at a duty-free shop and later in the jewellery industry. But as his tastes for an expensive lifestyle increased, his stomach for honest work declined.

He carried a handgun before he was old enough to drive and was always prepared to let people know he was armed. Regular drinkers at the Laurel Hotel in Ascot Vale tended to give young Moran a wide berth. He once followed a family friend into the toilet after a minor argument, pulling a gun and shoving the barrel into his head with the accompanying threat to blow it off. Lightweight criminals were frightened of him, while heavyweights did not react because of their respect for his father.

When Moran went to jail, his reputation for violence grew. One fellow inmate remembers the new boy in the (shower) block would tell anyone who bothered listening he was a force to be reckoned with. 'Do you know who the fuck I am?' he would ask. It was a rhetorical question.

Moran became a staunch ally of Alphonse Gangitano, self-proclaimed De Niro of Lygon Street. They shared interests: protection rackets, illegal gambling and violence.

Some of the violence was premeditated — some simply mindless. He bashed a stranger with a wheel brace in Punt Road because he believed the man had not used his indicator when passing.

No-one challenged him.

In 1995 police set up a video camera in the house of a family across the road from Moran's. When he found out, he is alleged to have responded by telling the family he would bomb their house and harm their children.

They sold the house, allegedly at a hefty loss, and launched a writ against the police force.

After Gangitano shot standover man Greg Workman at a St Kilda party, Moran helped get his then friend off the hook.

But it all changed after December 1995, when Moran and Gangitano went berserk in a bar in Melbourne's nightclub strip of King Street.

They were charged and the court case dragged on for years. Moran was caught on police listening devices saying Gangitano was out of control — a 'Lulu'.

On 16 January 1998, Gangitano was shot dead in his home in Templestowe. Police say Moran was the gunman and the murder weapon was thrown from the Westgate Bridge. Police divers were never able to find the gun at the bottom of the Yarra.

The Morans always denied involvement in the murder and kept a cross in their front yard as a tribute to Gangitano. Crocodile tears from gangsters in crocodile shoes, police say.

Alphonse's death should have shown Jason nobody was bulletproof. He failed to understand that his time would come.

In the underworld, the hunter can become the hunted overnight.

Moran was convicted of the King Street assault even though the judge remarked that his arrest, in which he received a fractured skull, was 'remarkably heavy handed'.

One of the police with the heavy hands later wandered into a Moonee Ponds pub for a drink. Standing at the other end of the bar was Moran with a group of heavies. A drink arrived for the policeman, care of Moran, who then walked over and said there were no hard feelings over the arrest, but as this was his area the copper should have his free drink and then 'fuck off.'

The policeman told Moran he would not accept the drink but would accept the advice. He left.

Mark was murdered while Jason was in jail. He was let out to attend the funeral. Many predicted he would plot the payback. A death notice he put in the *Herald Sun* strongly implied revenge.

But when he was released from jail in 2001, he applied to the parole board to travel overseas because of fears for his life.

Members of his family suggested he stay overseas, away from trouble.

He would receive regular payments from family enterprises, and could have lived a comfortable and somewhat anonymous life. But that would cramp his style. He wanted the notoriety of a gangster's life, apparently unaware he was doomed to the infamy of a gangster's death.

Against all advice, he returned to Melbourne within months.

FOR the homicide squad, all investigations start with looking for motive, means and opportunity. In most murder cases, the challenge is to find someone who wanted the victim dead. For homicide squad crew two, which was originally assigned the Jason Moran case, there were too many to choose from. It was a matter of trying to discount some of his enemies.

And in the Morans' social and business circles, enemies don't just cross you off their Christmas-card list.

There were many theories. One was it was a payback by Italian gangsters for Moran killing Gangitano.

Moran had many enemies, but the homicide squad quickly came to believe that Carl Williams was the most likely organiser. They certainly knew he was not the gunman — who was described as slim, fit and fast.

Police knew of Williams' hatred for the Morans and he was the number one suspect for Mark's murder. But who was the actual gunman this time?

Several names were mentioned and for once Andrew Veniamin's was not among them: he had a rock solid alibi. But one career crook was mentioned: a staunch friend of Carl's who had done jail time with him.

The former armed robber was known to be super fit, ruthless and violent. He became known as 'The Runner'.

He was considered one of the hard men of the prison system and diagnosed by a forensic psychologist as a full-on psychopath.

Little wonder, considering his past. Born into desperate domestic violence in the 1960s, he saw one of his sisters die young of heart failure. His mentally-disturbed father regularly beat him.

The young Runner came home from school to find his father stabbing his mother. He jumped in and saved her life.

He was first sent to Pentridge when he was 17, for assault. On his release he became one of Australia's most prolific armed robbers, always running from the scene for hundreds of metres to his waiting getaway car. He was an underworld soldier and did not need to be asked twice when Williams approached him in jail to kill Moran — a man he had never met.

'I said "yes" to show him my loyalty. I was aware of Carl's hatred of the Moran family. Carl told me about an incident in 1999 where Carl was shot by Jason Moran,' he later told police of the short-lived and murderous relationship that ended badly for all concerned.

Williams needed a new hit man, as he was becoming increasingly worried about Veniamin. While Williams and Benji appeared to be loyal to each other, Carl was beginning to have doubts.

He had wanted Veniamin to set up Moran but despite many promises had failed to deliver. Williams knew that Veniamin had once hero-worshiped Mick Gatto and began to think the hit man could be turned against Carl. He knew Veniamin had killed former friends such as Dino Dibra and Paul Kallipolitis, so why not Williams himself?

Williams had been shot once and had no intention of being shot again. So The Runner was ideal. Loyal, part mad and ruthless — the perfect CV for a paid killer.

Even before the bodies of Jason Moran and Barbaro were removed from the van, the dogs were barking: The Runner pulled the trigger.

He had a long and remarkable criminal history and was a former member of the ten most wanted by police.

In March 1990, he escaped from jail in South Australia where he had been serving a long sentence for armed robberies. The following month he was arrested in Melbourne and questioned over four armed robberies.

As he was being driven to the city watch-house, he jumped from an unmarked police car and escaped again. The sleepy policeman in the back seat did not have him handcuffed. (Many years later this detective was implicated for his alleged involvement in one of the underworld murders.) After his escape, The Runner was arrested near Kingaroy in Queensland in January 1991.

Associates of the Morans were to be dragged into the war as Melbourne gangsters were eventually forced to take sides. Some with no real interest in the feud would also end up as victims.

Ironically, the Williams and Moran children attended the same private school. It would have made for interesting parent-teacher nights.

Once, Roberta Williams complained to police that Jason had harassed her outside the school. She considered seeking an intervention order but later withdrew her complaint. She didn't mention Carl's plan to lie in wait for Moran outside the school, nor the idea of her picking a fight with Trish Moran to lure Jason to come out of hiding.

Never mind that, if it had come off, he would be shot in front of the Williams and Moran kids. Collateral damage.

After Mark's murder, Williams contacted one of the authors who had written that he was a suspect, saying 'You could get a man killed writing things like that.'

The double murder at the Auskick Clinic looked like a perfectly planned hit but it wasn't. For weeks, Williams and his partner had been trying to find Moran to ambush him.

Their efforts would have been considered laughable if not for their deadly intent. Much of it seemed inspired by bad Hollywood movies more than real cunning.

As mentioned earlier, they flirted with mad plans such as hiding in the boot of Moran's BMW or lying beneath shrubs outside the house where he was believed to be staying.

One problem was they couldn't find where he was living.

Of course, there was the idea lifted from *The Untouchables*, of The Runner dressing as a woman pushing a pram with a gun in it. He was many things but he was no Yummy Mummy.

Moran was on the move and hard to find. He knew he was hot, so he kept changing addresses. So when Williams and his sidekick spotted him at the Gladstone Park Red Rooster it was Jason, not them, who was armed. That's when they followed him and he flipped the latch on the hatchback and fired shots at them.

Finally, Williams was tipped off that Moran took his children to Auskick training every Saturday morning in Essendon North, near the Cross Keys Hotel.

But it was not the hit of choice. Williams wanted Moran killed at Fawkner Cemetery on the anniversary of Mark Moran's murder — but the hit team slept in and missed their Mark (or Jason).

It was then that the Auskick plan was set in stone for the following week.

During the week, The Runner and The Driver (of the getaway car) went to the Cross Keys ground to plan the murder. The Runner would be dropped at the hotel car park where Moran would be parked. He would run up, shoot Moran in the head and then run over a footbridge to the getaway van.

The hit men collected the guns stashed at the Pascoe Vale house of Andrew Krakouer, brother of former football champions Phil and Jimmy, and went to the Cross Keys carpark. Meanwhile, Williams had set up his blood-test alibi.

As expected, Moran arrived — but there was a problem. No-one had given the hit man a photo of his target. He saw a man he believed was Moran. 'I thought it might have been Jason because people were coming up to him, shaking his hand and generally paying attention to him. His behaviour was typical of a gangster.'

Williams and another member of the team drove by and gave the thumbs up — then headed off to the doctor's appointment.

'I then put on my balaclava and gloves and jumped out from the van, carrying the shotgun in my right hand. I had the two revolvers in a belt around my waist. I ran to the driver's side window of the blue van, aimed the shotgun at Jason Moran and fired through the closed window,' The Runner later told police.

Moran slumped forward and The Runner fired again. He dropped the shotgun, grabbed his long-barrelled revolver and fired at least another three shots. He then took off, running over the footbridge to the waiting van.

Moran was the target. Later, The Runner would tell police he was unaware there was a second man in the car and only learnt he had killed Little Pat when he heard it on the news.

'I did not even know that I had shot Pasquale Barbaro until later...I regret that happening.'

He had been promised $100,000 for killing Moran. He was paid just $2500.

JOHN William Moran was a good man and an upstanding citizen. He joined the army in 1941 during World War II to fight for his country. He died peacefully with his family on 22 June 2003. He was 81.

There were only a handful of death notices for John William Moran from his family and the Glenroy RSL, where he was a respected regular. He was also a member of the Glenroy Lawn Bowls Club, having been a player, selector and coach for 30 years.

About 60 people attended the quiet and dignified service for the former bootmaker at the Fawkner Crematorium.

Jason Matthew Patrick Moran (no relation) died the day before John Moran. He also 'passed away' in the company of members of his family — his six-year-old twins and their young cousins. But it was not peaceful.

For Jason Moran — gunman, drug dealer, standover man and killer — there were hundreds of death notices. In death he was accorded qualities he did not readily reveal in life. In the notices he was described as 'a gentleman ... a lovable rascal ... a special friend ... a good bloke ... a diamond'.

About 700 'mourners' attended his funeral at St Mary's Star of the Sea in West Melbourne — the same church where Gangitano had been farewelled. Police were required for traffic control. Floral tributes worth thousands were sent.

Moran's mother, Judith, a big blonde woman compared in her younger days with the former film star Diana Dors, spoke at the funeral and gave a not-so-cryptic message to those present. 'All will be dealt with, my darling,' she said.

Judy Moran would be a regular face in the media in the years ahead as she attended court hearings related to the deaths of her two sons and husband. She always dressed to impress and spent hours on her makeup and hair. At times she appeared to be a parody of herself, caught in some fantasy world — always denying her family's culpability while condemning others' violence. She called for the return of capital punishment — side stepping the fact that her Jason was a gunman and suspected murderer.

But there was one image of her at the Cross Keys slumped on a fence with no make-up and no outlandish outfit. A real mother weeping real tears for a son she adored but could not control.

Jason Moran was loved by his family and their grief was every bit as real as anyone feels when they lose someone close.

But the assorted mates, associates, crime groupies and downright fools who have tried to suggest he was anything but a callous thug must have been sampling the amphetamine-based products Moran peddled.

He was described as a 'family man' — yet he pursued a violent criminal career that constantly placed him, his wife and children under threat, and he was always happy to wreck someone else's family.

He was warned at least three weeks before his murder that his card had been marked, yet he still drove around with his children as though he (and they) were bullet proof.

The truth is that Moran was born into a life of violence and crime — and revelled in it. He showed no signs of wanting to change.

The tragedy is that the fascination exerted by gangsters is self-perpetuating. At one gangland funeral, two young children step from a funeral limousine. The boy, aged about six, is dressed in a little gangster suit and wears the mandatory gangster sunglasses, although the weather is bleak and overcast. The child looks directly at a press photographer and flips him 'the bird'. This was the next generation on display.

Most people in Melbourne know the names of Gangitano and Moran, but few recognise the names of the detectives who originally headed the investigation into their murders (for the record, they were Detective Senior Sergeants Charlie Bezzina and Rowland Legg).

Ned Kelly may be Australia's most recognisable name but few can recall the police killed at Stringybark Creek — Kelly's fellow Irishmen: Michael Scanlon, Thomas Lonigan and Michael Kennedy.

American author Damon Runyon once wrote: 'Legitimate guys are much interested in the doings of tough guys, and consider them romantic.'

But there was nothing romantic about Jason Moran. Beyond his own family and friends, he was no great loss. And he brought it on himself.

15

INSIDE JOB

Sometimes in the underworld
it is more dangerous
to be owed money
than to be in debt.

PEOPLE can strive all their lives to make money to guarantee their security. The irony for many Australian criminals is that as their illegal assets rise, so too do the risks to their long-term future.

The maxim that money can't buy health or happiness applies especially to criminals. In the case of a Melbourne couple shot dead in 2003, the money they made through the lucrative vice industry couldn't buy them good taste.

Steve Gulyas and his partner, Duang 'Tina' Nhonthachith, also known as 'Bing', had all the trappings of wealth, but were destined not to live long enough to enjoy them.

As with so many of the Melbourne underworld murder victims, they knew they were in danger, but did not grasp they would almost certainly be betrayed by someone close to them.

Steve Gulyas didn't see it until the moment he was shot on the hobby farm he had bought with dirty money. He and Tina had gone to their luxurious retreat near Sunbury for the weekend. He was lying on the couch, relaxed and secure, the remote control in his lap and a drink beside him when the killer placed the gun almost to his cheek and pressed the trigger.

Tina may have been able to get from her chair and run a few steps before she, too, was shot dead.

When the bodies were found on 20 October 2003, the television and the central heating were still on. Police believe the couple knew the killer and had invited him in.

They were security conscious. In their business they had to be. But the killer may have known that the couple's elaborate security systems would be flawed that weekend.

Electronic gates at the property were being installed but were not yet operational, and their guard dogs had been taken back to Melbourne earlier that day. The hit man was either incredibly lucky or, more likely, expertly briefed.

He would have known that vicious dogs, an iron fence and window shutters protected their home in Coburg. And that their 'introduction agency', Partner Search Australia, was also protected by a security system, including cameras.

But at their 30-hectare hobby farm in Wildwood Road, they were vulnerable because the gates and fence that would make their weekender a mini-fortress had not yet been finished.

Istvan 'Steve' Gulyas, 49, was born in Hungary, and Tina Nhonthachith, 47, in Thailand. Their bodies were found by an employee who went to the home after she became concerned for their safety. Police believe they had been dead at least 12 hours.

Partner Search Australia, in Sydney Road, Coburg, supposedly specialised in introductions to Russian and Asian women. But police say Gulyas had specialised in employing under-age Asian girls in the sex industry. Signs at the premises of Partner Search promote massage services — but it was unlikely the customers were looking for relief from bad backs.

It was well-known in the sex industry that Partner Search was an illegal brothel as well as an introduction service. Tina Nhonthachith became a director of the business just two months before her murder.

The Partner Search sex workers were kept in a weatherboard house across the road from the office. Conditions were basic. Introductions were offered as face-to-face meetings in the business offices or a more relaxed approach at cocktail parties held in the business's in-house, licensed function room.

Gulyas had an extensive business history and a questionable reputation, with company links in Sydney and Queensland. He was once known as 'The Birdman' until he sold a pet-bird business, also based in Coburg. He also owned a successful truck business with his son.

Some of his former customers believed themselves to be the victims of an arranged marriage scam and one complained that he had lost more than $10,000 after his 'bride' disappeared.

One customer looking for a wife was introduced to a woman he suspected was a prostitute. He said later, when he asked for his $5000 back, 'They just laughed. It was a total rip-off.'

No-one has been able to find one case where Partner Search helped anyone establish a meaningful relationship. When immigration officials raided the business in June 2000 they detained three Thai women who worked at the agency.

Tina Nhonthachith was a businesswoman in her own right and had her own fashion line, 'Tina's Trends'. But she and Gulyas ran the introduction agency for several years. Both often returned home: Gulyas to Hungary and Nhonthachith, whose three adult children live in Australia, to Thailand.

The house where the couple died is 500 metres from the road. It is well-hidden and surrounded by hills. The couple kept to themselves, and their neighbours liked it that way. 'They are not the type of people you would want to associate with,' one said.

Gulyas bought the Sunbury property about two years before his death, which proved he had plenty of money. He filled the house with his collection of stuffed animals, proving he had no taste.

In Melbourne, Gulyas had confided to neighbours he felt he was being watched. He was concerned about the Russian Mafia. His fears were well-founded.

On the weekend of the murders, the couple had planned some hard work on the Saturday to be followed by a relaxing Sunday. On Friday, Gulyas had picked up a stuffed polar bear from a Thomastown taxidermist to go with his lion and bison. On Saturday, a neighbour saw Gulyas shifting earth on a bobcat — the small machine, not the large cat.

There was a barbecue on Sunday and a mechanic who worked for Gulyas picked up a bottle of his boss's favourite Hungarian Golden Pear liqueur at Dan Murphy's in Ascot Vale.

The mechanic stayed for lunch with business associates, but agreed to take the couple's dogs to Coburg that night. He knew the dogs usually snarled and growled at motorists from the back of his ute, and did not want them acting up on the Tullamarine Freeway in Monday's traffic, so drove them to Coburg on Sunday afternoon. With the dogs gone and the gates not yet erected, the killer had open access.

If the dogs had stayed, there might have been no killing at all. Or a triple murder.

There was another man at the barbecue: a business associate who owed Gulyas around $500,000. He told detectives he had left the property but returned later that night, supposedly to have some papers signed.

The businessman was said to have ripped off banks for around $3 million and was found to have moved nearly $5 million through the casino.

He told police he had nothing to do with the murder. He has since moved overseas. But before he did, he bought the dead couple's Sunbury farm at auction for around $600,000 and sold it a few months later for about $1.1 million. A profit of $500,000 — the exact amount he owed Gulyas. Meaning, in effect, he was a total of a million dollars up on the deal.

Sometimes in the underworld it is more dangerous to be owed money than to be in debt.

16

THE TIDE TURNS

It was the beginning of the end
but it was not the end
of the killings.

THE kilometre-square block in the middle of South Yarra is one of the busiest in Melbourne. Traffic there regularly slows to a crawl. No-one would have noticed the late-model sedan that cruised the choked streets for days.

No-one, that is, except the police surveillance experts assigned to help Victoria's gangland taskforce, codenamed Purana.

Police were tracking two of the suspects in some of Melbourne's unsolved underworld murders. Both were known to police. Neither can be named but they were, at the time, loyal members of Carl Williams' rat pack. Much later they would rat on him. They were The Runner and The Driver and this would be their latest (and last) hit for the supermarket shelf stacker turned crime boss.

They drove around the block bounded by Chapel Street and Malvern, Toorak and Williams Roads, past the upmarket boutiques that thrive near the 1960s housing commission flats. They cruised by the 24-hour Prahran police complex in Malvern Road then turned left into Williams Road and past The Bush Inn Hotel, a favourite with local police. They pulled over, checked the side streets and studied the area as meticulously as town planners.

In one week in October 2003 they went to the block at least four times.

Experienced police knew these men were not sightseeing. They were there on business.

Detectives checked the area for likely targets and considered the possibility of a Spring Carnival raid on the Pub TAB at The Bush Inn. Two luxury car dealerships were also marked as susceptible. There was also a theory that the two suspects might have been planning an armed rip-off of a drug dealer in the area. But the investigators could only make educated guesses.

The detectives did have one big advantage — they had planted a tiny bugging device in the car being used by the suspects. But while it may have seemed that the men were researching a crime, they were not discussing details. Why would they? They knew what they were planning so there was no need to spell it out.

They also had another advantage. The hit team was stupid. They had to know police were close to them, but they continued on regardless. And Carl Williams, who now believed his own publicity, considered himself untouchable.

For the first time, Purana was ahead of the pack. Investigators had found the source of the gang's clean cars — untraceable sedans that could be used as getaway vehicles. The source was a close friend of The Driver — a backyard mechanic who re-birthed abandoned cars.

A police technical expert managed to plant a tracker in the car. All detectives had to do was wait.

But when The Driver picked up the car, he noticed the brake

light was flashing. He pulled over, checked the wiring, found the bug and ripped it out.

The police infiltration should have been blown but inexplicably the hit team didn't abort their plan.

The Driver wanted to pull out, but The Runner and Williams suspected he was fabricating the story to avoid the latest hit.

And The Runner was getting impatient to kill. He followed the target several times from his home in South Yarra to his business in Abbotsford. He knew his movements and was confident he could set up an ambush. The man who had been marked for death was Michael Marshall: hot dog salesman, kick boxer and drug dealer.

The Runner knew Marshall's movements. He knew he had a shop in Hoddle Street, picked up his rolls on Friday and Saturday afternoons and had a hot dog stand outside Motel nightclub.

He knew because Carl Williams told him. And he knew the information was right because it came from Tony Mokbel who, it is alleged, ordered the hit.

But police would not learn who was to die until it was too late.

According to The Runner, '(The Driver) mentioned to me that he had found what he thought was a tracker in the car. I dismissed the thought because my mind was focussed on doing the job...I decided to keep going without the clean car. In hindsight, it was sheer stupidity that I didn't take notice of the locating of a tracking device, but my mind was elsewhere and I was feeling the pressure of the job and that we had already wasted enough time'.

That night Williams backed The Runner and told them to push on.

At the last minute, The Driver decided to use his own silver Vectra, once owned by Williams. That car was already bugged by Purana.

So while police knew a crime was about to happen, they did not know *what* it was. All they could do was wait.

Four months before this surveillance exercise, on 21 June 2003, the same hit team had shot dead Jason Moran and Pasquale Barbaro.

On the day of the murders, detectives were tipped off that one of the men subsequently monitored in South Yarra was the likely gunman. Any chance of police having the advantage of surprise was lost when a television reporter rang the Moran family and nominated the suspect.

Now there would be a breakthrough — but it would come at a price.

The first job of police is to deter rather than apprehend. If detectives know a crime is to be committed, they have a duty to try to prevent it. But intercepting a major criminal and his sidekick because they appear to be driving suspiciously looks more like harassment than deterrence.

Police had not enough evidence to lay charges, and pulling the suspects over would only alert them to the electronic surveillance. There was no real choice but to let them run.

The then head of the Purana Taskforce, Detective Inspector Andrew Allen, was at work on the evening of Saturday 25 October, when he got the call from police monitoring the listening post. The suspects were on the move, but their intent was still unclear.

Then police started to get calls from the public. There had been a shooting in South Yarra. At gangland taskforce headquarters, investigators had a database of victims, suspects, potential targets and associates. They had established a core of around 100 and a second ring of about the same number. The man who was killed was not on the police list of possible targets — but he was on someone's list.

In underworld terms, Michael Ronald Marshall, 38, was a no-body with a minor criminal record — a former kickboxer turned self-employed hot dog vendor, selling mainly around nightclubs.

The fast-food business can be lucrative, but Marshall appeared to be flying. He lived in a big, double-storey house on the corner of Williams Road and Joy Street in South Yarra. He and his de facto wife had bought it from a Melbourne surgeon in December 1991, paying off their ANZ mortgage in just three years.

A three-metre-high brick fence and an electronic security camera at the gate on Williams Road protected the house. But it wasn't enough.

The men who had come for Marshall had done their home-work. The getaway car was parked in the next road, Howitt Street, facing Williams Road.

Marshall had been to a local bakery with his five-year-old son to buy rolls for his busiest night, Saturday.

Joy Street is a narrow road filled with blocks of flats and town-houses. Marshall parked his four-wheel-drive halfway down the short street, behind his hot dog van.

Although his house had a double garage, he preferred to park in the street. His second security camera, looking down on Joy Street, was not working.

As Marshall stepped from the car, at about 6.30pm, and be-fore he could open the back door to help his son from his har-ness, The Runner jogged up and shot him at least four times in the head.

But it was no clinical hit.

Just as in the Moran-Barbaro case, The Runner had no qualms about shooting a man in front of his children. And, as in the ear-lier case, the gunman had his escape route planned.

The killer ran down a partially hidden 50-metre path through a block of flats to Howitt Street. The Driver had the motor going and took off in the classic getaway style, making sure there was no need to cross traffic flows, turning left into Williams Road and left again into the next main street.

'I was jogging along the footpath towards Marshall's driver's side door as he hadn't got out yet. Just before I got to his car I pulled the balaclava down over my face. I was about three metres away from the driver's door, standing in the middle of the road when Marshall started to get out of the car.

'I had the gun in my right hand and Marshall was out of the car and noticed me. We looked at each other briefly and I started to raise the gun as he went to lunge at me. As he lunged, I fired a shot but I am unsure if this hit him. As the gun fired, the kick-back, along with the combination of me taking a step backwards from Marshall's lunge, caused me to fall over. I also think the ground may have been a bit wet. I quickly got up again and was face to face with Marshall. He was a large person, over six feet tall and I was aware he was a former kickboxer.

'I was concerned that he might overpower me, so I just began firing shots at him at close range to the head area. I am not sure how many shots I fired; I think it may have been three or four. Marshall started to fall to the ground and I think I fired one more shot into his head as he was going down towards my feet. At no stage during the altercation did I see or realise that Marshall's son was still with him.'

The young boy got out of the car and ran home to tell his mother his father had been shot. But, he later told police; he first looked right, then left and right again to make sure there was no traffic — exactly as his parents had taught him.

Later The Runner rang Williams to tell him, again, 'That horse has just been scratched'. It was the same code he'd used when he shot Jason Moran.

Again they were stupid. The Driver had found a police listening device in his house but did not want to alert police he had discovered it — working on the basis that he would avoid making incriminating statements within its range.

Unfortunately for that theory, the 'scratched' comment was made around 5pm — after the last race of the day. Williams just grunted when told — but it was enough.

Within hours, police arrested the pair near the Elsternwick Hotel. They were in a white Toyota Hiace van. Marshall was still alive in the Alfred Hospital but died about three hours later.

Williams was also grabbed and finally taken off the streets. It was the beginning of the end for him — but not the end of the killings.

MICHAEL Marshall had an interesting circle of friends and business associates. He trained at the same gym as Willie Thompson, another kickboxer connected to the nightclub business.

Thompson sold lollipops for vending machines at nightspots — although police suspected he was also involved in selling more lucrative products to clubbers. He had been shot dead in Chadstone three months earlier, on 21 July 2003.

The lives and deaths of Marshall and Thompson were remarkably similar. They were opportunists on the fringes of the nightclub industry — men who appeared to live well beyond their ostensible means and who paid with their lives when they finally alienated more powerful criminals.

Willie Thompson was shot dead as he sat at the wheel of his $81,000 Honda S-2000 sports car in Waverley Road, Chadstone about 9.30pm. He was ambushed by two gunmen who approached him from either side of the car, as he was about to pull out from his parking spot.

Thompson, 39, of Port Melbourne, had just left a martial arts class at the Extreme Jujitsu and Grappling gym when he was gunned down. The killers used their stolen car to block the sports car's possible escape route with a T-Bone manoeuvre.

Police found a bullet lodged in the wall of a bookshop in Waverley Road, two metres from Thompson's car. The killers were lucky not to have shot each other as they fired from opposite sides of the vehicle.

The two gunmen who ambushed Thompson's Honda had waited at a Red Rooster restaurant directly across the road for their target to leave the gym.

The gunmen's stolen Ford sedan was later found burnt out in Port Melbourne — two streets from where underworld figure Victor Peirce was murdered on 1 May 2002.

It was clear the killers knew Thompson's movements and while the job wasn't as 'clean' as some, it still showed the prerequisite planning.

Certainly this is one job where Veniamin had a rock solid alibi. But two other men close to Carl Williams did not. So was Carl behind the killing? Certainly some close to him believed he ordered the hit.

Thompson was another victim of the underworld war without a big reputation, although he had big enemies.

Drug dealer Nik Radev had firebombed Thompson's car about 18 months earlier. So in hindsight, replacing the destroyed car with a convertible was probably not one of Willie's better moves.

But it was clear Radev didn't kill Willie — because he himself was already dead.

Thompson was a familiar face at some of Melbourne's biggest nightclubs and a well-known bouncer for more than ten years.

Through his nightclub contacts he became involved in the film industry as a bit actor with roles in films partially financed by the owners of a city strip club.

He appeared in *The Nightclubber,* an alternative film shot at the Tunnel Nightclub and the Men's Gallery. It is a motion picture unlikely to be mentioned in dispatches at Cannes or even Cairns.

But none of these side interests could maintain Thompson's lifestyle.

Colourful Melbourne identity, Mick Gatto, placed a death notice in the *Herald Sun* for Thompson — a sure sign the dead man was connected to the underworld.

Friends said he was a 'gentleman' and well-liked. But, apparently, not by everyone. Like many who were gunned down in Melbourne's gangland feud, he lived like a drug dealer and ultimately died as one.

According to The Runner in a statement to police still to be tested in court, the hit on Marshall was mistakenly ordered by Tony Mokbel as a payback for the murder of Willie Thompson.

According to The Runner, Mokbel offered a massive bounty for Marshall's murder because he blamed the hot dog vendor for killing Thompson.

'Tony confirmed that he believed Michael Marshall was responsible for Willie's death and he wanted him dead. Tony offered Carl and I $300,000 to kill Marshall. When I shook hands with Tony he passed a piece of paper to me, which had the details of Marshall's address.'

'I was surprised, because I knew that Carl was behind Thompson's murder but it appeared that Tony had no idea of that.'

The Runner, who later pleaded guilty to the hit, told police he was paid $50,000 in advance and had three meetings with Mokbel where the murder was discussed. The Driver pleaded guilty and a Supreme Court jury found Carl as guilty as sin.

ANOTHER man who used his nightclub connections as a front for his drug activities was George Germanos.

George was a crowd controller with a reputation for losing self-control. While the venues varied, the story was always the same. The victims of his wrath were invariably smaller and helplessly intoxicated patrons.

There were complaints, and the former champion power lifter would be quietly moved on, but there were still enough Melbourne nightclubs keen to employ the big man with the bad attitude.

Even though the former national title-holder had retired from competition, had slimmed down and was now aged 41, he remained a menacing sight and continued to involve himself in violent clashes with paying customers.

One of those was on 21 October 2000 when a loud, drunk young man was taken outside a St Kilda nightclub, led around the back and flogged by Germanos.

The reports of the injuries suffered by the victim vary. According to some, the young man was left unconscious and badly hurt. Others say he recovered from the beating with few ill-effects.

But what is known is that the young man was the son of an influential member of the underworld — and the serious criminal was left seriously unhappy.

The man does not have a criminal record involving violence, but some of his friends do. His associates include well-known gangsters and one equally well-known former detective. He also has many friends in the outlaw motorcycle world.

For decades, the father has been successful in criminal endeavours and has influence in a world where anything can be done for a price. Of course, this might have had nothing to do with what happened to Germanos, who was involved in plenty of other things that could prove bad for his health.

For whatever reason, Germanos was in the cross hairs, and in the months following the beating he seemed to sense that time was running out. But, despite knowing he was a target and taking precautions, he was eventually set up.

And as in many of the Melbourne gangland murders, the victim was so busy trying to outflank his enemies he didn't see that a so-called friend would betray him.

After the beating, a man well-known to police became a friend of Germanos.

The friend is a major drug dealer and much older than the former power lifter. Despite the difference in ages and backgrounds, the two became inseparable and spoke almost daily.

The older man was later interviewed by police and has told them that while he would love to help, he has no idea why his new best friend was murdered.

Police remain unconvinced.

Germanos was more than a power-lifter on the wrong side of 40. He was ambitious, ruthless and determined to make money. But his best efforts to legitimately acquire wealth had routinely ended in tears — for his creditors.

His ultimate plan was to run a restaurant in Brighton, but his chequered business history suggested his ambitions often exceeded his abilities.

He had been in a partnership in a coffee shop but lost $30,000 and an automotive business where he lost $36,000.

But like many in the nightclub business, he had found a lucrative side interest — drugs. Germanos wasn't just a nightclub bouncer but a drug dealer, selling to patrons and selected staff at some of the nightspots where he worked. He also used his bulk and belligerence to intimidate other drug dealers.

Informally, he was blackballed from working at some nightspots but remained a favourite at three Melbourne nightclubs — although his reputation as being heavy handed was well known.

'He had been involved in some significant physical altercations . . . Some owners liked him, others didn't,' according to

Detective Senior Sergeant Rowland Legg, who would head the investigation into Germanos' killing.

In the weeks before his death, Germanos confided to members of his family that he was convinced 'something is coming.'

'He feared for his life and had become cautious,' says Legg.

Police found that on 21 March 2001 someone visited him at his parents' home in the late afternoon. The person was driving a late model, light coloured Toyota sedan, possibly a peach or apricot shade. The driver and Big George were seen having a discussion near the Toyota. The crowd controller was animated, possibly angry, while the other man remained calm.

On 22 March, about 9.30 pm he made a phone call. As far as police can tell, the call was to set up to confirm a meeting for later that night.

He left the house shortly afterwards. Police believe the meeting was scheduled for 10pm at Inverness Park in Armadale. The location was almost certainly picked by the other person, as Germanos did not appear to know the area well. His street directory was later found open in his car.

It may have seemed the perfect place for a private meeting, but it was also the ideal spot for an ambush.

The park intersects five streets, has several exit points, is covered with trees and is near a railway footbridge.

This meant there was cover for the gunman and a choice of escape routes. 'It was a perfect place for a hit,' according to Legg.

There is ample evidence that Germonos was expecting the meeting to go badly. He left his best jumper on the front seat, perhaps because he was anticipating trouble and did not want it ripped or stained.

He left his mobile phone and wallet at home — an old watch was found in the car that he used to check the time.

He was known to carry a gun, yet no firearm was found with

his body. He either went to the meeting unarmed, or, more likely, his killer took the gun after Germanos was shot dead.

He was wearing slacks, a dark sleeveless top and a jacket — regulation tough guy clothes.

He was also carrying black gloves. He was still clutching one and the second was about a metre behind where he fell. Police say he may have been wearing gloves because he expected a fight and wanted to protect his fists or because he thought he may have to shoot someone and wanted to protect his hand from gunshot residue. Or maybe he was just cold. It had been an unseasonably wet autumn day, so much so that the Tullamarine Freeway had been closed earlier that day due to flash floods.

Around 10.15 pm he was seen in a phone box in Wattletree Road near Glenferrie Road.

He appeared animated and was speaking half Greek and half English. His distinctive brown Valiant car was seen parked nearby in Wattletree Road.

Police believe he was talking to the man he was to meet, or an intermediary, perhaps complaining that there was no one at the park at the pre-arranged time. According to witnesses who saw him in the phone box, he seemed jumpy.

He then went to Cafe Lavia in Glenferrie Road, near High Street. He ordered a coffee and sat alone until about 10.30 pm. Police suspect the meeting had been postponed until 11 pm and he was killing time before the gunman would kill him.

Between 10.30 pm and 11 pm he was seen in Inverness Avenue, having parked 50 metres from the park in the dead end street, perhaps wanting to walk into the park in the hope that he would not warn the person he intended to meet.

He left his cigarettes and lighter in the car and walked in along a narrow tan bark covered path. He headed towards a wooden park bench next to children's swings and slides about ten metres away.

But the killer was already there, almost certainly hiding under a bush just to the right of the entrance.

Germanos walked in about five metres, and then turned, possibly hearing a noise or, just as likely, the killer called his name.

He was then shot in his barrel chest, then twice in the head from point blank range.

The killer then ran through the park and across a nearby railway footbridge. Legg says Germanos was the victim of a cold-blooded assassination.

'The killer was clearly forewarned about the victim's movements. We suspect he may have been set up by someone he trusted. There are indications he was anticipating trouble, but was ambushed.'

But who by? And why?

Sometimes people with a motive for a murder they didn't commit hint they might be behind it because they get the kudos with no prospect of being charged. Meanwhile, the real killer lies low.

17

QUARTER TO MIDNIGHT

> 'I haven't done anything.
> My conscience is clear.'

GRAHAM Allan Kinniburgh was a modest man. Although considered the most influential gangster in Victoria by some, he was always shy about acknowledging his achievements.

He preferred to conduct his business in private, though what that business was, few really knew.

His criminal record understates his influence on the underworld. It lists offences of dishonesty, bribery, possession of firearms, escape, resisting arrest and assaulting police.

But criminal records list only an offender's arrest history — his failures. The definition of a successful criminal is one that tends not to get caught.

Many wondered how he prospered. Sometimes even he struggled to explain. When he was interviewed soon after the 1998 murder of his friend and fellow gangster, Alphonse John Gangitano, he was uncharacteristically tongue-tied. Asked by homicide investigator Gavan Ryan what he did for a job, he responded:

'Occupation at the moment? It would be — I'm a — well, I'm still, I'm still, I'm still a rigger. I'm still a rigger, yeah.'

It could have been a Freudian slip. Whereas a lay person might assume he was referring to rigging in the construction industry, it was whispered that one of Kinniburgh's talents was to be an extremely well-informed punter. Although it was never proved, or even widely alleged, that he was involved in rigging horse races, people on both sides of the law — including a former assistant police commissioner — loved to get a tip from the man they called 'The Munster'. He was a great and good friend to more than one leading jockey.

'Rigging' had been kind to Kinniburgh, 62, right up until he was gunned down in front of his double-storey brick home in Kew just after midnight on 13 December 2003. Ryan — a member of the Victorian Police's Purana Taskforce — was immediately assigned to investigate the murder.

While Kinniburgh, a former shearer, had long given away paid employment, it didn't mean he would let a lucrative opportunity pass him by. He was late to his own wedding in 1967, telling his wife that he 'had to see a bloke'.

The shooting of 'The Munster' is the most telling — and probably the most ominous — of the underworld killings committed in Melbourne since 1995.

Nearly all the previous victims have been volatile and erratic men who saw violence as a weapon of first resort. There was an unspoken sense that they had it coming. But the older and wiser Kinniburgh was a tactician who saw gangland feuds as counterproductive.

While police are looking at a number of motives, two stand out as the most obvious. The raging favourite is that Carl Williams was out to kill anyone connected with the Morans and anyone he thought had the power to order a revenge attack.

What is known is that in 2003 Williams, frustrated at not being able to find Jason Moran, began preliminary work on launching a hit on Kinniburgh

The second — and increasingly unlikely — motive is he was killed as a payback for the murder of Alphonse Gangitano. It was his relationship with Gangitano that first forced the reticent Kinniburgh from the shadows. He was a close friend of Big Al — a relationship senior police found hard to understand.

Kinniburgh was wealthy, but tried to hide it — Gangitano was often struggling, but deliberately cultivated an image of affluence.

Kinniburgh kept a low profile, while Gangitano loved the headlines, although that high profile meant he was always the target of police investigations. But Kinniburgh's low profile was blown the night he went to visit the younger gangster on 16 January 1998, the night Alphonse was shot dead in his Templestowe home.

Police believe Jason Moran was at the house and argued with Gangitano. They say Moran opened fire on Alphonse without warning, killing him instantly.

The smart money says that a startled Kinniburgh ran to the front door of Gangitano's house, injuring his hand on the security mesh in his haste to throw it open. He then went upstairs, the theory goes, to grab the security video that could compromise him, before going to a nearby convenience store 'to buy cigarettes' — but in fact to concoct an alibi of sorts — before returning to 'discover' the body.

Some believe that Kinniburgh could have slipped away, but saw Gangitano's widow and children driving past and could not leave them to deal with the horrendous scene alone. But he also knew that touching the body in front of a witness would enable him to explain at a later time why his DNA was on the victim.

Kinniburgh didn't become a gangster heavyweight by losing his head when others (literally) lost theirs.

Either way, Coroner Iain West didn't buy his hastily-built alibi: 'I do not accept Graham Kinniburgh's version of events, as I am satisfied he was present at the time the deceased was shot.'

He said Kinniburgh went to the convenience store to be filmed on the security camera, 'thereby attempting to establish an alibi of being absent from the premises at the critical time.'

'I am satisfied that both Graham Allan Kinniburgh and Jason Matthew Patrick Moran were implicated in the death.'

The difference between Moran and Kinniburgh could be seen at the inquest.

The younger gangster wore a flash suit, while Kinniburgh dressed down for the occasion. He would do nothing to draw attention to himself.

While Kinniburgh could afford imported suits, he mostly preferred the casual clothes of an off-duty dock worker, even if in middle age he had acquired some expensive tastes and was a regular at the exquisitely expensive Flower Drum restaurant in Melbourne's Chinatown. At his funeral, his daughter, Susie, said, 'Restaurants all over Melbourne will not only miss his patronage but they'll be missing him. They used to fuss over him like he was a king. He didn't ask for it or seek out special favours, it was just bestowed upon him.'

A regular at Crown Casino, he also enjoyed trips to Las Vegas to try his luck at the spiritual home of The Mob. He also loved the atmosphere of old style pubs, where he would stand at the bar examining his form-guide and watching the races on television.

Kinniburgh lived in a large house in a quiet street in one of the better blocks of the prestigious Melbourne suburb of Kew, the natural haunt of doctors, lawyers, stockbrokers and media executives. But he drove a second-hand Ford, the car he drove home on the night he was shot. While Kinniburgh didn't flaunt his wealth, he managed to put his three children through private schools while not working in any legitimate job.

He was also an expert in picking police; trainee surveillance police were often sent to the street in Kew to try to follow him. It was a sharp learning curve.

In 1994, his son married a girl from a well-to-do Melbourne family. After the wedding, it was just a short walk from St Peter's Anglican Church to the reception in Melbourne's grand old established hotel, The Windsor.

During the stroll, an alert observer might have noticed photographers taking pictures not of the wedding party but of the guests. The photographers were intelligence police looking to upgrade their files.

As is the case in many weddings, the groom's friends and family had little in common with the bride's group.

One friend of the bride was mildly startled when introduced to Kinniburgh, not so much by the man himself as by the four who were standing around him. 'They were all wearing Ray-Bans and it was 10 at night,' she said later.

Dressed in a dinner suit, Kinniburgh welcomed his 100 guests with a speech that left an impression. One guest, who didn't know the colourful background of 'The Munster', later said: 'He reminded me of Marlon Brando.'

Weddings are emotional times and this one was no different.

A guest of the bride, a millionaire property developer, was dancing with a woman invited from the groom's side.

A friend of the groom, released from prison days after completing his sentence for biting a man's ear from his head, told the friend of the bride that he would be shot if he didn't immediately become a wall-flower.

The property developer lost interest in the music and retired to the bar. It was a sensible move.

Only a few months before Kinniburgh's death, his daughter married into a well-known Melbourne family with strong connections to Melbourne's legal and political establishment. The reception was held at the National Trust showpiece property, Ripponlea. The story circulates that when a friend asked the groom's mother how she had got along with the Kinniburghs in making the arrangements she just laughed and said: "No problems. We just agreed to everything they wanted."

For three decades Kinniburgh was connected with some of Australia's biggest crimes. Police say he was the mastermind behind the magnetic drill gang — Australia's best safebreaking crew — which grabbed $1.7 million from a NSW bank, a huge jewellery haul from a Lonsdale Street office and valuables from safety deposit boxes in Melbourne.

He was alleged to have been the organiser of a gold bullion snatch in Queensland and was also once charged over receiving stolen property from a burglary on the home of the well-known and fabulously wealthy trucking magnate, Lindsay Fox.

When police raided Kinniburgh's home, they found $4500 in a drawer and a rare pendant owned by Mrs Fox in a coat pocket. He told police they could keep the money if they didn't charge him over the burglary. This time he appeared to be out of luck. The detectives were honest and added attempted bribery to the other charges.

But 'The Munster' was nothing if not innovative. While he was convicted of bribery, he beat the theft charges by having an identical pendant made in Hong Kong to raise doubt about the unique nature of the jewellery.

In the 1990s he was charged over an attempt to import a record 15 tonnes of cannabis resin. Police flew to Sydney for the initial court hearing, in which Kinniburgh was granted bail.

Detectives flew back in economy seats only to see Kinniburgh in first class. The case against him later collapsed.

In his younger days Kinniburgh usually carried a gun. He was charged in the early 1980s after a parking officer saw a gun sticking out from under the driver's seat. The grey ghost turned a whiter shade of pale and contacted police, who arrested Kinniburgh when he returned to the car.

He was also charged after police found a gun stashed in a storm water drain opposite his house when he lived in Balwyn.

He once punched a detective outside a city nightclub, breaking his nose. A well-respected detective later went to his injured colleague and said Kinniburgh was upset at what he had done and would give 100 pounds — then several weeks' wages — as a peace offering if the charges were dropped. But the only thing bent about the battered policeman was his nose. He refused the bribe and the case continued.

In his later years Kinniburgh saw no value in exciting police, and other members of the underworld, by carrying a gun.

But in the weeks before his murder, he again began to carry a handgun. Friends say his mood became morose and they believe he knew he had been marked for death.

A few days before he died, he dined in Lygon Street, Carlton, with five colourful Melbourne identities. It can only be assumed none knew this would be the last time they would see their friend alive.

On the night of his murder he returned home to Belmont Avenue and parked on the street just past his driveway shortly after midnight. He walked about six steps, carrying a bag of groceries, before he was ambushed.

A pistol was found next to his body and the bag of groceries he dropped. He had been able to fire just one shot before he died in front of the house that crime built.

Kinniburgh was a careful man, but like many of the gangland victims he had become lazy. He had installed state of the art video security but it had broken down a year earlier and he had never bothered to repair it. He had a secure garage, but chose to park in the street. He had a special fortified door fitted inside the house so intruders could not get upstairs, but he wandered outside in the street rather than driving into his fortress.

And, a creature of habit, he always arrived home around midnight on Friday nights. You could set your watch by it. The killers obviously did.

Typically, the murder appeared to have been carried out by a hit team of two — a gunman and a driver. Witnesses who heard the shots say one gunman fired at least two volleys of bullets before fleeing in a car just after midnight.

Ambulance paramedics called at 12.07am found Kinniburgh dead at the scene.

The killing appears to have been meticulously planned. Within seconds, the hit team was driving north along Belmont Avenue towards Parkhill Road before doubling back to cross Cotham Road.

They were using a blue Ford Falcon. Any chance of the killers leaving clues in the car appeared to be destroyed when it was found burning about one kilometre from the scene soon after the murder. Residents among the million-dollar houses of nearby Doona Avenue reported the car had been dumped and set alight in a hidden driveway down a narrow, cobbled service lane.

The killers had certainly planned the hit for at least a week. The getaway car had been stolen from South Melbourne the previous Saturday and hidden until used in the attack.

Police also believe the gunmen had carefully scouted the local area before striking. The fact that the Falcon was dumped and burned in a tiny laneway not shown on any maps shows they had done their homework.

Detective Inspector Andrew Allen told the media that police would keep an open mind about motives but the fact that the murder was immediately referred to the Purana Taskforce and not left with the homicide squad showed that detectives accepted 'The Munster' was the victim of an underworld hit.

'There's a number of things that may have been attributed to this man in his past which may or may not relate to why this has happened,' he said.

'The fact that there's another execution-style murder is obviously impacting on the community; it impacts on lawlessness and quite clearly we are pulling out all stops to investigate this to our fullest ability,' he said. 'This sort of behaviour and this type of lawlessness must stop.'

While several million law-abiding citizens agreed with the policeman's sentiments, the people who really mattered — a handful of Melbourne gangsters — took no notice at all, as subsequent events were to prove.

And Kinniburgh? Long-time residents of Belmont Avenue said they knew of his reputation but said he was 'a quiet man who kept himself to himself'. There were no surprises here.

They said he had lived for at least fifteen years in his red brick house, which is fronted by a high brick fence and sprouts several video security cameras. Neighbours said he was occasionally seen walking a small, white fluffy dog.

Kinniburgh had many friends. One of them was the ill-fated Lewis Moran, father of the late Jason and Mark.

When evidence was led at one court hearing that Lewis had been caught on police telephone intercepts talking about crime, Kinniburgh just shook his head as if perplexed that his old friend could be so stupid.

Perhaps Graham Kinniburgh was killed because of his wide network of friends; it may have been his Godfather-like reputation that made him a target.

Some elements in the underworld are convinced they know who did it. They say he is a former armed robber who once tried to organise a million-dollar raid but ended up suffering the wrath of the Special Operations Group. Police have been told that Williams once approached the gunman to ask if he would accept the contract to kill Kinniburgh. They believe he was at first reluctant but later agreed to carry out the hit.

No-one has been charged and investigations are continuing.

A MONTH before Kinniburgh's death the Purana Taskforce arrested Williams over making threats to kill a detective and the man's wife.

Police hoped that with Williams in jail the murders would stop, but two weeks before the Kew killing, Carl was freed on bail.

So when Kinniburgh was murdered, the Williams name was on top of the suspect list. But the day after the killing he told one of the authors he was not violent and could not explain why so many of his associates had been killed over the past six years. He denied claims he was trying to take over the illicit drug market and said he was not systematically killing any opposition. He also said he did not know 'The Munster'.

'I've never met him and I've never heard a bad thing said about him. I have nothing to profit from his death. It's a mystery to me.

'I haven't done anything. My conscience is clear.'

Seemingly relaxed, he and family members met one of the authors in a city coffee shop about 36 hours after Kinniburgh's murder. He said he did not carry a gun, had never owned one and did not employ any form of security.

Carl's wife, Roberta, said Williams had the perfect alibi. 'It was his lawyer's birthday and he was out with him. He got Chinese and came home drunk as a skunk. They can't blame him for this one.'

The food wasn't from the Flower Drum. That was 'The Munster's' hangout.

Williams says he knew dead gangsters Jason Moran, Mark Moran, Mark Mallia, Dino Dibra, Willie Thompson and Richard Mladenich. 'That doesn't mean I know what happened to them,' he says. 'People die ... that's life. I have known people who have died in car crashes and overdoses. I also know people who have been shot.'

Immediately after Kinniburgh's death, the speculation began that close friend Lewis Moran was on an underworld death list.

But Williams claimed he had no grudge against Moran Senior. 'I've only met Lewis once,' he said before the latter's death. 'I haven't got a problem with Lewis. If he thinks he has a problem with me I can say he can sleep peacefully.'

So it would now appear that Carl told pork pies as well as eating them.

A few months later Lewis was put to sleep — permanently. Williams later pleaded guilty to the murder — one of many he had ordered since he was shot in the stomach in October 1999.

Williams said he was a close friend of The Runner — one of the men charged with the murder of former kickboxer and hot dog seller, Michael Marshall, who was shot dead outside his South Yarra home on 25 October.

'(He) is a good friend but I don't ask him about his business. I'll stick by him now.' Later the good friend gave evidence against him and Williams was convicted of the murder.

At the time the former supermarket shelf stacker said he was between jobs although he dabbled in property development and was a lucky punter. 'I did well over the spring carnival.'

He said he couldn't understand why Melbourne's gangsters were killing each other. 'I don't know how this started and I don't know where it will end. All I know is that I have had nothing to do with it. This should all stop. It is only hurting everybody else.'

He said public speculation was putting his life at risk. 'They can have a go if they like. They know I'm unarmed. If it happens I won't know about it.'

In the office of the Purana Taskforce in St Kilda Road there was a short list of potential victims. The name of Graham Allan Kinniburgh was on that list. The name of Lewis Moran was also there. So was Andrew Veniamin's.

It would turn out to be three out of three.

18

COUNTERPUNCH

I was trying to kill him.
He was trying to kill me.

MICK GATTO has made a career out of grabbing his chances as they come along. From boxer to enforcer to the more sophisticated title 'industrial mediator', Gatto has methodically crafted a reputation as a man who can persuade others to see his point of view. Circumstances outside his control during the underworld war have led to that reputation becoming bigger than he might wish.

Media reports suggest the Melbourne identity first came to prominence as a boxer who was close to winning the national heavyweight title. Some say he won fifteen fights by knockout.

The truth, always elusive at ringside, is that as a heavyweight boxer Mick Gatto was never going to be a genuine headliner. But he would make page one much later for actions more violent than those inside the square ring. He was tough, with a knockout punch and a big heart, but too slow to make the big time and too smart to allow himself to become another punching bag for young, faster fighters.

247

Gatto's official record is modest. Over seven years he fought under Queensberry rules just nine times. The records do not record what happened in the streets. In 1973 he had five bouts, losing one when Mark Ecimovic — a boxer who later fought for the Australian heavyweight crown — knocked him out in the first round.

The following year he fought twice, losing once on points and winning the other by knockout. Strictly a preliminary fighter, he did little for three years until a main event on the then popular *TV Ringside* threatened to fall over when one of the boxers withdrew.

Enter Big Mick, who entertained the crowd by going the distance in a ten-round fight with Reno Zurek — later to be crowned NSW heavyweight champion. Two years later he again fought Zurek, this time in Griffith in an eight-rounder. Again Mick lost on points but went the distance. It was Gatto's last big fight, but he was the main event.

Mick Gatto learned much in his journeyman boxing years. He learned that if you are wounded never let your opponent know he has the upper hand. He learned that when cornered it is best to cover up. He learned that the clinch can be the boxer's best friend because when you are holding an opponent he can do less damage than if he has room to swing. He saw that big fights are rarely won with one punch and good boxers don't fight out of anger or fear. They do their homework and anticipate their opponent's likely moves. In seconds they can calculate the risks and rewards of every option and choose their moment to launch an attack. Hotheads get the crowds cheering but it is the cool ones who more often take home the purse. Unless, of course, the fight is fixed.

Gatto knew that local boys win more than their fair share and so, given the chance, you should fight on your home turf with trusted friends in your corner. He also learned that the men who are truly feared and respected — from lightweights to heavyweights — have one thing in common. When faced with danger they never blink.

MORE than 25 years after leaving the ring, Gatto would enter another gladiatorial arena where there could only be one winner — the Supreme Court of Victoria — to face the charge of murdering a hit man named Andrew Veniamin, who had gone from obscurity to notoriety in a few murderous months before copping a fatal dose of his own medicine. Melbourne — made up of sprawling suburbia with a low crime rate, a respected police force and a tendency towards self-congratulation — had been the centre of a vicious, and unusually public underworld war.

Colourful men with strange nicknames, no jobs and unexplained wealth were turning up dead. A man like Nik 'The Bulgarian' Radev — a refugee who hadn't held a legitimate job for twenty years yet managed to maintain a five-star lifestyle — was typical of the victims.

Virtually unknown until his very public murder, Radev was shot next to his luxury Mercedes in Coburg in April 2003. Shortly before his execution he had paid a dentist $55,000 in cash to whiten and crown his teeth, turning them from basic Bulgarian to glitzy Hollywood. It was a waste of money: he was shot up to seven times in the head and body. Fittingly, he was later buried in a gold casket with what was left of his million-dollar smile.

Usually, Melbourne's main players in the criminal world watched the flashy ones like Radev come in full-on and go out feet first. But this time it was different.

First, the war was public and embarrassing. The police force, which had long fancied itself the best in the country, was beginning to look silly.

The then Assistant Commissioner (crime) Simon Overland would later admit police had dropped the ball in investigating organised crime. This meant — as police hate to look silly — there would be a major reaction. They would form a taskforce called Purana, and it would prove to be more effective than many thought possible. The taskforce would crack the gangland code of silence and charge 157 offenders with 485 separate offences including 25 counts of murder.

The war had also made the state government look silly. Politicians seen as 'soft on crime' can imagine themselves losing their seats, so the government gave police new powers to call suspects to secret hearings and seize hidden assets. All of this was bad for business in Mick Gatto's circle.

It had long been a standing joke that for decades Gatto had spent a fortune on flowers and death notices as friends and foes lost their lives in violent circumstances. Some cynics suggest he had the death notice number of the *Herald Sun* classifieds on speed dial, often ringing before the latest victim's name had been made public. In the early 1970s and '80s he paid his respects as gangsters such as brothers Brian and Les Kane were gunned down. But by the 1990s many of his own network were targeted.

Alphonse Gangitano was a close associate of Gatto's and police often saw them together. Both belonged to the Carlton Crew. Of Italian origin, but raised in Australia, they had some of the mannerisms of the so-called mafia but would spend their Saturdays like many other Aussies, sipping a drink, watching the races and having a punt. When invited to the Collingwood President's Room at Victoria Park, Gatto spent more time out the back watching the races on television than the football in front of him. Gatto and Gangitano both had an interest in Italian food, imported suits, gambling and boxing. In fact, Alphonse was a fight promoter and boxing manager for a short time, although his form for negotiating deals bordered on the eccentric. Heavily in the camp of local boxer Lester Ellis, he once attacked, bashed and bit champion Barry Michael — an Ellis rival — in a city nightclub in 1987. Even a shark like Don King didn't chew on his opponents. He left that to Mike Tyson.

While Gatto and Gangitano were friends, they were not as close as many thought. Gangitano liked his reputation as the Black Prince of Lygon Street and spent a decade in the headlines. Gatto preferred to remain out of the glare of media attention. Gangitano was the show pony, Gatto the stayer. Repeated police investigations found that while Gangitano was a professional criminal he did not have the asset base to justify his reputation as a Mr Big. More style than substance, they believed. But that didn't mean he wasn't dangerous.

IT has become part of gang war lore that on 6 February 1995, Gangitano was at a party in Wando Grove, East St Kilda. And that at 4.40am, he went outside with another colourful Melbourne identity, Gregory John Workman. There was an argument, and Workman was shot seven times in the back and once in the chest, which meant he lost both the debate and his life. After Gangitano persuaded two key female witnesses to change their stories and then rewarded them with long overseas vacations, the murder case against him collapsed. But he didn't take his second chance and continued to participate in high-profile criminal activities until his own violent death. He was shot dead inside his Templestowe home on 16 January 1998.

Present, but not directly involved in the shooting of Gangitano, was Graham 'The Munster' Kinniburgh — a father figure to Mick Gatto. The shooter was said to be Jason Moran, himself soon on the list of gangland murder victims.

Some say Gatto and Gangitano had grown apart in the years before the shooting. Alphonse drew the attention of the media and police to business matters that people like Gatto felt were best left private. However, in a rare interview, Gatto said later they were still friends at the time of the murder but he had grown tired of his name always being linked to the dead gangster. 'Why can't they let him rest in peace?'

LIKE Gangitano, Mick Gatto did not hanker for a nine- to-five job. He has been described over the years as a standover man (a claim he hotly denies) a landscape gardener, a professional punter and a gambling identity connected to Melbourne's once profitable illegal two-up school. These days he is a consultant for the building industry — a highly-paid problem solver. He also has an interest in industrial cranes. Combining business with pleasure his company, Elite Cranes, is a prominent sponsor of young boxers in Victoria.

Gatto has convictions for burglary, assaulting police, possessing firearms, and obtaining financial advantage by deception. He was also charged with extortion, blackmail and making threats to kill, but these annoying matters were struck out at committal.

Big Mick says such immature behaviour is all in the past. He maintains that these days he is as straight as a gun barrel.

In February 2002, he was invited, via a subpoena, to appear at the royal commission into the building industry to discuss his role as an industrial relations consultant on Melbourne building sites. The commission was interested in an alleged payment of $250,000 to solve some sticky industrial problems for a company that did not want extended labour conflicts. Inquiring minds at the commission found that $189,750 was paid to a company controlled by Mick Gatto and his business partner and good friend, Dave 'The Rock' Hedgcock.

When he gave evidence, Gatto appeared offended that people could suggest he used threats of violence to solve problems. 'I'm not a standover man. I'm not a man of ill repute. Fair enough

I've got a chequered past ... but I paid for ... whatever I have done wrong.'

Police who know Gatto say he is unfailingly courteous, slow to anger and always in control. He uses body language to ensure that people around him are aware that he remains a physically imposing man. 'It is not so much what he says, but what he leaves unsaid,' one detective said.

His unofficial office was La Porcella, an Italian restaurant on the corner of Faraday and Rathdowne Streets, Carlton. Most weekdays he was there, often in the company of men with healthy appetites and colourful pasts. But he was rarely there at weekends. That was time for his family. It is said that people with problems were prepared to pay $5000 to sit at the table with Mick and discuss solutions. Sometimes he could help and other times he couldn't. But it would always be a pleasant and entertaining luncheon. The scaloppini was to die for.

Many police and criminals dine out on Gatto stories and it is hard to distil reality from myth because those close to the big man are staunchly loyal — and silent. Those not so close seem to believe it would not be wise to tell tales out of the old school.

But there are several stories to indicate that while Gatto is charming and does not use violence indiscriminately, he succeeds because people fear the consequences of not seeing his point of view.

In one case he was able to jolt the memory of a businessman who owed an associate $75,000. The debt was paid and Gatto was said to have kept $25,000 as his commission. Everyone was a winner. The man who owed the money is still able to walk without a limp, the businessman did not have to write off the entire sum as a bad debt and Gatto was handsomely paid for two phone calls.

One solicitor once used Gatto's name to threaten someone who owed him $15,000 and then asked Big Mick to collect the debt. A policeman says Gatto did as he was asked, but pocketed the full amount as a fine for the lawyer using his name without permission. Again everyone was a winner — one man learned to pay his debts, another not to use people's names to make idle threats and Mick's bank balance received a healthy injection. That is, of course, if he put such a small amount in the bank. A detective said he knew a case of a man who was dancing at a nightclub when he had a nail punched into his shoulder. The reason? He owed Gatto $400.

Yet another policeman said he believed Gatto once shot a man in the leg in Carlton. When police tried to get a statement from the victim, the man not only denied that he knew who had shot him but denied he had been shot at all. When asked why he was sitting in casualty with blood seeping from the wound, he said he didn't know why his leg was 'leaking'.

Another time a man came asking for help but Mick's advice was to deal with the matter rather than employ others who might lack the subtlety to solve the problem. This was not a time for the use of a sledgehammer to crack a walnut — or in this case two walnuts. Years later the man could see the wisdom of the advice. Many police had a grudging respect for Gatto as a man who did not go looking for trouble and saw him as 'old school'.

But the underworld landscape was changing and Melbourne's criminal establishment was being drawn into a gangland war not entirely of their making. When the Moran boys shot Williams over a drug business, it was nothing to do with Gatto — whose colourful background does not include drug charges. But it would become his business by default as his friends and associates continued to be picked off.

Some of those who were shot seemed to become fatalistic. Lewis Moran and Kinniburgh knew they were on a death list, yet took few precautions. Gatto was different. A good friend but a dangerous enemy, he was never going to let himself be stalked in the shadows.

It was the ambush killing of Graham 'The Munster' Kinniburgh in late 2003 that hit him the hardest.

The death of an old and respected friend distressed Gatto and made him realise that the dominoes around him were falling and he could be next. Within hours of the murder the dogs were barking (wrongly as it turned out) that one of the men who killed 'The Munster' was the hot-headed streetfighter turned hit man called Andrew 'Benji' Veniamin.

VENIAMIN was a small man with a growing reputation for violence. Like Mick Gatto, he was a former boxer, although they were from different eras — and vastly different ends of the weight divisions. Any chances of Veniamin making a name as a boxer ended when at nineteen he badly broke his leg and damaged his knee in a motorbike accident. But all this meant was that he could channel his violent inclinations to activities outside the ring.

Heavily tattooed, with a close-cropped haircut and a bullet-shaped head, the brooding Veniamin looked like a man who could take offence easily and was only a glance away from yet another over-reaction.

According to Purana Taskforce investigators, Veniamin's criminal career could be broken into three phases. In the beginning, he was a street thug in Melbourne's west. He ran with two other would-be gangsters, old schoolmates Paul Kallipolitis and Dino Dibra, and specialised in run-throughs, ripping off and robbing drug dealers who grew hydroponic marijuana crops in rented houses.

Veniamin had a criminal record that began in 1992 with a $50 fine for the theft of a motor car. In 1993, he was convicted of intentionally or recklessly causing injury and sentenced to 200 hours of unpaid community work. Over the next decade he was found guilty of theft, robbery, false imprisonment, assaulting police, arson, deception and threatening to cause serious injury.

The nature of the modern underworld is that access to drugs — and drug money — means relatively minor players can become influential figures in a matter of months.

While Gatto tended to look for amicable solutions, Veniamin saw violence as the first resort. Pasquale Zaffina was an old friend of Veniamin but that didn't stop the gangster trying to move in on his girlfriend. When Zaffina objected, Veniamin responded with a surprising lack of contrition. He fired shots into Zaffina's parents' house and, apparently unimpressed with the results, left a bomb at the residence and threatened to kill Zaffina's sister.

To settle matters they agreed to meet for a fight in a park in Melbourne's western suburbs with seconds to back them up — as though conducting an old-fashioned duel. They agreed it would be fists and no guns. But as they shaped up, Veniamin produced a .38 calibre handgun and aimed it at Zaffina, who managed to push the gun towards the ground. Three shots hit him in the leg but he lived to tell the story — at Gatto's trial, as it would turn out.

The defence would make much of the Zaffina story, claiming it showed Veniamin could conceal a .38, would ambush and attempt to kill people and did not care if witnesses were present. But that would be much later.

Soon Veniamin saw himself as a man of substance (as well as substances) and felt he could associate with men with established reputations. These included members of the so-called Carlton Crew and Mick Gatto, in particular.

The younger gun exhibited all the signs of being starstruck and appeared to hero worship the man who was a household name in a certain type of household.

Gatto saw Veniamin as dangerous but extended his big hand of friendship, working on the principle that you keep your friends close and your enemies closer. He knew the new boy was vicious but Veniamin was a rising power in the west and Gatto thought that if he needed muscle in the Sunshine area 'Benji' could be handy.

Gatto loved to build networks — some good, some bad. Veniamin — twenty years younger — was high maintenance and at times was only just tolerated by the Carlton blue bloods. He was said to have asked Gatto to provide him with firearms and on more than one occasion the older man had to intervene after Veniamin involved himself in mindless violence at nightclubs.

Gatto said in evidence, 'Well, I remember just one occasion, that he asked me if I could get guns for him, revolvers and, you know, I said I'd ask, but I mean I had no intention of doing that, to be honest, because it's a no-win situation. And the other occasion I can't really remember, but he was forever getting himself into trouble at nightclubs and what have you, and I was always sort of getting involved, sort of patching things up.'

But Veniamin was more than just a camp follower. He was already a killer. Police now believe he killed seven men in just four years. He killed friends, enemies and strangers for a price. He was Australia's most dangerous hit man, but he would never have the chance to retire in anonymity. He would be shot dead, aged just 28.

THE Melbourne fruit and vegetable market has always been connected to a resilient strain of organised crime. The cash economy and Australia-wide transport network has sometimes been used for gambling, drug and protection rackets.

From the market murders of 1963–64 through to the cannabis boom of the 1970s and 1980s there has been money to be made on the side.

By the 1990s, tensions were again building with massive kick-backs by major retail outlets, bribery and battles to control the lucrative black economy.

Alfonso Muratore was steeped in the tradition. His father, Vince, was a senior member of the so-called Italian organized crime group, The Honored Society, and was shot dead outside his Hampton home in 1964.

Alfonso would later marry into the powerful Benvenuto family. His brother-in-law was Frank Benvenuto, the son of Liborio Benvenuto, the former Godfather of the mafia-like crime group the Honoured Society, who died of natural causes in 1988. Frank and his brother, Vince, became powerful figures at the market.

But Alfonso tried to rock the family boat. He left his wife for his mistress and at a secret meeting told the giant Coles-Myer group of a kickback scheme.

This was not a move to strengthen family bonds and on 4 August 1992, he was shot dead as he was about to hop into his car in Hampton in a virtual repeat of the ambush killing of his father 28 years earlier.

Frank Benvenuto was one of the main suspects for ordering Alfonso's death.

At different times Frank employed two Melbourne gunmen with him at the market. One at the time was notorious, the other hardly known.

Accused police killer and armed robber Victor George Peirce was well known as a vicious gunman but Andrew Veniamin was yet to build his reputation. It didn't take long.

Frank Benvenuto was shot dead outside his Beaumaris home on 8 May 2000.

Police say Veniamin was the killer but it wasn't his first paid hit. In May 1999 another Italian fruit and vegetable identity, Joe Quadara, was shot outside a Toorak supermarket. Investigators are convinced Benji did it.

They also say he was the gunman who killed his former friends and criminal associates — Dino Dibra, shot dead near his West Sunshine home on 14 October 2000, and Paul Kallipolitis, whose body was found in his West Sunshine home on 25 October 2002. Veniamin was the hot suspect in the murder of standover man Nik Radev, shot dead on 15 April 2003. And he was part of the torture team that grabbed and killed Mark Mallia in August 2003. And police say he shot Victor Peirce in May 2002.

The dates, and the nationalities of the victims, suggest that Benji worked for more than one crime syndicate. The first two victims were clearly connected to Italian organised crime while many of the later ones were enemies of Carl Williams.

It now appears that Veniamin killed for a price — not a cause — and he was not too fussed who paid the bills.

In November 2002, Veniamin's allegiances to the Carlton Crew began to drift. He swapped camps, moving to become Williams' high-profile bodyguard and close friend.

The story goes that Tony Mokbel was bashed in Lygon Street by a Perth bikie during what was supposed to be a meeting set up by Carlton Crew heavy Mario Condello. It is said that when violence broke out, Gatto did nothing to protect Mokbel. It wasn't his fight.

Veniamin drove the badly-injured Mokbel to hospital and, indignant at what had happened, changed sides. That is one version. There are others. But, for whatever reason, Veniamin became the constant companion of Carl Williams.

Weeks after the Radev shooting, police established the Purana Taskforce. The taskforce called for all intelligence holdings on suspects such as Veniamin and was stunned to find how little was known about the vicious killer. Assistant Commissioner (crime) Simon Overland would later use Veniamin as an example of how police had failed to monitor organised crime in Victoria.

In the last year of his life he seemed to think he was above the law. A suburban detective once drove past him in an unmarked car. Veniamin gave chase and confronted the policeman in a petrol station demanding to know if he was being followed. Veniamin, well-built but not much bigger than a jockey, seemed comfortable trying to intimidate the detective. In just a few months he managed to acquire more than 40 speeding and parking fines.

Police approached Veniamin in 2003 with a message to 'pull up' — warning him his activities meant he was now also a potential victim. It was no idle statement, as at that point at least five shooters in Melbourne's gangland war had already been murdered. When detectives told him he was likely to die violently, Benji didn't seem fazed. He told them he knew the risks and had already told his parents that if he was killed they should honour the underworld code of silence and refuse to co-operate with police. He wrote to one of the authors suggesting publicity at such a delicate time could 'endanger my life'.

Having changed camps, Benji appeared blindly loyal to Williams, who was committed to kill all his perceived enemies. But there were certain perks in becoming a family friend and constant bodyguard to the new breed gangster. He was invited to share a family holiday with Williams, staying in a five-star resort in Queensland. It was a case of the boy from Sunshine spending up big in the Sunshine state. Never the master of measuring risks, he took to dog paddling in the surf, even though he could hardly swim. By late 2003 he had moved into a city penthouse and drove a borrowed $200,000 car said to belong to a bus line owner. And he was still registered to pick up the dole.

But even Williams, who claimed Benji was his best friend, had begun to distance himself because he feared the little killer could turn on him. When he had failed to deliver Jason Moran for an ambush, Williams began to wonder if Veniamin might have been recruited back to the Carlton Crew.

Eventually Williams stopped meeting Benji alone for fear of an ambush. But Roberta Williams didn't share her husband's concern and, in a touching show of faithlessness, remained close to Veniamin to the end.

Veniamin was one of the first principal targets of the Purana Taskforce and police developed a strategy of trying to harass and disrupt his routine so he would not have the freedom to continue to kill. Purana investigator Boris Buick (a passionate investigator and red wine connoisseur) gave evidence at the Gatto trial that police were constantly pulling Veniamin's car and raiding his home and those of his friends and relatives. He said this curtailed his criminal activities:

'To the best of my knowledge, and as I said, we had saturated coverage of him, he was no longer committing acts of violence and was well aware of our interest in him. As well as essentially saturating the deceased by means of surveillance, personal surveillance and electronic surveillance, we also commenced regularly intercepting him and his associates, specifically seeking to disrupt their criminal activities.

'We searched vehicles and other persons, of associates of his, and some other premises that he was associated with. And he was well aware at that stage, and we essentially made it aware to him that we were targeting him and his associates ... to prevent further offending, in particular to prevent offences of a violent nature and involving firearms.'

Police bugged his home and car and had a court order to bug his telephones. The court order covered the period from 20 July 2003, to 19 May 2004 — coincidentally just four days before he was killed. Veniamin knew he was bugged and complained to Gatto that anyone he spoke to was raided a short time later. But the constant police surveillance helped clear him in at least one case. When Graeme Kinniburgh was shot dead, police were quickly able to establish Benji was near Taylors Lakes at the time

— on the opposite side of Melbourne from the murder scene in Kew.

Veniamin loved guns and was always trying to find more, allegedly keeping one cache of weapons at a friendly kebab shop. But with police always near him, he could not always carry a weapon. According to Purana investigator Detective Senior Constable Stephen Baird (who was to die suddenly just months after the trial): 'Veniamin became paranoid, in fact, about being surveilled by police, both physical and electronic, and also paranoid about being intercepted by police at any time and both his person searched and any vehicle he was being in searched for firearms.'

So why then did he carry a .38 revolver with him to meet Mick Gatto in a Carlton restaurant on 23 March 2004?

ON 22 December 2003, nine days after Graham Kinniburgh's murder, Gatto met Veniamin and others at the Crown Casino in what police claim was an attempted peace conference. For police it was an ideal spot as the area was saturated with security cameras and the meeting could be monitored. For the main players, who did not trust each other, it was also an ideal place for the meeting for the same reasons: it was neutral ground where the cameras ensured there could be no ambush. The Atrium Bar at Crown is much safer than from a dead-end corridor at the back of a Carlton restaurant.

The cameras even picked up the jockey-sized Veniamin kissing the much larger Gatto with the traditional mafia-style peck on the cheek as a respectful welcome.

Detectives later employed a lip reader to discover what the suspects said. According to the lip reader, Gatto chatted to Williams — who remains the main suspect for organising Kinniburgh's murder.

Gatto said, 'It's not my war. You walk away from this and mind your own business. If someone comes up to you for that sort of shit, if someone comes up to me with the same sort of shit I'll do the same thing. I'll be careful with you. You be careful with me. I believe you. You believe me. Now we're even.'

And walk away they did. But no-one was even.

Williams thought about Gatto's words. Could this be the end? He sought advice from his lieutenant who said: 'Ask Benji. He knows him (Gatto) better than me.' Veniamin was insistent: 'Kill him.' There would be no truce.

Gatto's sharp instincts would told him that it was not a matter of if, only when, there would be an attempt on his life.

The nature of his phone calls to Veniamin changed. The prosecution argued that telephone intercepts showed 'a growing menace in Gatto's voice' that Veniamin failed to pick up. Gatto later argued his phone conversations were never threatening. 'I just wanted to know what he was doing, what he was up to, and you know, keep your friends close and your enemies closer, you know. It was that sort of thing.'

On 29 December Gatto saw two men drive near his house. The passenger, he said, was a dead ringer for Veniamin. And more disturbingly, the passenger ducked when Gatto looked in his direction. The next day he rang Benji and was relieved when he found he was in Port Douglas rather than Doncaster. So were a group from Purana sent to monitor Williams and Benji. Sometimes investigating major crime figures has its fringe benefits, including tropical fruits and beers at the Court House Hotel.

Police telephone intercepts showed that Gatto and Veniamin spoke regularly, often referring to each other as 'buddy' and 'champ'. An example was a call from Veniamin to Gatto on Friday 19 March — the last day Benji's phones were tapped.

Veniamin: *What's doin', buddy?*

Gatto says he hasn't heard from him in a month and Veniamin replies: *You know, I swear to you, mate, every bloke I've rung off this phone has been raided.*

Veniamin tells Gatto: *Mate, I'm still there, mate.*

Gatto: *Well, mate, that's assuring. I fuckin' hope you're here a long time, buddy.* As Gatto probably was not overly concerned with Veniamin's long-term health it is likely the comment was laced with irony and possibly even menace.

Veniamin, always a literal type, either ignores or is unaware of the subtext: *I've been meaning to drop into that ... that joint when you're there.*

Gatto: *Mate, I'm there every day, buddy. Every day we're there.*

Veniamin: *I promise you, mate, I swear to you, I'm gonna come. I want to come.*

Gatto: *Mate, any time you want to, buddy, you know where we are.*

Veniamin, who has only days earlier been released from hospital after an attack of pancreatitis, says: *I've just been a bit stressed, I've been in and out of hospital the last two weeks, you know.*

Gatto: *I heard, mate, I heard.* He adds: *Mate, stay quiet, buddy.*

Veniamin: *Oh mate, I am, mate.*

Gatto: *Stay quiet.*

Veniamin: *But I'm still there, mate.*

Gatto: *Yeah.*

Veniamin: *Don't forget.*

Gatto: *I know that. I know. All right.*

Veniamin: *All right, buddy.*

Gatto: *Take care of yourself, mate, keep in touch.*

Veniamin: *I'll drop in there.*

Gatto: *You're welcome any time, mate.*

Veniamin: *Thanks very much, buddy.*

Gatto: *Take care, Andrew.*

Veniamin: *See you, buddy. Bye, mate.*

Gatto: *See you, mate, thanks.*

Police would ask later whether the 'Stay quiet, buddy' comment was well-meaning advice or a veiled threat. Certainly it is unlikely that Veniamin would have considered that when he said 'I'm still there, mate' that four days later he wouldn't be.

On 23 March, Gatto rang Veniamin's mobile phone and asked him to come to the restaurant. It was about 2pm. What detectives can establish is that Veniamin was in the Melbourne Magistrates' Court that morning and that when he received the phone call he was in the borrowed silver Mercedes that was bugged by police. A few minutes later he called someone else and said he was about to 'catch up with someone ... the big bloke'. He double-parked the car and walked into the restaurant and sat with Gatto and others at a raised table. Both were in their trademark attire — Gatto was wearing a suit, Veniamin a T-shirt and track pants.

Later he and Gatto walked to the back of the restaurant and entered a dead end corridor for a private chat. One side of the corridor running to the fridge was stacked with cartons of tinned tomatoes. The width was just wide enough for the shoulders of the former heavyweight. Gatto had handed his mobile phone to his friend Ron Bongetti and Veniamin left the keys to his car on the table.

Next moment five shots were fired and Gatto walked out leaving Veniamin dead on the floor. Three shots hit Veniamin at point blank range. One smashed the main artery in his neck, the second severed his spinal cord and the third entered his head near the right ear. There were powder burns on Gatto's suit showing the two men were next to each other when the shots were fired, the gun virtually pressed against the victim. Gatto later had short-term hearing problems from the shots and thought he may have been nicked on the left ear by one of the bullets.

Police were called and a remarkably calm Gatto explained to them that it was self-defence — that Veniamin had drawn a gun and in the struggle the smaller man was shot. 'He pulled a gun out ... he pulled out a gun and he tried to shoot me and he finished second best,' he told police at the scene. Gatto was taken back to the homicide squad offices in St Kilda Road, given a legal caution and told he could have access to a solicitor. He didn't need to be told he needed legal representation. He had phoned a solicitor from the restaurant — and he didn't need to check the Yellow Pages for the number.

He was swabbed for gunshot residue and later for DNA. Around 11pm a short formal interview began. Mr Gatto said: 'I've had some legal advice and I just wish to say that I've done nothing wrong and I've acted in complete self-defence, and I'd like to make no further comment at this stage.'

Purana investigator Boris Buick asked: 'Is that the extent of the statement that you wish to make?' Gatto said: 'That's it.' Police were faced with a dilemma. They had one very brief version of events — Gatto's self-defence argument.

The case for murder was weak and relied exclusively on circumstantial evidence. But what if police had freed Gatto and allowed the matter to go to inquest at the Coroner's Court? There would have been allegations that because Veniamin was out of control and because police lacked the evidence to charge him with the seven murders he was suspected of, they had 'greenlighted' Gatto to kill him. It would have been hard to explain how the warrant to bug Veniamin's telephones lapsed just four days before he was killed. Besides, there were issues worth exploring in front of a Supreme Court jury.

Why did Gatto, a self-described industrial mediator, have a body bag in the boot of his Mercedes outside the restaurant? If Veniamin planned to murder Gatto, why would he do it in a restaurant filled with Gatto's friends, almost guaranteeing retribution? Why kill a man in a place frequented by police and often under surveillance? Veniamin was unaware his phone was no longer bugged and would have believed police had recorded that last conversation with Gatto before he arrived. If it was a planned hit he had virtually no chance of fabricating an alibi. Why did he leave his keys on the table, meaning he would have to return to confront the rest of Gatto's team before he could escape? Veniamin had stopped carrying guns because police had repeatedly raided him in the previous year. He had been in court and unarmed that morning. When and where did he get the .38 before his meeting with Gatto? Why did he choose a tiny corridor for the confrontation where the much bigger and stronger Gatto could so easily overpower him?

There were many theories, including one that Gatto, using the lessons learned in the ring, chose the precise moment to counterattack. One where there were no witnesses to dispute his version of events. There was a feeling that Gatto was too proud to sneak in the dark to ambush an enemy or pay others to do his dirty work.

Another theory was that such a public killing was a statement to others that if the war was to continue, he would come after them. Or did Veniamin, increasingly erratic and more drug-dependent, just lose it, as he had before? Did he react in a way he would not live to regret? Was it, as Gatto has always maintained, a clear-cut case of self-defence?

Certainly, those close to Veniamin had trouble with the self-defence theory. The day after his funeral, Lewis Moran, an old-school criminal and friend of Gatto, was shot dead in the Brunswick Club in what was a direct payback.

IT would take more than a year for the trial to begin and it was a very different Mick Gatto who arrived in court from solitary confinement. Unable to eat in restaurants, he had embarked on a fitness campaign, shadow boxing for hours in his cell. He had lost 30 kilos and was back to his old fighting weight.

The Supreme Court can diminish a man. Men with reputations as tough guys can seem intimidated in the dock. They must look up to the judge, bow when he enters and wonder about the twelve strangers who will decide their fate. They are led in and out by prison guards and those who are aggressive soon learn to at least behave passively.

But Mick Gatto was not diminished. Well dressed, he seemed at home in the combative environment and far from intimidated. He was moving on the balls of his feet. During breaks, when the jury was not present, he would wander to the back of the court to talk to friends and family who attended. It was almost like a royal walk as he chatted to his subjects.

He would talk to reporters and compliment them if he thought their coverage was a fair representation of the evidence so far, evidence that would decide his future. Mick Gatto was 49. If found guilty of a gangland murder he would be looking at about sixteen years minimum prison sentence. If that happened, he would be 65 when released and yesterday's man.

Robert Richter QC is used to representing big names, from John Elliott to Steve Vizard to Geoff Clark. Those who can afford the best often turn to the wily silk. Regardless if the alleged offences are indiscretions in the boardroom or gangland killings, Richter's advice tends to be the same: In court he is the boss and the client is just there for the ride. He believes that patients don't tell surgeons how to operate and clients shouldn't try to run complex criminal trials. When it comes to murder, he is of the view that in nearly every case the accused is better off letting the defence lawyers do the talking. Sit up straight and look attentive, engage the jury without intimidating them, don't look bored and don't look angry. And, most importantly, shut up.

Richter's strategy, as with most defence lawyers, is based on counter punching. The prosecution must prove a case beyond reasonable doubt but the defence must only find a weak link in the argument. But that strategy can collapse when defendants get in the witness box. They are wild cards. No matter how well briefed, they can lose a case with one wrong answer. A man charged with murder can lose his temper during rigorous cross-examination and juries can take more notice of reactions than actual words. Much better to leave it to the experts.

In scores of murder trials Richter has allowed maybe only two clients to take the walk from the criminal dock at the back of the court to the box twelve paces away. One of the two was Mick Gatto.

'He somewhat insisted,' the barrister later remarked. Gatto likes to get his own way. The risk was that as Gatto tried to explain to the jury how he shot Veniamin in that tight corridor he might also shoot himself in the foot. But at least there were no eyewitnesses to contradict his version of events. The only other person present had lost interest in proceedings fourteen months earlier.

At first, the defence team gently took Gatto through his story about how he called Veniamin at 2.01 pm on 23 March, and how the little hit man arrived at the restaurant a few minutes later. According to Gatto, he was having lunch at his unofficial Carlton office, La Porcella, and intended to visit his sick cousin at the Royal Melbourne Hospital in the afternoon:

> Well, when he first come in I was actually shocked that he arrived so quick because it only took him like eight or ten minutes to get there. I actually yelled out to him, 'Hello stranger', or something like that. Anyway, he come and sat next to me and there was just general talk about him being in court that day. He was at the court case there in the Melbourne Magistrates' Court and he was just going through all that.

He said that despite his concerns about the erratic killer he didn't check Veniamin to see if he had a concealed weapon, no doubt believing he was safe in such a public venue. The two sat with others at a table on the higher level of the two-tiered, large restaurant.

He actually kicked my foot under the table, and he motioned with his head like that, that he wanted to have a chat. And I said, 'Do you want to have a chat?' and he said, 'Yes, I do'. I remember pushing my chair in and walking around and giving the phone to Ron (his good friend Ron Bongetti) in case anyone rang while I was having a chat and I'm not sure whether ... I thought he led the way but I'm not 100 per cent sure. And why I say that is I thought we were going to go outside, and actually he pointed into the kitchen, and I said 'wherever you want to go', and we walked in there.

Question: Who suggested the corridor?

Answer: He walked in. I just followed him ... he turned round and he was just looking at me. I said, 'What's doing, mate?' And he said, 'I'm sick of hearing this shit.' And I said, 'What do you mean?' And he said, 'I'm still hearing that you know, you think that I'm responsible for your mate.' And I said, 'Well, I have to be honest with you, mate, that's what I keep hearing, that's what people keep saying.'

Question: How did he respond to that?

Answer: Well, there was no argument. I mean, we were just talking. Veniamin said, 'I wouldn't interfere with you because you're a mate.' I said to him, 'Well, Dino Dibra and PK were your mates, you fucking killed them.' He said, 'Well, they deserved it, they were dogs', or something like that. I said, 'Look, Andrew, I think it's better if you stay out of our company. You know, I really don't believe that you can be trusted. I'd just rather you not come around near us at all.' He just said, 'I'm sorry to hear that', or, 'I'm sorry to hear', something like that, you know, and I was looking at him in the eyes, and his face went all funny and he sort of stepped back and he said, 'We had to kill Graham, we had to fucking kill Graham. Fuck him and fuck you.'...I didn't see where he pulled it from, but he stepped back and he had a gun and I just lunged at him, and I grabbed his arm, grabbed his arm with my hand, and the gun went off past my head. Went past my left. Actually I thought it hit me. (Grazing his left ear) It was just the loudest thing I've ever heard in my life.'

Question: After the gun went off you thought you'd been hit. What happened then?

Answer: Well, I had hold of his hand with both my hands and I sort of pushed it towards him and I ... with my hands I sort of ... I forced ... he had his hands on the trigger and I just forced his hands, squeezed his hands to force him to pull the trigger and ...

Question: How many times did the gun go off?

Answer: I know how many times it's gone off because I've heard it in evidence, but at the time I didn't know.

Question: How fast was all this?

Answer: Just like a few seconds. I mean, I remember nearly falling on the ground on top of him. He sort of pulled me over off balance.

Question: At some point did you finally get control of the weapon?

Answer: I did.

Question: After a number of shots went off what happened?

Answer: Well, I'll just explain it. When I pushed the gun towards him and I was squeezing his hand he sort of pulled me off balance and I nearly fell over on top of him and the gun was going off. It was just bang, bang. And I mean I don't know where it went or whatever. I've got to be honest, I thought I was a dead duck anyway, I thought I was gone. And like I've said, I remember nearly stumbling, landing on top of him. And I just pulled the gun out of his hand because he still had it in his hand. I pulled it out of the grip of his hand and I ran out of the hallway there, out of the corridor, into the restaurant.

Question: From entering that corridor to when you ran out, so from the moment you went in to the time you left that corridor, how long would you estimate that incident lasted?

Answer: A couple of minutes, a minute, it wasn't that long, you know. I mean, it was just that brief talk and then, you know, he just ... I've never seen anyone sort of just change so quick. He just went from one extreme to another. I couldn't believe it.

Question: When you ran out were you holding anything?

Answer: I had the gun in my hand.

Question: Which gun is that?

Answer: The .38.

Question: It was suggested by Mr Buick (taskforce investigator) in evidence he had a working hypothesis that you fired a cover-up shot; what do you say to that?

Answer: That's completely ridiculous.

Question: It was suggested by Mr Horgan (prosecutor) in opening that you shot Mr Veniamin a fourth time as he lay dying on the floor of the passageway. Did you shoot Andrew Veniamin while he lay dying on the floor of the passageway?

Answer: No, I certainly did not. I certainly did not. He always had hold of the gun.

In Gatto's version of events he then stepped out of the corridor and spoke to the owner of the restaurant.

Question: Do you remember having a discussion with Michael at that point?

Answer: I do, yes. As we met each other, he said, 'What happened?' And I said, 'He just tried to fuckin' kill me like he killed Graham.' I said, 'Am I all right?' And at that point I put the gun in my pants, and I said, 'Is my ear all right, because I think he hit me or something?' And Michael said, 'It looks a bit red.' And then we stepped back into the kitchen. Because I was so fat, I had a big stomach; the gun nearly fell out anyway. I grabbed it and I gave it to him, and I said, 'You'd better take that.' I gave him the gun and he went and wrapped it in a towel or something; I don't know what he done with it; and put it on the bench in the kitchen area. I thought I was actually shot, you know, I thought the bullet hit me ... After that happened, I walked out of the restaurant, and as I walked over to the high level, where the boys ... they were all standing up, they didn't know what was going on ... Michael Choucair walked out of the kitchen at that point and he said, 'What'll I do?' And I said, 'You'd better ring the police and ring an ambulance.' And then I turned around and grabbed my phone off Ronnie, and I said, 'You wouldn't believe what happened. He just tried to fuckin' kill me, this bloke. He just tried to kill me like he killed ... like he tried to kill Graham', or something like that. 'He just tried to kill me like he said he killed Graham', words to that effect.

He said that when the police arrived he told them: 'He pulled a gun out ... he pulled out a gun and he tried to shoot me and he finished second best.'

Question: After the shooting, how did you feel?

Answer: Just didn't know where I was. I was in a state of shock. I mean, I couldn't believe that I was still alive, you know. It was just my life flashed before me. The whole world was just ... it was all over, you know. I thought I was a dead duck.

He explained that he had a gun in his pocket but did not have a chance to grab it when Veniamin launched his sudden attack.

I would've been a statistic if I'd done that. If I'd tried to pull it out of my pocket, he would've shot me straight in the head. I mean, I never had time, it was just that quick. I never had a chance to go for my pocket. If I hadn't have lunged at him and grabbed him, his arm, mate, I wouldn't be here today to tell the story. I'd be a statistic.

Fearing that he would be charged with having an unlicensed gun, Gatto gave his .25 handgun to his good friend Brian Finn saying:

Do me a favour, get rid of that.' And I gave him the gun, and he put it in his pocket, which is a .25 that I had on me, and he just left ... I used to carry it in my right pocket from time to time, the pocket of my trousers.

The final three questions by his lawyer were designed to leave an impression on the jury and to cut through the mass of conflicting expert testimony of the events of more than a year earlier.

Mr Gatto, you've been charged with the murder of Andrew Veniamin?

Answer: That's right.

Question: Did you murder Andrew Veniamin?

Answer: Christ, no way known. What I done is stopped him from murdering me.

Question: How did Andrew Veniamin die?

Answer: He died because he just pulled a gun at me. He went ballistic. He tried to kill me and I stopped him from doing that and he got shot rather than me. Thank God he did.

At no stage did Gatto make the mistake of trying to disguise his mistrust of Veniamin. As he was to say elsewhere:

If it was anyone else in my position, they'd get a key to the city. It's just unfortunate that it's me.

This frankness made it all the harder for the prosecution to undermine him. There was not much left to expose. When it was the turn of prosecutor Geoff Horgan, SC, to try to bring down the old heavyweight, Gatto would stand in the box, big fists grasping the wooden rail on either side of the elevated box, pushing his silver-framed glasses back to the top of the bridge of his nose. Refusing the traditional yes-no answers, he would take any opportunity to remind the jury of the lack of forensic evidence or what he believed were the perceived weaknesses in the prosecution case. For a slugger, he was boxing clever.

Asked why he wanted to meet Veniamin in the Carlton restaurant, he said:

Just to see his demeanour. Just to get my finger on the pulse with him, just to keep my finger on the pulse with him ... there were all these rumours going around that I was going to be next and there was a possibility that he was going to do it. That's the only reason.

He said he believed Veniamin had killed four or five times before and Horgan asked:

But you're happy to have an acquaintanceship with such a man?

Answer: That's right ... Let me say this, Mr Horgan, I've got hundreds of friends and ... or hundreds of acquaintances. I'm very well known, and he just fitted that category. I mean, I don't like to burn bridges; I like to establish networks of people. It always comes ...

Question: What networks would you establish with Andrew Veni-amin, this man you believed to be a killer multiple times?

Answer: Well, it comes in handy with the work that I do.

Question: Does it?

Answer: It might be a building-type scenario in the western suburbs and he might know someone that's there. He runs that part of town. I mean, it's always … you know, it's always handy to sort of … I like to know as many people as I can.

Horgan then wanted Gatto to say he hated Veniamin because he believed the hit man had killed his best friend, 'The Munster'. He wanted to establish a motive to back the claim that Gatto lured his enemy to the restaurant, took him to the corridor where there were with no witnesses and murdered him before setting up the self-defence scenario.

Question: After Graham Kinniburgh was murdered you were deeply affected by that, weren't you?

Answer: I was.

Question: Because he was a man, I think you told us yesterday, you loved?

Answer: Yes, I did, I still do.

Question: Did you believe that Andrew Veniamin was responsible for that?

Answer: I did at the time.

Question: Did you come to believe that he'd done it?

Answer: Come to believe, yes, within days. I did believe that.

Question: Believed that he was the murderer?

Answer: Yes.

Question: Of your dear, dear friend?

Answer: That's exactly right.

Question: And because you believed it, did you have a very strong animosity towards Andrew Veniamin?

Answer: Yes, probably you could say that.

Question: You had that same animosity up until the time of his death?

Answer: No, I don't agree.

Question: What's wrong with that?

Answer: Well, because we had two or three meetings where he emphatically told me that it wasn't him ... And on two or three or four occasions I was satisfied that it wasn't him and had an open mind about it.

Question: You would loathe him?

Answer: I wouldn't have been happy with him, no.

Question: Let's not beat around the bush ... You would have loathed him?

Answer: Yes, that's right.

Question: So, let's just clarify the situation. As at 23 March 2004 you did loathe Andrew Veniamin or not?

Answer: I wasn't sure. I wasn't sure.

Question: What weren't you sure about, whether you loathed (him) or whether he killed Kinniburgh?

Answer: Well, I wasn't sure whether he killed Graham, I wasn't sure, but as far away ... as far as the way I felt about him, yes, it was certainly changed, yes.

Horgan also wanted the jury to see that the accused man was more likely to try to take justice into his own hands than leave the investigation to police, even though Gatto's own life was in danger. According to Gatto, taskforce detectives had asked him about the series of unsolved murders and added, 'Mick, be careful, you could be next' — a statement police denied.

I said, 'I don't know anything and if I did I wouldn't tell you anyway ... I'm not an informer. I'm not a police informer. I pride myself on minding my own business.'

Question: You mean you don't believe that if a brutal murder has occurred where someone has been executed, and you know something about it, and you know the person responsible who's still running around the community executing people, you wouldn't tell the police about it?

Answer: Well, you never get into trouble minding your own business.

In response to a series of questions Gatto replied:

You keep twisting it and changing it ... I've told you that when I lunged at him I grabbed at his arm and his hand, but, you know, it happened that quick, the gun went off in my face. I mean, you know, I wouldn't wish upon anyone what happened to me, and I mean, to try and remember for the last fourteen months, I wake up in a cold sweat every night of the week reliving exactly what took place that day. It goes through my head every night of the week. I wake up in a cold sweat thinking about it ... I was squeezing his hand. I was trying to kill him. He was trying to kill me, I was trying to kill him.

Question: So you've trapped his hand on the gun, so that you're capable of squeezing his finger around the gun so that he kills himself?

Answer: That's right, that's exactly how it happened.

Question: You've got control of his hand which was holding the gun?

Answer: That's right, I'm squeezing his hand, squeezing his fingers to press the trigger.

Question: So he will press the trigger?

Answer: That's right.

Question: And your intention was to squeeze his hand till the gun went off, causing him to shoot himself. Was that your intention?

Answer: Of course it was. There's no dispute about that. I'm very happy about it, to be honest.

JUSTICE 'Fabulous Phil' Cummins shows two signs of his personality in the big criminal trials. A judge who does not wear the traditional wig and probably the only one in Australia who wears a sparkling stud in his left earlobe, he imposes himself on trials — much to the chagrin of various defence lawyers. Some judges tend to watch passively, allowing the prosecution and defence to battle in front of the bench — speaking only when asked for a legal ruling. Their turn comes when they address the jury at the completion of the evidence. But Phil Cummins is much more a participant, through pre-trial arguments, cross-examination and closing arguments. An experienced trial advocate before he moved to the bench, he reminds a watcher of a footballer turned coach who would rather still be getting a kick than making the moves from the sidelines.

When the jury is out of the room, Cummins will question lawyers on the direction they are taking, warn them when he disagrees with their tactics and occasionally rebuke them when he feels the need. Some experienced barristers think they are kept on too tight a leash in a Cummins trial.

But when the jury enters his court, the judge's manner changes. He is both charming and protective of the twelve strangers who make up the jury, and over the weeks or months that trials can run, he develops a bond with those selected to represent the community. He appears to try to build a protective bubble for the jury, repeatedly reinforcing that only they have the common sense to deal with the issues at hand. His well-practised intimacy with strangers appears to be designed to remove the intimidation of the court setting. It is as if he and the jury have stumbled upon some bizarre circus act being performed in front of them by lawyers and witnesses. He sometimes appears to be a tour guide showing visitors the interesting spots in what can often be a dull landscape.

One of the most entertaining distractions in a high-profile trial is jury watching. Lawyers, police and neutral observers gossip about the jury members — how they sit, how they react, how they look at the accused, and how they relate to each other. Like veteran track watchers studying horses before they race, they look for the tiniest sign that could help them back a winner. But juries, like horses, can't talk so it always ends as guesswork. During the long court days some jury members are obviously bored — only half listening to hours of seemingly irrelevant evidence.

Like students in a classroom, some only truly switch on at the last minute as if preparing for their final exams. In court, the final swotting is listening to the judge's summary. While the judge is supposed to sum up the law, many jury members look for messages in the judge's charge to see which way they should jump.

Like contestants on *Who Wants To Be A Millionaire?* they hope there is a message in the delivery that can guide them to the right answer. The judge stresses that he will not and cannot do their job. He will tell them the law, but they must decide the facts.

On 8 June 2005, after a trial lasting nearly seven weeks — short by modern standards — Justice Cummins finally cut to the chase. He spoke to the jury for more than two days — reviewing the evidence and explaining the law. But it was early on day one of the summary that he explained the basis of the case, pure and simple. Who pulled the gun in the corridor? If it were Veniamin he copped his right whack and it was self-defence. If it were Gatto, it was murder:

> In your decision-making, ladies and gentlemen, you must put aside sympathy and you must put aside prejudice and decide the case solely on the evidence led here in court. Put aside completely any previous publicity. You must not decide the case on prejudice or on extraneous considerations or on sympathy but solely on the evidence led here in front of you in this court, just as you have sworn or affirmed to do.
>
> Proceed in your decision-making, ladies and gentlemen, as you would expect and wish a judge to proceed, because each of you now is a judge, fairly, calmly, analytically and solely on the evidence. ... In this case, ladies and gentlemen, the accused Mr Gatto, gave evidence in front of you and was cross-examined. Mr Gatto could have remained silent throughout this case and not come forward to give evidence and be cross-examined, and that is because, as I will come to in a moment, an accused person has no burden to prove anything in a criminal trial. The person who has the burden to prove in a criminal trial is the prosecution because the prosecution has brought the charge. So when you are assessing the evidence of Mr Gatto, you apply the same principles as you apply to other witnesses in the case: Is the witness telling the truth or lying? And is the witness accurate

and reliable or not? But with Mr Gatto, the accused, you also are entitled to take into account in his favour that he gave evidence in front of you when he had no obligation to do so.

To be convicted of murder, the accused has to kill another person. There is no dispute about that in this case. The accused Mr Gatto says he did kill Andrew Veniamin by forcing Andrew Veniamin's finger to pull the trigger, forced by Mr Gatto by squeezing Veniamin's hand and that killed Mr Veniamin. There is no dispute about element number one, ladies and gentlemen. ... The issue here is: Who had the .38? The prosecution says Mr Gatto had the .38, he took the deceased out the back, Gatto produced the .38 and shot the deceased repeatedly with it. That is the prosecution case. The defence says the .38 was Veniamin's. Veniamin arrived at La Porcella with the .38 hidden, and when they both went out the back, Veniamin produced the .38 and was going to shoot Mr Gatto with it. So that is the issue in a nutshell, ladies and gentlemen. No-one has suggested in this case, ladies and gentlemen, that if Veniamin had the gun and Veniamin pulled the gun on Gatto, threatening to kill him, that Gatto was not entitled to act in self-defence. No-one suggested that. If Veniamin had the gun and Veniamin pulled the gun on Gatto and threatened him, you must acquit Mr Gatto of murder. So the issue is: Who had and pulled the gun?

The accused does not have to prove he acted in self-defence. The prosecution has to prove he did not act in self-defence at the time he killed the deceased and must so prove beyond reasonable doubt. That is the burden of proof, ladies and gentlemen. Despite the use of the words 'self-defence', the accused does not have to prove he acted in self-defence. The prosecution has to prove, and prove beyond reasonable doubt, that the accused did not act in self-defence.

So, what does that all come down to, ladies and gentlemen? Who had the .38? And that is what this case has been about, ladies and gentlemen. For a conviction of murder, the prosecution must prove beyond reasonable doubt that the accused Mr Gatto produced the .38 at the restaurant and shot the deceased with it. ... So, that is what it all comes down to ladies and gentlemen. Has the prosecution

Art imitates life
... the paid actors
are the ones
in the bottom
picture.

Mark Moran: shot near his home in
mid-2000.

Callan Mulvey as Moran.

Graham 'The Munster' Kinniburgh dresses down at
Alphonse Gangitano's inquest.

Veteran Gerard Kennedy as 'The Munster'.

Graham Kinniburgh's funeral in leafy Kew ... Mick Gatto
(back, right) is one of the pallbearers

Pallbearers play
their part.

Detective Sen Sgt Stuart Bateson leads members of the
Purana Taskforce away from the Melbourne Magistrates Court
after winning an order to interview a murder suspect.

Actor Rodger Corser channels detective 'Steve Owen'.

Purana Taskforce members led by dogged detective inspector
Gavan Ryan (centre) just after Williams had been sentenced to
35 years. This time, police held the press conference.

Frank Holden plays a character uncannily similar to Ryan.

Mario Condello ... a man of means by no means.

Changing places: Martin Sacks tries the dark side.

Every dog has its day: Carl Williams in happier times, when he gave the press conference and the police said 'no comment'. It didn't last.

Red Rooster or KFC? ... Gyton Grantley's 'Carl' ponders
the big questions.

Roberta Williams
with family friend
Andrew 'Benji'
Veniamin. A short
time later he was
shot dead.

Below: Kat Stewart
as Roberta.

proved beyond reasonable doubt that Mr Gatto had the .38? If the prosecution has proved beyond reasonable doubt that Mr Gatto had the .38 you would convict Mr Gatto of murder. If the prosecution has failed to prove that beyond reasonable doubt you must acquit him of murder.

The jury returned with a verdict on 15 June 2005, after less than 24 hours. Gatto stood in the dock, plucking at a thread that had come away from his elegant grey tie in the long minutes before the jury members returned to decide his future. His wife and daughter were in the public gallery behind him. He told them repeatedly that he loved them. He spoke calmly, quietly, assuring them everything would be all right. He and his wife, a pleasant-looking and charming woman, spoke warmly. He appeared to be more concerned for them than for himself. He made an obvious effort to control his emotions, not wanting to increase their concerns. He talked to his daughter gently about domestic matters. She said despite her father's absence some things hadn't changed — her room at home was still messy. He laughed.

When his son arrived, nervous and distressed, Gatto smiled again, telling him everything would work out fine, trying to remove the building tension. It was hard not to be impressed. If a measure of a man is how he deals with life-defining moments, there was no myth about Gatto that day. He told them that the most important words he would ever hear would be from the jury. The foreman would say either one word or two — 'Guilty' or 'Not Guilty'. One of the authors who happened to be sitting with the Gatto family speculated that it would be two. Gatto responded, 'I hope you're right.' To his family downstairs and his friends upstairs he repeatedly gave a Roman-like salute, right clenched fist across the heart, then fingers to the lips.

The jury of six women and six men filed in. Some were smiling, others emotional. His son had his head in his hands, shaking and close to tears. His daughter's right leg bounced with nerves.

His wife just looked at her husband. As the jury came in he smiled. When the foreman announced the verdict of 'not guilty' Gatto showed emotion for the first time, pushing his glasses back as his eyes welled with relief. He then turned to his family. He thanked the judge twice as he was told he was free to go. One lawyer had previously asked him how he had remained so strong during the trial. He said he feared his family would collapse if he gave way.

Outside was the usual media throng and backslappers. Gatto told them, 'Thank God for the jury system, thank God for Robert Richter, a top barrister.' His lawyers had every reason to thank their client in return. The rumoured fee for the defence team was $400,000. That night Gatto's many supporters returned to his house for a celebration with wine, beer and pizza, ending Gatto's fourteen-month prison-inspired diet. A few days later he posed for a *Herald Sun* photographer as he relaxed in Queensland. The picture did not impress some friends of the late Andrew Veniamin.

Gatto was inundated with media requests and said he was prepared to talk for a fee to be donated to the Royal Children's Hospital. For years he had donated to the Good Friday Appeal — he even managed to contribute $5000 from his prison cell while in solitary confinement. He told 3AW's award-winning breakfast team and budding investigative duo, Ross Stevenson and John Burns, 'If there is a media outlet or a talkback show that is prepared to pay a six-figure sum that goes directly to the Children's Hospital I would be more than happy to give my input and have a chat — no problem'. He confirmed he had lost 30 kilograms in jail but said he doubted if people would like to follow the program. 'I have always maintained I would rather have been fat and free. I used to shadow box in my cell because as you know I was locked up for 23 hours a day. They were calling me Hurricane Carter in there. I did it to keep focused and my mind right, otherwise you just go off your head.

'There are plenty of people in there who lost the plot and went mad. Imagine being locked in your bathroom for 23 hours then you'll sort of understand. A lot of people didn't recognise me. Some thought I had fallen ill, but I intended to lose the weight. It was the only good that came out of it. He said that following the verdict he wanted to keep out of the headlines. 'I just want to be low key and be left alone to do my own little thing. I'm going to concentrate on the building industry ... it's been pretty good to me. I want to forget about all this other nonsense. It's really got nothing to do with me anyway.'

He said he didn't feel he needed to look over his shoulder in the future and did not feel in danger while in prison. 'No, I was never in fear. That was all trumped up. There was never a problem there. I was happy to go out in the mainstream handcuffed. I said "Send me out in the mainstream handcuffed". I didn't want to be a hero but I just knew that all this nonsense was blown out of proportion. I've got no enemies. I've done nothing wrong. The bloke tried to kill me. What am I supposed to do, let him kill me? So at the end of the day I can walk around with my head held high. I'm not worried about anyone.'

Two months after his acquittal he chanced to meet one of the authors in Lygon Street. He looked at peace with the world. He smiled and pulled back his jacket to show his stomach and said he'd put on ten kilograms.

19

COOL BEER, COLD BLOOD

> He tried to carry a gun but
> his arthritis meant it
> was more of a liability
> than an asset.

LEWIS Moran was a traditional criminal with traditional tastes. And that, in part, led to his violent end in the front bar of the Brunswick Club on 31 March 2004.

For many years Moran's regular pub had been the Laurel Hotel in Mount Alexander Road in the inner western suburb of Ascot Vale, strategically placed mid-way between Moonee Valley and Flemington racecourses.

The Laurel was a pub of choice for gangsters of discernment. Moran's son Jason once pulled a gun on another drinker there. Graham 'The Munster' Kinniburgh popped in for a drink in the bar there before he headed to a meeting with Alphonse Gangitano in January 1998 on the night Big Al was murdered.

But when the old style pub turned trendy and began to serve foreign Tooheys beer, Lewis was disgusted.

The Moran clan had drunk at The Laurel for years and while Lewis was comfortable surrounded by friends and associates there, he decided that if the pub didn't have his favourite Carlton United product on tap it was time to try the Brunswick Club in Sydney Road — a few hundred metres from the local police station and near a proposed redevelopment Tony Mokbel claimed would turn the tired shopping strip into a little piece of Paris Down Under. Which piece he didn't say.

Melbourne is known for its exclusive establishment men's clubs but the Brunswick Club is not one of them. Moran the elder felt welcome there and became a fixture. Several times a week, he would turn to the left when he walked in and stand at the bar to sip seven-ounce glasses of beer.

All his friends knew they could find Lewis at his favourite spot, known in the trade as his 'lean'. The trouble was, so did his enemies. In fact, they could see him through the window from the street.

Lewis Moran knew he was marked for death but, according to friends, he 'was too stubborn to take any notice'. The elder statesman of the crumbling Moran crime dynasty was facing serious drug charges and police had already tried to keep him in jail for his own protection. When he insisted on being released on bail, police tried again: varying the reporting conditions to make his movements harder for a hit man to track. But all their good work was wasted because he could always be found at the Brunswick Club.

Lewis Moran may have wanted a quiet life but crime was all he knew. Detectives had given evidence in the Melbourne Magistrates' Court that he had been involved in drug deals worth $10 million over the previous four years.

Senior Detective Victor Anastasiadis told the court one informer gave Moran $5.5 million in pseudoephedrine-based tablets, used to make amphetamines, and was to receive a share of the amphetamines in the deal with Moran. That's why the 57-year-old grandfather was facing 17 charges, including trafficking commercial quantities of amphetamine, hashish, ecstasy and pseudoephedrine.

He had been charged with his old friend, Bertie Wrout, a senior citizen and likeable rogue who later had heavy calibre reasons to wish he hadn't been Lewis' drinking mate.

Senior Detective Anastasiadis said he feared for the informer's safety if the accused pair was released. But the informer was not in as much danger as the pair of old crooks.

On 22 July 2003 — after nine months on remand — Lewis was granted bail despite police opposing it, officially on grounds he would seek retribution for his son's murder and pose a threat to a police informer. He was released on condition he reported daily to police, obeyed a night curfew and would not contact witnesses.

His lawyer also argued he should be freed so he could act as a father figure for his murdered sons' children.

Violent death ran through the generations on both sides.

In October 1978 Leslie Herbert Kane had been shot dead in his Wantirna unit. His body was never found. But it was one of his children, Trish, who eventually moved in with her childhood sweetheart — Jason Moran — and had children with him.

Les Kane's brother, Brian, was also shot dead — in a Brunswick hotel in November 1982, apparently as revenge for the brazen shooting of Raymond Patrick 'Chuck' Bennett in Melbourne Magistrates' Court three years earlier.

Among the mourners for Brian Kane was a young Jason Moran.

In the same month, in an unrelated shooting, Mark Moran's natural father, Les 'Johnny' Cole, was shot dead in Sydney as part of a NSW underworld feud.

When the decision to kill Lewis was made is still a matter of speculation, but police believe it was probably at a reception centre near Keilor Cemetery the previous evening.

It was there that many of the western suburbs' most dangerous criminals gathered for a wake for Andrew 'Benji' Veniamin, shot dead in a Carlton restaurant on 23 March 2004.

After all, straight after Benji was shot dead, Williams had said, 'Here we go again, fasten your seatbelts' and he was not planning a trip at the time.

Police tried to protect Lewis but he had lost his will to live. His arthritis meant carrying a gun was now more of a liability than an asset. The former light-fingered pickpocket could no longer make his fingers work.

He gave up the gun idea after firing a shot through the floor of a car while trying to load his new weapon.

Someone who had known Moran for years said of him: 'Lewis loved money. He was rich but he didn't know how to have a good time.'

He had been introduced to the drug business by his sons and embraced the wealth it generated. Friends said he liked to watch cooking shows during the day, do a little business in the late afternoon and drink from about 6pm. He was notorious for hiding money, much of which has never been found.

Once he hid $14,000 in an oven and was shattered when someone turned it on — shrinking the notes to the size of Monopoly money. But there was a happy ending. His well-connected mate Kinniburgh found a compliant bank manager in Sydney who would accept the cash.

Moran had little formal education but, as an experienced SP bookmaker, was sharp with numbers. After Kinniburgh was murdered he knew his own survival was a long shot.

Despite that, he went to the Brunswick Club every night — regular as clockwork — until time ran out.

He was killed and his mate Bertie Wrout badly wounded the day after Veniamin's wake. It was no coincidence. Some say revenge is a dish best eaten cold, but Carl was a fast food boy from way back.

Moran saw the gunmen enter the club and said, 'I think we're off here.'

'Off' is an underworld expression for dead.

Lewis ran in an arc trying to escape. He didn't have a chance and was shot dead a few metres from where he had been enjoying a quiet beer just seconds earlier. The moments leading up to the murder were caught on the Brunswick Club's security camera, but the killers were wearing balaclavas.

Club staff were deeply traumatised and were said to be worried when a wake was planned at the bar where Lewis was murdered.

A few years earlier, Lewis had still been a powerful figure with powerful friends. When his stepson Mark was killed he was bent on revenge. He refused to help police with their investigations because he still believed he had the pull to deal with his enemies. At first he wasn't sure who was behind the hit, but eventually all roads seemed to lead to Carl Williams.

A secret police report, later to be leaked to the underworld with disastrous consequences, claimed police informer Terence Hodson was offered $50,000 to kill Williams. The offer was allegedly made in May 2001 in the name of Lewis Moran.

Lewis, always careful with the money he stole from other people, was well under the odds with his contract offer. Moran senior was easily trumped when it came to murder by tender.

The man who would later plead guilty to Lewis's murder said he was offered $150,000 to kill Moran although he said he was short-changed $10,000 on settlement.

It's a bit hard to go to the Small Claims Tribunal to argue you've been short changed in an underworld contract killing. And you can't even claim it as a tax deduction.

The killer, known as The Journeyman, talked so that he could get a minimum sentence rather than life with no chance of release. And as he talked he warmed to the task, implicating himself in a murder where he wasn't even a listed suspect.

The Journeyman claimed that the money for the Moran hit came from Carl Williams and Tony Mokbel. Williams would later plead guilty to the murder, while Mokbel continued to declare he was not involved.

Once almost untouchable, in his final year Lewis Moran was close to a spent force. The boys were gone, his friend, Graham Kinniburgh, was dead and his respected associate, Mick Gatto, was in jail.

Isolated and without a power base, Lewis, 58, let it be known he no longer wanted to fight back. Crippled by grief and illness, he was no longer a threat. But his enemies were not sure and they wanted to be. Dead sure.

Lewis was no fool. Shattered by the death of Mark and Jason, the death of his mate was the final straw. He was safe in jail but still fought for bail. When he was bailed on drug charges his former lawyer, an old mate, Andrew Fraser, who was in the same prison on drug charges, farewelled him with the traditional 'See ya later.' Moran shook his head and said he wouldn't. He knew he'd be gone by the time Fraser was freed.

In the few weeks before the final hit police had been hearing that some would-be-gangsters were offering their services to kill Williams.

Williams maintained he could not imagine why anyone would wish him harm. Carl, nicknamed The Truth by Tony Mokbel, was telling little lies.

There was a confrontation in a western-suburbs Tabaret not long before Lewis Moran's death, when the old crook was called outside by Williams. With no back-up, no guns, arthritis, a 25-year age gap and a 30 kilo handicap, Lewis wisely declined.

Lewis was said to have lost his personal taste for violence, although he did not seem to mind when Mark and Jason Moran used guns, baseball bats, fists and feet to exact revenge against real and perceived enemies.

Lewis was another of Melbourne's old-style crooks who seemed to sail through life with few financial concerns and no pressing need to work for a living.

His crime record charts post-war criminal history. In the early days he was chased from a circus when he was discovered to have lifted valuables from members of the audience.

He was said to be involved in protecting backyard abortionists, SP bookmaking and steal-to-order break-in rings before moving into modern crime and, inevitably, drug trafficking.

When his sons were running hot he moved into semi-retirement, but his notorious love of a dollar drew him back into the drug business with its rivers of cash.

For Lewis, the day would begin by checking the form, placing a few bets and then turning on the cable TV. But he would not spend his time glued to the racing channel. Like many of his generation of gangsters, he was besotted by the cooking channel.

Even during the middle of the underworld war Lewis would sit and watch good, bad and indifferent television chefs cooking up international dishes.

Then, between 4pm and 6pm, he would often visit associates to talk business before heading to the pub. There the subject would revert to the day's television recipes.

Gunmen, drug dealers, former armed robbers and try-hards would exchange tips on how to avoid gluggy risotto or overcooking crispy skinned salmon.

It was a long way from a pie at the races.

Police say there was no need to shoot Moran's friend, Bertie Wrout. At 62, tall, thin, popular and relatively harmless, he could not have been seen as a threat by the two gunmen who walked into the Brunswick Club and opened fire.

Wrout survived the gunshot wounds but doctors were puzzled when they found one more entry wound than bullets. The puzzle was solved in a painful way for Bertie. Much later, while going to the toilet he felt burning pains more usually felt by brothel clients who insist on unprotected sex — and that wasn't Bertie's caper. When he heard a metallic noise at the bottom of the urinal, the pain stopped. Bertie had passed shrapnel. It is not known if police collected the vital evidence.

Less than an hour after Lewis Moran's murder, Williams was not his chatty self, saying: 'I've got no more to say.' When asked if he feared for his life he said: 'I'm all right.'

But Roberta was more animated. 'My heart goes out to them (the Morans),' she said. 'I don't know anything about it. This is insane. It just has to stop.'

While police and politicians expressed outrage over the Moran murder, Melbourne citizens seemed to have become accustomed to bloodshed on their doorsteps.

Upstairs at the Brunswick Club is a billiard room. Hours after the murder, two snooker players tried to pass the police lines to head upstairs for a game.

Even though Moran's body was visible, they twice argued with police that they should be allowed inside to play.

After all, life goes on. For some.

From his prison cell, Gatto was able to organise a death notice for his mate. It read: 'Lewis, you knew it was coming, you just didn't care ... Deepest condolences to Tuppence (Lewis's brother) and the Moran family. Rest in peace my Mate and a big hello to Pa. (Kinniburgh) — Mick Gatto.'

The funeral was not a lavish affair, but Judy Moran would not let the story die with her estranged second husband.

'Lewis and I were both worried about his safety, but he didn't care; he was sick and tired of it all. I was horrified when I found out he'd been murdered, about three minutes after it happened.

'But I am outraged that my family has been portrayed in the way they have. They were good people, not bad people, but they keep calling Lewis a drug baron — which is not true.

'I am doing this for my grandchildren as a legacy to their grandfather.'

In her acknowledgements at the end of her book she thanked several people, including her photographer, the lady who helped her chose her outfits 'at a very difficult time' and a gentleman in the fashion industry for providing her with 'lovely shoes.'

She thanked her hairdresser, 'for all the hairstyles you created for me for the funerals of all my family.'

However, she omitted to thank the Purana Taskforce that was working to solve the murders of her family.

20

THE DOUBLE CROSS

> He was off to have a drink
> with some mates.
> Or at least he thought
> they were mates.

LEWIS Caine was tough, confident and at the peak of his powers until he found too late that in the underworld tough guys often end up dead.

Good looking and with piercing eyes, Caine could have been mistaken as a former sportsman on a gradual decline — the type who is past his best but remains a formidable opponent.

But fellow crooks and police knew without asking that he had done some serious jail time — the giveaway was the way he moved. He had a cocky, almost confrontational walk that some men pick up in prison. A cross between a boxer's strut and a street brawler's stride. It gave a message that he was always ready for action and was confident he could handle any challenge. He was wrong.

Caine, a self-proclaimed karate expert, kicked a man to death outside a Melbourne nightclub in 1988. He was convicted of murder and was considered dangerous enough to spend most of his ten years inside in maximum security.

Caine, 39, was a friend of Mick Gatto but also an associate of Carl Williams. It was enormously difficult to remain neutral and Caine was from Tasmania, not Switzerland (although he would end up looking a little like Swiss-cheese). People in the underworld were expected to pick sides. It may be that Caine chose the wrong one.

Roberta Williams said she saw Caine only days before his murder. Both Williams and Caine had abandoned anonymous suburban life, choosing to live in central Melbourne high-rise apartments. It may have been the nightlife, but more likely they knew that secure city buildings with lockup underground car parks, swipe card doors and working state-of-the-art closed circuit recorders were sizeable obstacles to would-be hit men.

It was a sound argument. Certainly Mark Moran, Frank Benvenuto, Mario Condello, Charlie Hegyalji, Dino Dibra, Graham Kinniburgh and Michael Marshall were in no position to dispute the logic — they were all killed outside their suburban homes.

Roberta Williams told the author, 'He came over to say hi. We didn't know him well. He seemed like such a nice person.'

She said Caine's killing was 'just another kick in the guts' and added: 'When is this all going to end?'

It was a rhetorical question. She should have asked her husband.

Most criminals go bad by degrees. They start with minor property offences as kids, graduate to theft and then become violent. These are the building blocks of the gangster.

But Caine was not your average 'crim'. He went from indecent language to carrying a gun to murder — with little in between.

The son of a Tasmanian police inspector, he loved the idea of being a hard man but lacked the discipline to prove himself in a legitimate way. According to a confidential police report, he joined the army on 11 May 1982, but went AWOL five months later and was discharged.

He was born Adrian Bruce Bligh in Devonport, Tasmania, on 22 April 1965. His parents divorced and his mother moved to Queensland. According to police he had 'an intense hatred of his father'. He claimed to be a martial arts expert but police found it was a lie. 'He did some classes, but was only a beginner,' one officer noted. But he knew enough to kick a harmless man to death.

It was obvious Caine was fascinated by death and destruction. When he was arrested for murder he was found to have books on terrorism, Special Forces tactics and weaponry. Earlier he had been found with a book on explosives.

He was a courier who once injured both wrists in a motorbike accident. According to a police report, at the time of his arrest, 'Caine was under suspicion of being a large drug dealer, using his employment as a courier as a cover for his trafficking activities.' It was believed that Caine's position in the syndicate was one under the actual importer. He would not sell to street addicts, only to other heroin dealers.

In the early hours of 18 September 1988, two lives collided: one of the man who courted violence and the other of a bloke just out for a good time.

David Templeton was 34 years old when he crossed Caine. He lived with his parents in Williamstown until he married in 1978 and moved to Essendon. In 1984 he separated and later divorced. He then returned to live with his parents until 1985, when he bought a house in Newport.

Templeton was always gainfully employed and regularly promoted. After leaving Williamstown Technical School, he had worked for three years as a bank teller. He then moved to Medibank where he started as a clerk and was later promoted to branch manager.

After 10 years with Medibank he decided he needed a change and became a sales representative.

His family described him as honest, hardworking and community minded. He was an active member of the North Melbourne and Point Gellibrand Rotary Clubs.

But on the night of Saturday 17 September 1988, the likeable and responsible Templeton was for once a pain in the neck.

He had been admitted to the Melbourne nightclub, Lazar, and after a few too many drinks proceeded to make a scene.

Caine had arrived at the same nightclub at 10.30pm to see a friend who worked as a bouncer and to catch up with a woman he had met the previous day at a motorcycle dealership in Elizabeth Street.

As they stood at the bar, Templeton and Caine were to have the briefest of conversations.

The salesman had grabbed a policewoman friend's badge and, without her knowledge, used it to pretend he was in the job. It is an offence to masquerade as a policeman, but Templeton's antics were immature rather than malicious.

He was guilty of being a show-off, and probably a drunk one. He should have woken up the next morning with a sore head and an attack of guilt. But he was never to wake up.

Templeton and Caine appeared to show a sudden interest in one girl and an instant dislike for each other.

Caine was seen to be loud and aggressive and Templeton, still pretending to be a policeman, complained to a bouncer, who happened to be Caine's friend.

Caine was taken outside and told there had been a complaint and that he was no longer welcome inside. He took it badly, swearing and kicking a parked car.

He continued to yell and swear, claiming a policeman was trying to steal his girlfriend. Twenty minutes later Templeton came out and Caine attacked him. Templeton ran away, but Caine jumped into a cab already occupied by four people and hunted him down in Spencer Street.

According to a witness, 'The victim was lying on the ground and Caine was punching and kicking him in the head and body.'

A police report said later: 'Caine pursued Templeton and subjected him to a savage and merciless beating and kicking, causing multiple abrasions, lacerations, contusions, and fracturing of skull.' He died on the footpath.

Caine went back to the nightclub and was seen with blood on his hands. According to police he was heard to say, 'That bloke copped it; I knew I'd get him. Don't fuck with the Wing Chun boys.' He was also heard boasting in triumph: 'I got the guy who got my girl.'

He was arrested around 3am. He showed no concern for his victim and no regard for his future, glaring and trying to intimidate the arresting police. When he was handed over to homicide detectives, one told him that staring might work in the schoolyard but not in the interview room.

The days of homicide detectives giving offenders short and violent lessons in manners were long gone. These days they want to gain convictions rather than inflict concussions.

Manslaughter and murder convictions are not easy to get in prosecuting alcohol-related fatal assaults. But in the Templeton case the jury was so horrified by the cold-blooded nature of the attack, they were prepared to convict Caine of murder. Not once, but twice.

He was convicted in November 1989, appealed and was convicted again in August 1990.

During his appeal, Caine managed to slip his handcuffs and escape from court. He was caught close by, after falling over. Police who grabbed him saw him trying to get rid of a knife. 'How Caine came to arm himself with a knife and avoid detection of same is not known,' a policeman noted.

A police summary said, 'Caine is a loner with no strong family ties. He is a keen and regular exerciser who maintains an excellent standard of fitness. He is fit and healthy. He has an unpredictable nature and to this day has shown little or no remorse for his conduct.'

A detective who interviewed Caine had no doubt he was already a lost cause: 'In my opinion he is capable of killing again either whilst in custody or when released. Members should exercise extreme caution when dealing with him.'

Far from being mortified that he had killed a man, Caine, also known as Sean Vincent, became a hard man inside prison.

When moved to a less violent part of the prison system, he asked to move back. He loved the dog-eat-dog nature of the violent jail culture. In 1997 he was one of five prisoners subdued with tear gas after a three-day standoff in the top-security unit in the Barwon Prison.

The inmates, led by Caine and double murderer and escapee, John William Lindrea, were demanding contact visits, extra time in their cells, access to recreational equipment and a more 'relaxed regime' in the management unit.

On the first day of their protest in July 1997, an emergency response team went into the cells and forcibly carried the inmates out into the exercise yard. The following day the prisoners again refused to move and the head of the jail's emergency response team issued a series of progressive warnings telling the inmates they could be subjected to force unless they complied.

After two hours the inmates were told they would be given no more warnings. The team then moved in and ordered the inmates to lie on their cell floors with their hands behind their backs.

When the inmates refused the team used an aerosol tear gas spray, but the prisoners went to the air intake valves in their cells to breathe fresh air.

The team then dropped two tear gas grenades, each the size of an egg, through the door slots of Lindrea and Caine's cells.

The wing filled with tear gas and prison officers, wearing gas masks, stormed the area, grabbed the five inmates and forced them into the open air. They were stripped, showered and taken to an exercise yard. Prison sources said the inmates declared they would refuse to dress as a continued protest.

'After two hours in the nude in the cold they decided that discretion was the better part of valour and dressed,' a prison source said.

Caine was violent before he went to jail. He was cold-blooded by the time he left and he walked into an underworld war where cold killers were a valued commodity.

Caine had a tough guy's glare but underworld survivors need to be able to keep one eye behind them.

He had mastered prison power plays but was out of his depth in the streets of Melbourne. Caine left his city apartment about 8pm on the night of his murder. He was off to have a drink with some mates.

Or at least he thought they were mates.

CAINE was not the only underworld shark circling with the smell of blood in the water. He began to drink with two others, one who had turned betrayal into an art form.

Caine would have been confident he could confide in his new hardened drinking buddies. He would have known the word was out they had killed Lewis Moran in the Brunswick Club just weeks earlier on behalf of Carl Williams and, it is alleged, Tony Mokbel.

Williams had been on a hit man recruiting drive. His first choice, Benji Veniamin, was dead and his second, The Runner, was in jail.

It was time to replace the casualties of war.

He had first turned to a group of old school gangsters with a family history in the notorious painter and docker union. He persuaded one, The Journeyman, to take the contract to kill Lewis Moran for $150,000.

Now he recruited the volatile Lewis Caine.

Williams was frightened that after the murder of Moran Senior, the Carlton Crew would hit back and he was now committed to an extermination policy. He would kill all the key men close to Mick Gatto and then the Don himself.

The first target would be Mario Condello, the smooth former lawyer who was Gatto's best friend. It was Condello that Mick entrusted to run business while he was in jail for 14 months waiting for his murder trial over the death of Veniamin.

Williams reasoned that with Gatto inside, Condello was hopelessly exposed. It was the perfect opportunity to launch a hit and he offered the job to Caine, who accepted. Caine then tried to recruit The Journeyman to his team.

It was an error of judgement. A fatal one.

The Journeyman not only had links to Williams, but to the Carlton Crew. Police believe he flipped on Carl's team and told Condello of the contract.

Mario outbid the contract and The Journeyman swapped sides.

On 8 May 2004 The Journeyman and his off-sider called for a meeting at a Carlton hotel to discuss the Condello hit. Other drinkers in the bar said the three seemed friendly and relaxed. What exactly was said will never be known but the three hopped into a four-wheel drive and headed off.

Caine was in the back seat. He'd had a little to drink and a small amount of cocaine but he was functional. The Journeyman's offsider turned around from the front seat and without warning shot Caine under the right eye, killing him instantly.

The body was dumped nearby in a dead-end street called Katawa Grove, in Brunswick.

Police say no attempt was made to conceal the body because Condello wanted to make a public statement of what he would do to anyone who came after him.

The Journeyman told the *Herald Sun* he had seen Caine since his release. 'I thought he was trying to lead a normal lifestyle. I don't think he was a gangster or a big-timer.'

Certainly the man's views on Caine were of interest to the Purana Taskforce. The Journeyman tried to cover his tracks by leaving messages on the dead man's mobile phone hours after the killing, but all roads led to him and within weeks he was arrested and charged.

He was convicted of the murder and later became a prosecution witness and would talk about the murders police knew he had committed and one they didn't — one that would raise serious allegations of police corruption.

Caine may well have been a nasty standover man with connections in the drug world, but away from business he had an attractive and devoted live-in lover from the other side of the legal tracks.

He was living in the city with a solicitor from a well-known Melbourne criminal law firm.

The solicitor, the controversial Zarah Garde-Wilson, who lived with Caine for almost three years, was shattered by his death and made a request to the Coroner's Court to have sperm taken from his body and frozen. The request was made after Caine's body was released following the autopsy.

The sperm had to be taken from the body within four days of death to ensure it remained fertile. The Supreme Court would have to approve the release of the sperm before Garde-Wilson could use it to become pregnant.

She had told friends before the murder she planned to marry Caine, but his relatives said he was not ready to wed and didn't want children.

Underworld sources said the pair had only recently postponed plans for a lavish wedding with guests expected to fly in from around Australia and overseas.

The couple first met when she was assigned to represent Caine over a routine .05 charge. Love bloomed among the lawyer's briefs.

The irony is that, like most crims, Caine fought to stop police getting body samples from him that could be used to link him to unsolved crimes. But after his death, he had no say in the matter.

You may not be able to get blood from a stone, but you can get sperm from a dead gangster.

21

RATS IN THE RANKS

'I may not be an angel,
your honour, but I pride myself
as being a police officer
who hates crooks ... For me
to pass on that type of
(murder) information,
I'm sorry, I would never,
ever do it.'

SENIOR SERGEANT PAUL MULLETT TO THE OFFICE OF POLICE INTEGRITY.

OF all the murders during the gangland war, the shooting of male prostitute Shane Chartres-Abbott was one that failed to generate more than a flicker of public interest.

He was not a colourful underworld figure, nor an innocent victim. He was just an opportunistic weirdo who specialised in sado-masochism and, from all reports, liked his work.

The case would sit dormant for nearly four years as police, the courts and the media concentrated on the high-profile murders involving the Morans, Carl Williams and the so-called Carlton Crew.

But the murder of Shane Chartres-Abbott was a time bomb that finally exploded to create high profile casualties and substantial collateral damage.

The breakthrough, when it came, exposed a litany of alleged corruption, cover-ups, leaks, disloyalty and attempted sabotage that would severely damage the reputation of the Victoria Police.

The case looked destined to remain unsolved until the hit man known as The Journeyman confessed to a senior Purana detective that he was the gunman.

By this time, many killers and bit players in the war had done deals to avoid life sentences, but The Journeyman's admission still came as a shock.

He had already been sentenced to a minimum of nineteen years for his role in two contract killings and was not even considered a suspect for the male prostitute's death.

If he had shut up, he would never have been a suspect for gunning down Chartres-Abbott. But was he credible?

In four decades in the underworld, The Journeyman had been motivated by self-interest. He had avoided several murder charges by forcing members of his gang to plead guilty on his behalf. He was a liar, a killer, and a manipulator.

Yet his explosive statement implicating himself in the Chartres-Abbott murder did not appear to be driven (at least on the surface) by self-preservation. Ultimately, he would go much further — implicating one serving and one former detective in an alleged monstrous conspiracy.

He named Detective Sergeant Peter 'Stash' Lalor and former Detective Sergeant David 'Docket' Waters. Even though The Journeyman was rightly considered a habitual liar, so much of his statement was corroborated that senior police set up a special taskforce, code-named Briars, to investigate any alleged links between a bent victim, supposedly bent cops and a bent hit man.

It is hard to feel much sympathy for the murder victim. At the time he was killed he was standing trial for raping, bashing and biting a female client.

Chartres-Abbott's defence on the charge was as bizarre as his lifestyle. In 2002, he went to the Saville Hotel in South Yarra to a booking. He was to see a Thai woman — it was not their first meeting but it would be their last.

What was supposed to be a session of commercial sex-on-the-edge descended into dangerous violence.

When staff found the woman around 5am she was covered in bruises and bite-marks, had been raped, and part of her tongue was missing.

Chartres-Abbott was immediately the obvious suspect and was soon arrested.

If the case weren't weird enough, it got worse when the victim told police the male prostitute had informed her he was a 200-year-old vampire. This would severely limit his chance of accepting any daytime bookings.

The suspect's defence began as a traditional one. Yes, he had been to the hotel, but when he left the woman had not been attacked and raped. From there the defence case spiraled from the bizarre to the unbelievable. He claimed the victim told him he was being set up. He also claimed she warned him that vice bosses had cast him as the victim in a snuff movie so he fled the hotel before he could be grabbed.

His defence was somewhat weakened when it was revealed that when he was arrested he had the victim's blood on his pants and her phone in his bag.

A few days into his County Court trial, his legal team successfully sought removal of the accused's home address from any paperwork on security grounds.

It was too late. The killers already knew where to get him. Within 24 hours he was dead.

As he left his home on 4 June 2003, to head to Court, two men appeared. One attacked Chartres-Abbott's pregnant girlfriend and her father to distract them while the second shot and killed him.

He was shot in the neck. Vampires hate that.

There were many theories, the most popular being that his bosses in the vice world, concerned he might do a deal and tell all to authorities about their racket, ordered his execution.

But it now appears the motive was much simpler. Someone very close to the victim was not prepared to leave justice to the system and offered a contract to kill the baby-faced, sado-masochistic prostitute.

The Journeyman, acting as a freelance hit man, would tell police he accepted the offer. But what mattered most was that he also told them he was helped from within police ranks.

He told detectives he drank with the serving policeman Lalor and the former policeman Waters in a Carlton hotel and discussed the hit with them. He made a statement that he asked Lalor to help find the address of the target and assist him with an alibi.

He claims the policeman did provide the address and also helped set up, if not an alibi, at least a set of circumstances designed to confuse investigators.

The Journeyman had outstanding warrants for a spate of driving offences. He walked into the Prahran police station to give himself up just eight hours after the shooting. The theory being that a killer would want to make himself scarce after a shooting and not walk into the lion's den.

The man who arrested the Journeyman at the station over the warrants was 'Stash' Lalor, though in itself this was not necessarily proof Lalor was a party to a murder plot.

The Journeyman is violent, disingenuous and disloyal so why

would Waters and Lalor choose to drink with him, if indeed either of them had? Or perhaps only one had.

Intriguingly, 'Docket' Waters had been charged and acquitted of drug offences in a case where a key witness had refused to testify.

Investigators believe a jailhouse deal resulted in the key witness in the case refusing to testify in exchange for a guarantee that a major witness in his upcoming murder trial also remained silent.

In both cases the witnesses refused to co-operate.

The prisoner who was said to have set up the deal on behalf of police charged with drug offences was The Journeyman.

Still waters can run deep.

WHEN The Journeyman made his confession, senior police set up Operation Briars in May 2007. It was to be the most secret taskforce in Victoria.

Until it wasn't.

Age investigative journalist Nick McKenzie learned of the Briars investigation and approached Deputy Commissioner Simon Overland for comment.

Overland spoke to McKenzie and told him if he ran a story it would tip off the targets and destroy the infant investigation.

McKenzie agreed to sit on the story until there was a breakthrough or until Lalor and Waters became aware they were under investigation.

But the fact that the information had leaked to the media disturbed Briars investigators, senior police and the Office of Police Integrity.

At some point (the date remains unclear) the OPI Director, George Brouwer, became so concerned that confidential police information continued to leak that he ordered another secret investigation.

And what that probe was to find would expose a hidden world of backstabbing, Machiavellian empire building and questionable personal relationships that led to the very heart of police command.

In November 2007 the OPI activated its rarely used powers to hold public hearings where witnesses are compelled to give evidence and may be called to account for previous sworn testimony delivered in secret sessions.

In just six days those public hearings exposed, humiliated and discarded two trusted senior police officials and left the head of the powerful police union fighting for his career.

The fallout was long and bloody, with prolonged faction fighting, industrial unrest, protracted legal action and damaged morale.

But the main allegation on the table, and the supposed real reason for open hearings, remained unproven.

The central claim made in the opening address by Counsel assisting the inquiry, Doctor Greg Lyon, SC, was that a sinister chain that began with senior police and ended with a maverick police union boss had effectively nobbled Briars.

The hearings provided plenty of smoke and mirrors — without finding the smoking gun. The OPI believes the murder investigation was deliberately sabotaged — an act of cold-blooded betrayal that if proven would result in an unprecedented corruption scandal and certain jail time for the offenders.

The chain, as alleged within the hearings, was that police media director Stephen Linnell improperly passed information on the investigation to assistant commissioner Noel Ashby, who told Police Association secretary Paul Mullett, who passed it to association president Brian Rix. The chain had allegedly ended with the target, Detective Sergeant Peter Lalor.

Linnell and Ashby were the first casualties — both resigning after their damning telephone conversations showed how they lied to private OPI hearings, improperly discussed the hearings, played poisonous internal politics and leaked information.

The head of the police media unit, Inspector Glen Weir (previously Ashby's staff officer), was suspended after it was alleged he discussed the private OPI hearings. Weir was a bit-player who maintains he did nothing wrong but was swept away in a tidal wave of allegations and intrigue.

Meanwhile the major target — Senior Sergeant Mullett — was suspended from the police force while maintaining his innocence and holding onto his position as association secretary.

All may face criminal charges — not for derailing Briars, but for talking about the hearings, an offence that carries a maximum penalty of a year in jail. Another possible breach included the Telecommunications Interception Act, which prohibits discussing possible phone taps, an offence that carries a maximum of two years jail.

Plus Linnell and Ashby may face the additional — and much more serious — perjury charges.

To understand how the claims of a conspiracy to sabotage a murder investigation became public it is necessary to understand the agendas of three complex organisations — the Police Association, the police force and the OPI itself. Then it is necessary to examine how three separate investigations ended up concentrating on the same group of characters.

PAUL Mullett may be the most powerful union boss in Australia — although his workforce does not strike. He has the ear of senior politicians and while he can be a loyal friend, he is an unrelenting enemy.

Both sides of Parliament have duchessed him. He was sounded out to be a Liberal candidate — then former Premier, Steve

Bracks, signed a secret deal with him to try to neutralise the association as a political lobby group during the 2006 state election. When he rings politicians, senior police or top-level bureaucrats, they rarely put him on hold.

Mullett believes that Chief Commissioner Christine Nixon has improperly used her power behind the scenes to try to unseat him — an allegation she rejects. His response, as it always is when threatened, is to attack — first in public and later in the back room.

'Fish' Mullett is an old-style detective with two police valour awards who has never shied from a fight. Those who know him claim he thinks the Marquess of Queensberry rules are for the fainthearted, the weak-kneed and the sexually confused. He fights to win at all costs.

Believing Nixon was favouring an anti-Mullett Police Association faction, Mullett contributed to a covert campaign against the union's then president, Sergeant Janet Mitchell.

Mullett called on an old mate from his St Kilda days and associate delegate, Detective Sergeant Peter 'Stash' Lalor, to be his hatchet man.

Lalor became 'Kit Walker' (The comic book super hero The Phantom's 'real' name), a notorious emailer who wrote false and defamatory reports on Mitchell that were distributed on the police computer system.

So why 'Kit Walker'? Both Stash and Fish had worked in the armed robbery squad in the 1980s and one of the squad's highest profile scalps was notorious gunman and escapee Russell 'Mad Dog' Cox, arrested at Doncaster Shopping Town with the equally dangerous Raymond John Denning in 1988.

Cox had spent eleven years on the run after escaping from the infamous Katingal maximum-security division of Sydney's Long Bay Jail in 1977.

Perhaps coincidentally, while Cox was on the run he also adopted The Phantom's name of 'Mr Walker'.

The Lalor campaign so enraged the then Police Association executive member, the head of Purana, Detective Inspector Gavan Ryan, that he said: 'I've worked homicide for a long time and I've dealt with a lot of crooks, bad crooks. Most of them have more morals than the cowards that send out these malicious, defamatory emails against her.'

At the time Lalor was suspected of being just a character assassinator. Later Briars would link him to a paid assassin.

During the faction fighting, Mullett was on the verge of losing his power base. He started to look for another job, thinking his time was up. And then in May 2006 his enemy unwittingly handed him a lifeline. Nixon announced she had ordered a bullying inquiry into Mullett, saying she was obligated at law to examine the allegation.

But rather than spearing the 'Fish', it shored up his position because he astutely suggested the inquiry was an attack on the independence of the police union rather than a lawful investigation.

While his relationship with Nixon descended into hatred and vitriol he cultivated assistant commissioner Ashby — the man overlooked for the top job in 2001 and who still harboured ambitions to be chief.

Ashby was assigned to deal with Mullett over pay-rise negotiations and the two spoke nearly every day. They talked work and gossiped. Ashby passed on information that he thought could damage his main rival, Simon Overland.

But the OPI claims that Ashby did more, that he improperly discussed OPI hearings, warned Mullett his phone could be tapped and leaked information on Operation Briars, including the names of the two targets.

What is known is that after Ashby told Mullett that his phones were tapped the union boss told Brian Rix to warn Lalor. Mullett says he asked Rix, a former head of the homicide squad, to tell Lalor to 'be careful who he talked to'.

But he said his warning related to the bullying allegations and the Walker investigations, not Operation Briars.

But within five minutes of Lalor being warned, he rang Waters to say they needed to meet. The question that remains unanswered is why he needed to meet Waters urgently when the former policeman did not appear to be involved in the Kit Walker matter.

Before the tip-off, Lalor and Waters were taped chirping on their phones regularly. But, according to the OPI, their demeanour on the phone changed — as if they knew someone could be listening.

But what was also discovered was that both men had wide-ranging contacts within policing although both had questionable reputations. Waters had twice been charged (and acquitted) of serious criminal charges.

The most generous description of 'Docket' in his policing days was that he was a colourful rogue. But once he left policing he began to associate with gangland figures who were the subject of organised crime investigations.

In his annual report, OPI Director, George Brouwer, wrote: 'Sometimes, the most influential member of a (corrupt) group is a former police officer who continues to connect with, and exert influence over, current serving members who are willing to engage in corrupt conduct. Many of these former police resigned from Victoria Police while they were under investigation.'

The OPI sought and was granted warrants to tap the phones of Mullett, Ashby and Linnell. The timing and the evidence provided to justify the taps remains secret.

It was a bold and crucial move. As union secretary, Mullett

was deep in complex pay negotiations with senior police at the time his phone was monitored. If it had become public that his phone was bugged or if information on union strategy was improperly used, the negotiations would have collapsed.

Mullett says the OPI targeted him because of the Kit Walker claims. The truth is that an experienced policeman like him would have known that such a minor offence could not legally justify tapping telephones.

The OPI says its probe was into high-level leaks and that is how Mullett became involved. But if so, why was the OPI investigation given the code Diana — the name of The Phantom's long time girlfriend?

It was through the recorded conversations of Ashby and Linnell rather than Mullett that it became clear there was a serious problem. It was quickly established the media director had inappropriately given the assistant commissioner information on Briars. But there is no suggestion that either wanted to damage the investigation.

Linnell was then set up from within and fed information to see if he would leak. He did — within eleven seconds. It was the perfect trap: Doctor Lyon told the hearings it was 'flushing dye through the pipes, so to speak'.

The Briars investigation was so secret that the taskforce, made up of trusted homicide and ethical standards detectives, was sent to a separate building, away from prying eyes.

In September, Lalor was suspended but not charged. This presumably means that the taskforce was unable to find sufficient evidence to support the hit man's version of events. So while Lalor is entitled to the presumption of innocence, his career might still be over. Even if he is never charged over the murder, the Kit Walker allegations and his questionable relationship with the hit man via 'Docket' Waters are sackable offences. And those who had time for 'Stash' may look at him in a different light when they consider his alleged links with a career criminal who once shot and crippled a policeman.

On 14 September 2007, he spoke on the phone (knowing it was bugged) saying, 'Yeah, they've suspended me with pay for the time being. Overland wanted me charged . . . and I'm told — well, you don't know whether it's true or not, but it says Ron Iddles is lead — is the lead investigator in this. He and Ron had an argument over the fact that I should have been charged, and the story goes that Ron didn't think there was sufficient evidence at this stage to do that.'

The rumour that swept policing (falsely, as it would turn out) was that there had been a dispute between Simon Overland and Detective Senior Sergeant Ron Iddles over the handling of the case.

The truth was there had been discussions about charging Lalor but it was decided there was not enough evidence.

Mullett claims the investigation into him was personally and politically driven. Intriguingly, Lalor was suspended on 12 September — the same day Mullett finally signed off on the Enterprise Bargaining Agreement. Senior police say it is a coincidence.

The OPI investigations have shown that at the very least, both Mullett and Nixon had flawed judgment when it came to confidantes. Nixon appointed Linnell, subsequently exposed as secretly supporting Ashby's unofficial dirty tricks campaign as the senior policeman pushed to become the next chief commissioner. And Mullett relied on Lalor, whose deep flaws have also been exposed.

The OPI inquiry also exposed that Ashby was jealous of Overland and resented Nixon. The phone taps showed he was prepared to leak damaging material to further his own ambitions.

The fact that Nixon could not rely on all her senior officers was no surprise to her. When appointed for her second term in February 2006 she told *The Age* she was determined to outlast her enemies in the force who expected her to leave after one term. She said many had already left but 'there are a few more who won't outlast me as time goes on'.

IN the end he had no choice.

His reputation in tatters after two days of humiliating cross-examination in Office of Police Integrity hearings, Assistant Commissioner Noel Ashby, 51, saw his future hopes collapse as his past overtook him.

On 9 November 2007, he offered his resignation to his boss Christine Nixon. It was accepted without hesitation.

Having joined the force at sixteen as a cadet, Ashby had risen through the ranks and was eligible to retire with superannuation worth well over $1 million.

But had he been charged and convicted of a criminal offence, courts would have the power to review his payout.

As the assistant commissioner in charge of traffic, Ashby was one of the best-known faces in the force. A hard worker and notorious gossip, he was driven by the desire to one day be chief commissioner.

He worked his way up through the ranks in tough areas such as homicide and moved from investigator to manager as he built an impressive CV, always with an eye to the next rung on the ladder. He gained academic qualifications at Monash University, was promoted to assistant commissioner in 1998 and later awarded the prestigious Australian Police Medal.

Having been beaten for the chief commissioner's job by Ms Nixon in 2001 he was to successfully run a region as an assistant commissioner before working his way back to the inner sanctum.

A smooth networker, he courted colleagues, journalists and politicians, always with an eye to the top police job.

But he saw his colleague Simon Overland as his main rival. Overland, four years younger, a former federal policeman with a Bachelor of Arts in administration, a Bachelor of Laws with first-class honours and a Graduate Diploma in Legal Studies, was given the high-profile job of Assistant Commissioner (Crime) and oversaw the successful Purana Taskforce that investigated the gangland killings.

Selected by Nixon and then promoted to Deputy Commissioner, Overland was clearly the frontrunner to be the next chief. And Ashby was angry. He believed he had been shafted and began to run his own campaign for the top. 'Don't always put your money on frontrunners,' he once said. He schmoozed Mullett (a man with powerful political allies) and persuaded police media director Steve Linnell to act as his unofficial campaign manager.

Ashby continued to believe he could one day be chief. His taped phone calls were peppered with references to political networking. He never missed a chance to remind listeners that (unlike Overland and Nixon) he was a local and that he could deal with Mullett and the police association, whereas Overland and Mullett had fallen out. He believed the government would want a chief commissioner who knew which strings to pull to provide industrial peace.

And the phone taps showed how the canny Mullett played on Ashby's blatant personal agenda.

In one call, Mullett stokes Ashby's ambition with just a few sly words: 'Yeah mate, er, I heard though that your stocks are rising, er, in the, er, in front of the premier.'

Ashby: 'Oh, are they?'

Mullett: 'Yeah, yeah, significantly, apparently.'

The OPI hearings were to examine whether the Briars investigation had been undermined but ended by showing that Nixon had been betrayed by two of her insiders.

The tapes exposed an ugly side of the police hierarchy but it was the sort of office politics that exists in nearly all large corporations. The difference, in this case, was only that it was caught on tape and aired in public.

Both men persisted in talking on telephones even when they suspected they were bugged. Even gangland killer Carl Williams knew better than to talk on suspect mobiles — and he ended up getting 35 years jail.

What is clear is that when both men realised they were under investigation, they panicked and tried to patch together a protective quilt of half-truths and optimistic alibis. It was never going to work, and the very attempt may have left them open to criminal charges.

It is possible they are innocent of the original allegation of leaking but, like Richard Nixon facing the Watergate scandal, they could be sunk by the attempted cover-up.

Despite the fruitless search for an escape, Ashby would have known that when call after recorded call was played back to him in the hearings that he was finished.

On 15 August Linnell warned Ashby to 'be careful', implying Mullett's phone was tapped. On 25 September, Linnell warned Ashby he could be called to give evidence at a closed session of the OPI — a direct breach of secrecy provisions. Then the two talked tactics. It was a recipe for disaster — or more accurately, the formula for a poisoned pill.

STEVE Linnell was always more interested in political intrigue than cops and robbers. He was a cloak-and-dagger rather than a blood-and-guts man.

As a successful football writer with *The Age*, he slowly lost interest in the game itself as he became fascinated by powerbrokers behind the scenes.

He cultivated highly-placed sources within the AFL and those relationships were mutually beneficial. Linnell had plenty of scoops and his sources' points of view were always well represented.

After reaching the top in the sports section, he was eventually appointed general news editor. He was popular, hard-working, irreverent and always up to date with the latest office politics.

His decision to abandon daily journalism in 2003 for the highly-paid police media director's job came as a surprise. During the selection process, one senior officer was warned that Linnell was a 'wild card' who lacked the experience for the job and was liable to be manipulated.

Before he left *The Age* he was warned to be wary of cut-throat police politics because it could be career-ending and to try to temper his locker-room language because it could be used against him. He ignored the advice. Former media director Bruce Tobin offered to provide a background briefing on the job and the key players in the force. Linnell declined, preferring to wander into the minefield without a map.

He soon forged a strong relationship with Chief Commissioner Christine Nixon and became responsible for a staff of 101. He became Media and Corporate Communications Director and controlled not only dealings with the media but publications such as *Police Life* and the police website. Behind the scenes, Linnell wanted to be a kingmaker. He became increasingly distant from the working media and appeared to embrace a role as a political numbers man.

He also started to champion his 'best friend and mentor', Noel Ashby, as a future chief commissioner. Linnell and Ashby gossiped regularly, plotted privately, talked footy and bagged colleagues, sometimes light-heartedly and at other times viciously. But it was perhaps a one-sided relationship.

Ashby, consumed with ambition, saw his colleague Simon Overland as his main rival and believed Nixon was giving the former federal policeman the inside running for the top job. He used his friendship with Linnell to further his own ends.

When Nixon appointed Overland and Kieran Walshe to become the two deputy commissioners, Ashby felt snubbed and rejected. This further fed his burning jealousy and he rarely resisted a chance to privately criticise Overland as naive and inflexible.

Overland had become the public face of the Purana gangland taskforce and, while he didn't court publicity, it followed him: with each murder and, later, with each arrest, his media profile grew.

Overland worked out of the St Kilda Road crime complex, while the media director's office was in the Victoria Police Centre in Flinders Street, well away from the real action. Linnell felt snubbed and complained that he was being kept out of the loop.

Ironically, when he was brought into the loop he managed to wrap it around his own neck. When he was given explosive confidential information, it would destroy his career.

A committee to oversee the Briars taskforce was set up. It consisted of Nixon, Overland, Ethical Standards Department Assistant Commissioner Luke Cornelius and Linnell. Senior investigators were concerned that Linnell would be privy to the inner workings of the taskforce, but because of the explosive nature of the claims Nixon wanted a media strategy for the firestorm that would erupt when the allegations broke.

The targets of Briars — Lalor and former detective sergeant Waters — continued on their daily routines, apparently unaware they were the subjects of the highest priority investigation in Victoria.

And then the phones went cold. The two targets appeared to have been tipped off. On 15 August, Linnell showed Ashby the confidential terms of reference from Operation Briars. The same day, Linnell warned Ashby that Police Association Secretary Paul Mullett's phone might be bugged.

LINNELL: Did you talk to Mullett on the phone yesterday?
ASHBY: Yes.
LINNELL: Right.
ASHBY: I speak to him probably quite regularly, why?
LINNELL: Just got to be careful, that's all.
ASHBY: Why, is he being recorded?
LINNELL: Just be careful.
ASHBY: Is he being recorded?
LINNELL: Um, I can't say.
ASHBY: He might be?
LINNELL: I can't — I'm not — I can't say. Talk to you later.
ASHBY: Fuck. Can you come and see me? I did talk to him yesterday, right?
LINNELL: Um, come and ...
ASHBY: I'll ring you on a hard line.

On the same day the two talked about Overland.

LINNELL: You know, it's not as — it's certainly not as though you've had a fucking easy ride, like that c... (Deputy Commissioner Simon) Overland. That's what shits me.
ASHBY: Yeah, I ...
LINNELL: You know, all — all the shit you've had to deal with over the years ...
ASHBY: Yeah, and ...
LINNELL: and there would be fucking shit that I wouldn't even be able to dream of, and the hard f...ing yards, and that c... swans in at age fucking 45 or whatever he is ...
ASHBY: And straight to a deputy's job.

In September, Linnell was subpoenaed to appear at the OPI for secret hearings. A series of recorded phone calls show how he veered from outright panic to false bravado and was hopelessly out of his depth.

Linnell's lack of understanding of the law, the separation of powers and the secrecy provisions of the OPI can be illustrated by his ham-fisted approach to Premier John Brumby's senior adviser, Sharon McCrohan, at the Geelong-Collingwood preliminary final on 21 September.

In a recorded conversation with Ashby, Linnell said he spoke to her about his appointment with the OPI. 'And I said, "I'm going to a place soon that I can't talk to you about"'.'

He claimed McCrohan asked what it was about and he replied, 'I can't tell ya'.

He said she asked: 'You have been called up (to the OPI)?' Linnell said he replied: 'Yeah, and I'm not happy.'

On 25 September, he spoke to Ashby about the evidence he had given at a secret OPI hearing that day — a clear breach of the secrecy provisions.

If he felt his private conversation with his mentor would remain that way, he was mistaken. Just two days later, Mullett rang Ashby. It was no fishing expedition, as the police union boss clearly already knew of the OPI probe. Mullett asked: 'Did your mate attend at that location?', and Ashby did not hesitate: 'Oh, yeah, absolutely.'

On Sunday, 30 September, Ashby met Mullett in a shopping centre and handed him an application to rejoin the Police Association five years after he had quit — a clear sign he wanted the powerful union's deep pockets to assist with his looming legal liabilities.

It would appear that Ashby had begun to lower the lifeboat, but there would be room for only one on board.

Having stabbed some of his senior colleagues in the back out of misguided loyalty to his mentor and then being betrayed himself, Linnell finally fell on his sword. He resigned and admitted he had misled the OPI.

He had no choice but to admit that he had told Ashby details of Operation Briars. But there has been no suggestion that he did so to sabotage the operation or warn the targets.

According to a former colleague, Linnell 'lived the job. He took everything personally and tended to panic under pressure. It could be seven in the morning when he would start swearing about the latest drama and I would say, "Hey, are we going to be paid this week? Just calm down."'

He said the 39-year-old Linnell had aged markedly in the previous two years. 'Despite what was on those tapes, he is a good bloke. He just got sucked into the politics. What has happened to him is a real tragedy.'

For the OPI the sensational public hearings did not produce hard evidence that the chain of Linnell to Ashby to Mullett to Rix led to the Briars tip-off.

In fact they haven't proved that Lalor was tipped off at all. The alternative theory pushed by Mullett in the hearings was that Lalor went quiet because he thought he was under investigation for the Kit Walker material.

In evidence Mullett was adamant. 'I may not be an angel, your honour, but I pride myself as being a police officer who hates crooks ... For me to pass on that type of (murder) information, I'm sorry, I would never, ever do it.'

But while the OPI failed to prove its original claim, it did expose a culture where mateship and misplaced loyalty displaced sworn duty. And its use of public hearings has helped deflect the criticism that the body was a toothless tiger.

The next time a police officer is called to a secret hearing to give evidence before the OPI he or she will know that any attempt to lie is potentially career-ending and could be publicly humiliating.

Just ask Noel Ashby.

THE double execution of Terence Hodson and his wife Christine in their own home was shocking, but it was also sinister because it was more than an example of criminal brutality spiraling out of control. It had a deeper significance — it linked allegedly corrupt cops with the underworld war.

The murders caused many, including the Liberal Opposition in Victoria, to call for a royal commission into the police. The Labor Government responded with a raft of reforms, including a revamped Ombudsman's office, coercive powers for the Chief Commissioner and new asset seizure laws.

But as the crisis deepened and it was revealed that possible police involvement in the murders was being investigated, former Queensland Royal Commissioner Tony Fitzgerald was called in to inquire why confidential police documents about Hodson's role as a drug informer had been leaked to violent gangsters.

Terry Hodson was a drug dealer turned drug squad informer who provided information on friends and competitors to a detective at the drug squad.

Hodson was charged in December 2003, with two detectives from the major drug investigation division, over an alleged conspiracy to steal drugs worth $1.3 million from a house in East Oakleigh in September.

On the surface, the attempt by Hodson and Senior Detective Dave Miechel, 33, to complete the massive drug rip-off was spectacularly inept.

The house had been under surveillance for months when the two arrived to burgle the property. Both knew there was about to be a police raid and the drugs inside would soon become a court exhibit before being destroyed. They reasoned that if they moved now — just before the raid — the crooks would never squeal and the raiding party would never know.

But greed had smothered common sense. The video camera caught them smashing the overhead light on the porch so they could break into the house in darkness.

A neighbour heard the noise and called police. It was astonishingly bad luck for the crooked detective and his informer that two police dog units were in the area.

Miechel tried to bluff, telling one dog operator he was 'in the job'. He then threw a punch — another bad move.

The dog didn't like his handler being manhandled and attacked, taking a massive chunk out of Miechel's thigh. For good measure the dog handler hit him an equally massive blow with his metal torch. Miechel, as the saying goes, lost interest.

Earlier he had sprayed himself with dog repellent because he had been told there were guard dogs on the property. It is not known if he received a refund.

Hodson was found nearby hiding in the dark. Both men were empty handed but a search found $1.3 million in cash and drugs that had been thrown over the back fence.

They were both charged, along with Miechel's immediate boss, Detective Sergeant Paul Dale.

Police later raided the house as part of the biggest ecstasy bust in Victoria's history.

In 2006 Justice Betty King sentenced Senior Detective Miechel to fifteen years with a non-parole term of twelve, saying 'You have sworn an oath to uphold the law and the community has acted upon that oath you swore and placed its trust in you. You have abused that trust.'

Hodson had been a drug squad informer since August 2001,

but after his arrest in 2003 he agreed to inform for the police anti-corruption taskforce, codenamed Ceja.

Christine Hodson had no convictions and had not been charged with any offences. She was an innocent victim of Melbourne's underworld war.

Her tragedy was that many in the criminal world knew her husband was an informer. Their suspicions were confirmed when the leaked police documents began to circulate in the Melbourne underworld in early May 2004.

A month earlier, lawyers for Hodson indicated in the Supreme Court that he would plead guilty. It became obvious he was prepared to give evidence against the two police charged with him. Police sources say he had originally agreed to be an informer to try to protect family members also facing drug charges.

He acted as the inside man for police on at least six drug squad operations — specialising in helping police expose cocaine and ecstasy networks.

Charismatic and likeable, Hodson knew most major crime figures in Melbourne. A carpenter by trade, he had built secret cupboards and storage areas for some of Melbourne's biggest drug dealers, according to police.

According to an old friend, the Hodsons arrived in Perth in 1974 from Britain. They had married in July 1967, in the city of Wolverhampton. Hodson used his carpentry skills to land a job as a maintenance officer looking after rental properties. He was said to have had a deal with an insurance assessor to rip off the company by submitting over-inflated bills for damaged kitchens.

He began his own building business and was successful enough to buy a luxury home.

The friend said the couple became obsessed with possessions. 'She (Christine) would vacuum three times a day.'

Hodson was a bookmaker's son but he had struggled at school and was barely literate. When he made money in Perth, he hired a private tutor to help him with reading and writing. He didn't need any help with arithmetic, especially counting money.

He built a small business empire in Perth and became involved in a partnership dealing with prestige cars. The story goes that he believed his partner was ripping him off so he hired some oxy-acetylene blowtorch gear and found a safebreaker to get into his partner's safe. But a neighbour came by to feed the cat and the safebreaker left suddenly, leaving the gear behind.

Police were able to trace the fact that Hodson had hired the gear and he was convicted, only to later escape amidst unproven claims he paid someone to turn a blind eye.

He later moved to Melbourne. The old friend recalls: 'I lost track of him until I got a call from his wife asking for $50,000 for bail. I said no.'

Hodson loved the idea of being a gangster, he says. 'He wanted to be a flamboyant type; I guess he didn't make it. Every time there was a murder of a crook in Melbourne I thought it would be Terry. In the end it was.'

The Hodsons' bodies were found by their son in the lounge room of their home in East Kew on Sunday 16 May 2004.

Hodson almost certainly knew the gunman. Like most drug dealers he was security conscious and no-one entered his home without an invitation.

He also had two large and loud german shepherd dogs to deter intruders.

One theory is that Hodson knew the killer, let him in to the heavily fortified house, and was ambushed in the lounge room; his wife was then killed because she could identify the gunman, probably a business associate or 'friend' of her husband.

It is believed Hodson was smoking a roll-your-own cigarette when his guest produced a handgun and ordered the couple to kneel on the floor, where their hands were bound behind their backs before they were shot in the back of the head.

The couple was killed some time after Saturday evening. Their guard dogs were locked in the garage, either by the killer or by the couple when they welcomed their guest.

One neighbour said: 'I didn't hear the german shepherds, so I wondered what had happened. I heard what sounded like a shot about 6.15pm, but didn't pay any attention.'

Hodson had been offered protection but had declined it. Being in protection would have meant he couldn't keep seeing his grandchildren. Although he knew his life was in danger, he had decided to carry on as normal.

Ethical standards police had installed a state of the art security system and the Hodsons used it diligently. They had seven tapes each labelled with a day of the week and each day the correct tape was inserted. When investigators checked, only one tape was missing. The one labelled Saturday — the day of the murder.

If a covert camera had also been installed perhaps the killer could have been identified but such a security precaution was considered too expensive.

Investigators wanted to know why the police information report, written in May 2002, had mysteriously begun to circulate two years later.

It contained many allegations. Amongst them was the claim Hodson had been offered $50,000 by Lewis Moran to kill Carl Williams.

By the time the information became public Moran was already dead, but it could be interpreted as placing Hodson on one side of the fence in the underworld war.

On 14 May 2004, a story in the *Herald Sun* repeated some of the information from the leaked report, including the contract offer.

The following day Hodson and his wife were murdered. Some might draw conclusions about cause and effect.

Was it death by newspaper? The leaking of the confidential police document was a massive breach of security — but homicide squad detectives had to investigate not only *whether* the leak caused the murders but if that was the intention behind the leak.

Certain members of the underworld had seen the police report before the newspaper story was published. George Williams confirmed he had seen the document in the previous few weeks.

In fact, many members of the underworld didn't need to see Hodson's name as a police informer on an official document. They had suspected it for years.

Lewis Moran believed Hodson was an informer but found him entertaining company. He just made sure Terry was not close by when business was discussed.

Both Miechel and Dale were interviewed by homicide squad detectives and provided alibis.

But with Hodson dead, charges against Dale were dropped because of lack of evidence. Dale has always denied any connection with either the drug rip-off or the double murder. He resigned and took over a country service station, moving from pumping people for information to pumping petrol. And from giving suspects the hamburger with the lot to providing the same service for hungry truck-drivers.

For investigators, the Hodson double murder became even more important because of the suggestion of bent police involvement.

So much so that it was the one case with the potential to get multiple killer Carl Williams a decent discount on his sentence providing he talked about what he knew — and then was prepared to give evidence.

In the months before Williams agreed to plead guilty he suggested he had such information. In fact, he told police he had a man inside the drug squad who provided him with secret information. Perhaps that is why, when Williams was arrested for drug trafficking, the investigators were suburban detectives and not from the specialist drug squad.

Williams also suggested a policeman had told him Hodson had to go and that Carl should think about possible options. Williams, it is alleged, later came back to say he would deal with it but the policeman said the matter was in hand. A short time later the Hodsons were murdered.

But the value of Williams' statement was destroyed when he chose to give self-serving evidence at his plea hearing. He deliberately destroyed his credibility as a potential witness in any future trials, earning a further two years for his efforts.

But while the court dismissed Williams, somebody must have been listening. Certainly, shortly after Carl made his statement, police launched a fresh taskforce, code named Petra, to investigate the Hodson double murder.

Deputy Commissioner Simon Overland said 'This is a priority investigation. And we are making progress.'

So who pulled the trigger that night in Kew?

Many of Melboune's hit men developed huge profiles during the underworld war. But there is one with links to the Mokbel-Williams camp who refused to move from the shadows.

Ruthless and deadly, the man known as The Duke has been mentioned as the possible hit man for the murder of Brian Kane, who was gunned down in the Quarry Hotel in Brunswick in November 1982. He has previously been charged with murder but acquitted.

He was also investigated over his alleged connection to the killing of Mike 'Lucky' Schievella, 44, and his partner, Heather McDonald, 36, at their St Andrews home in 1990. The couple, connected to the drug world, were forced to kneel, then bound and gagged before they were slaughtered in their own home. Just like the Hodsons.

It is not the first time a selective leak might have contributed to murder after finding its way into print.

Observers with long memories recall that Isabel and Douglas Wilson were drug couriers for the notorious Mr Asia heroin syndicate in the 1970s. When the pair decided to talk to police about drug running that fact soon appeared in the *Brisbane Sun* newspaper.

The Wilsons' bodies were later found in Rye, Victoria, on 18 May 1979. They had been shot on the orders of the syndicate boss, Terry Clark, because they had been talking.

The Wilsons, too, were dog lovers: their pet was found wandering in the suburbs because the hit man wouldn't kill it. But, as with the Hodsons, it didn't save them.

22

BODY BLOW

Police say that while Williams
was planning to kill him,
Mario was trying to set up his
triple hit counter attack.

THE big man strolling through the city's legal precinct didn't look like someone on the underworld equivalent of death row. He had no idea that within days he would become yet another victim of Melbourne's vicious gangland war.

Mario Condello was deep in conversation with a member of his legal team when he stopped mid-stride and beckoned. He wanted a chat.

It began badly. Then went downhill.

'I'm not fucking happy with you,' he opened. He was not in the mood for idle chit-chat.

The author, unused to such robust language in a public street, asked the reason for his apparent concern.

It was his picture that had appeared in the most excellent crime book *Leadbelly — Inside Australia's Underworld Wars* (available at all good book stores).

The caption read, 'Mario Condello ... a man of means by no means.'

'What's that supposed to mean?' he demanded. It was a rhetorical question.

For a nano-second, the author considered responding that it was a clever play on words to illustrate that Condello was a disbarred lawyer living a million-dollar lifestyle without actually working.

But he wisely decided to remain silent on the grounds of self-preservation.

Condello, dressed casually but expensively, was also offended by the word 'shady' appearing in a caption under another of his photos in the seminal work *Underbelly 8*.

The author quietly suggested that it was a fair comment given Condello's record, which includes convictions for arson, fraud and drug matters.

Years earlier, Condello was the target of a police taskforce code-named Zulu that investigated his alleged criminal links to drug trafficking, arson, fraud and attempted murder.

The author suggested that since Mario had been sentenced to 13 years' jail, the term shady was fair and apt, perhaps even understated.

Condello, always the argumentative (if disbarred) lawyer, instantly responded that he had served only six years and furthermore, 'It should have been two ... we all make mistakes'.

During the chat in Lonsdale Street, just days before he was due in court to face an incitement to murder charge, Condello was in vintage form. He moved from threatening to entertaining and, finally, charming.

He wanted his name kept out of the papers as he didn't need the publicity or the notoriety. Headlines were bad for business, he said. He did not expand on what that business might be. When it was pointed out to him that his arrest for attempting to incite the murder of a rival underworld figure, Carl Williams, his father, George, and a Williams' team member, was of more than passing interest, he graciously acknowledged that such headlines were inevitable. He said of the so-called rival, Carl Williams: 'I hardly knew him. I met him once at Crown (casino). That was it.' Certainly, Mario had been a frequent and welcomed guest at Crown where he had unfettered access to the high-rollers' Mahogany Room and was said to turn over more than $7 million a year.

No wonder they gave him free finger food.

Money may open doors, but bad reputations can close them. Both Condello and Williams were later deemed undesirables and banned from the casino by order of Chief Commissioner Christine Nixon.

Condello's trial before a Supreme Court jury was due to begin in early February 2006. The court was to hear allegations that he offered a contract of $500,000 for the triple hit and would organise a fake passport to get the killer out of the country.

The case was simple, relying on a police informer and secret tapes that appear to indicate Condello would pay for the murders.

The prosecution claimed Condello had purchased an arsenal of weapons from South Australian porn king, Bill Nash.

A police informer said Nash provided 15 weapons including an Uzi 9mm sub-machinegun, a Colt .357 Magnum, a Bentley 12 gauge pump-action shotgun plus handguns and ammunition. The first shipment arrived in March 2003.

Police used a wire on the informer and claim they taped Condello saying he wanted the hit man to gun down Williams in Lonsdale Street with the Uzi from a passing motorcycle.

'You'll have the fuckin' money to cover you, 150 a fuckin' head. Do ya understand? We don't want to go around hurting innocent fuckin' people ... but some of these blokes from the western districts or western suburbs ... they just want to take action ...

'Until they're fuckin' gone, mate, there's always going to be trouble.'

The conversations and the alleged plot occurred in March 2004 — when the cool-headed Gatto was in prison waiting for his trial over the Veniamin trial, leaving Condello in charge.

Condello and his lawyers remained confident they could defend the charges. But they didn't get the chance.

To those who wanted Condello dead, time was running out. If he were found guilty, he would have been jailed and put in maximum security, where he would have been untouchable. If he won, he would be able to move where he wanted, when he wanted, free of the bail restrictions that threatened to turn the sitting duck into the dead variety.

Condello said the underworld war was a media myth as it was not two sides fighting, but one side determined to kill its perceived enemies. He said Williams was 'out of control' and wanted to destroy the established network known as the 'Carlton Crew.'

'They were out to kill anyone connected with Mick (Gatto).'

It was a reasonable assessment. Two of Gatto's closest mates had been shot dead — Graham 'The Munster' Kinniburgh on 13 December 2003, and Lewis Moran on 31 March the following year.

'It would have been Ronnie (Gatto's friend Ron Bongetti who died in 2005 of natural causes), Steve (Kaya, who gave evidence for Gatto) or me.'

Gatto and Condello had been close and loyal friends for years. In a letter written by Mick Gatto while in jail on remand and offered for sale to the media by a mystery broker, Mick appears to ask Condello to assume control while he is out of action.

'I tell you what Mario, it's [jail] changed a lot since the days of old. I have to be honest; they treat you with the greatest of respect. I feel a bit like Hannibal Lector.

'I am good as gold Mario, I can't believe what has happened to me the last couple of days, but so be it.

'I can't believe for a bloke that prides himself on not getting involved in all the bullshit, I can't believe how trouble finds me. I can't believe that little maggot tried to kill me, anyway he is in his place.

'Mario give the old bloke my regards and all our team — tell them I am going all right and I will be in touch in the near future.

'Keep your eyes wide opened; you can't trust any of these rats. I would hate to see anything happen to any of ours.'

When Gatto was acquitted, he took his usual place at the head of the table but the table had moved.

Once a fixture in Lygon Street, they had been forced over the past few years to move their social base to the upmarket Society Cafe in Bourke Street to avoid well-wishers and crime groupies. There was the added bonus that the Parliament end of the city has plenty of security cameras, making life harder for would-be assassins.

Gatto and his friends could be found playing cards and chatting upstairs at Society most days. Condello had an early dinner at the restaurant on Monday, 6 February, eating simply and tipping big. He left shortly after 7pm. His bail curfew meant he had to be home by 10pm and he pulled into the driveway of his North Brighton home with minutes to spare. Punctuality and premeditation go hand in hand. His killer was waiting, and despite the electronic security, he was shot dead in his garage just before 10pm.

Gatto, one of the first to hear, was devastated by the loss of his friend.

Within hours he said: 'I know nothing about it. I don't believe it is gangland connected ... no way. I believe whatever the reason, it will come out in the wash.'

He said he would not speculate as his friend 'was a very private person. He wouldn't want me to talk about it'.

Gatto, a former heavyweight boxer, later threw eggs at the media flock gathered outside his home, quickly establishing he was not prepared to be interviewed and that he had not lost power in his right arm.

During his chat with the author just days before he was shot, Condello admitted he had carried a gun during the underworld war but said it was for self-defence as there had been three plots to kill him.

During the height of the gangland killings, Condello said he moved from his North Brighton home, not to hide from his potential killers, but to draw them away from his family.

'Why should they be dragged into this?'

For that moment, Condello dropped his tough-guy façade and became just another concerned and proud father. His daughter, he explained, was heading to America for post-graduate medical studies at a world-renowned hospital and his sons were working hard in a well-known Melbourne private school.

While Gatto was in jail, Williams decided to kill Condello as a payback for the death of Veniamin. Running out of hit men, his first plan came a cropper when Lewis Caine confided to the wrong people he was going to kill Mario. His friends flipped him and Caine was swiftly disabled.

The word is that Mario paid for the double cross, outbidding Williams' kill fee.

But Williams would not give up, even though the talent pool of potential hit men was starting to dry up. He employed a new group who lacked the cunning and the caution to last long.

On 9 June 2004, the Special Operations Group arrested two armed men outside the Brighton Cemetery where they were waiting to ambush Condello. Four men — including Carl Williams — were arrested. It was a major turning point and the first time Purana was clearly ahead of the game.

Williams would not be granted bail and most of his loyal soldiers eventually made statements against him.

Days after the hit was foiled, Condello told Channel Nine: 'For the first time, I've heard the birds singing in the trees. So let's hope these birds continue to sing and everything becomes more peaceful than it has over the last ... however many years ... because, after all, we are not going to be here forever.' (He was right about that).

But Peaceful Mario didn't last long: 'I hope it doesn't continue to others or to myself for that matter because, as I said, I am prepared to forgive once and that's as far as it goes. No more.'

Police say that while Williams was planning to kill him, Mario was trying to set up his triple hit counter attack.

On 13 June 2004 Condello was arrested for conspiracy to murder.

But on the eve of his hearing he said he was relaxed and looking forward to his trial, where he intended to finally clear his name.

He also said he believed his life was no longer in danger.

When he was released on his fourth bail attempt in March 2005, he looked up at the magistrate and promised, 'I can assure you of one thing: I won't let you down.' Deputy Chief Magistrate Jelena Popovic, no stranger to controversy, didn't need to be told that some hardliners would see her ruling as unnecessarily lenient.

'I've gone out on a significant limb here. This will not be a popular decision,' she told the man she was setting free. Then she gave what was intended to be a friendly warning but which turned out to be tragically accurate: 'You will be very closely watched.' Popovic had no idea how right she would be.

For Condello, his release ended nearly nine months in solitary confinement on charges of conspiracy to murder. It would also effectively end his life.

Condello had survived two decades in the underworld, a long jail stint and various plots against his life by developing a highly-tuned sense of survival.

But when he was bailed on a surety of $700,000 and ordered to obey a 10pm to 7am curfew, he showed no signs of knowing that the clock was already ticking. Condello was shot repeatedly in his garage as he stepped from his car on 6 February. It was 9.50pm, just 10 minutes before his court-ordered curfew deadline to be home. Apparently the hit man was able to slip in as the door opened, shoot his victim and slip out before the door closed. He was no amateur.

Those close to Condello say the nine months he spent in jail in virtual solitary confinement scarred him deeply. During his bail hearing, the court heard that since his arrest, the one-time tough guy had suffered depression, high blood pressure and bad migraines. A prison psychologist went so far as to say he had become 'stir crazy'.

His time on remand appeared to change Condello. He emerged stooped and not as big as he once was. His family said he had rediscovered religion and had re-assessed his life.

But a few days before his murder, he appeared to be the old Mario — upbeat, combative and confident. He said the charges against him had already been downgraded. The conspiracy-to-murder charge had been dropped, he had pleaded guilty to possessing a firearm (during a time in Melbourne where for people in his line of work it was almost a crime of stupidity not to carry a gun) and he was convinced that he would be acquitted of the incitement charge.

'I have not asked for the charges to be dropped. I want them dealt with in open court.'

The former lawyer said that after he was exonerated in court, he would call for a judicial inquiry into the use of informers rewarded for giving prosecution evidence.

The conversation with the author was terminated with handshakes, compliments and expressions of mutual respect. Condello was pushed for time as he wished to talk further with his lawyers.

He agreed to conduct a full and frank interview two days later. But when contacted as agreed, he said his lawyers had persuaded him that this was not a good idea, but that as soon as his trial was over he would sit down for a long chat.

Through circumstances beyond his control, he was not able to make it.

Carl Williams had wanted Condello dead and was prepared to pay up to $140,000 for the contract. But when Mario was murdered, Williams was yesterday's man — without the pull, money or connections to organise another hit.

But he was not the only man in town who liked to pay cash for killings. On 14 March 2007, Purana detectives failed in a court bid to take Tony Mokbel's brother, Mlad, from jail to interview him over Condello's murder.

They claimed he told a friend he should 'make himself scarce,' because Condello was about to be shot. Forty-five minutes later Mario was gunned down.

Lucky guess?

MARIO Condello should have known better. His partner in crime — one tough enough to give evidence against him later, and survive — was busy cutting premium Lebanese hashish into something less pure and more profitable at an empty Carlton factory when Condello arrived with a stranger.

This was no ordinary stranger. He was a federal politician, his face known even to a dope-running, gun-toting knuckleman, schooled on the street and more wary than Condello, then a young bent lawyer.

'Mario lifted the roller door and there was the senator sitting in the car! I said, "What the fuck did you bring him for?"' The answer — Condello was showing off. A consummate middle man, he wanted to introduce the tough guy to the politician, aiming to impress both and make himself look good. It wasn't such a smart move.

The tough guy was furious that Condello would risk exposing their racket to someone who could attract so much trouble. He soon found out why Condello was so cocky. The politician, then comparatively young, was 'a smoker'. Condello supplied him with the best 'buddha sticks' — potent 'heads' picked from the middle of every 'brick' of 100 sticks they smuggled through the docks then steamed apart to sell.

That was Condello. Vain and manipulative, he had a knack for finding the politician, policeman or parking officer, perhaps even university lecturer, who could be charmed — and compromised. Around him was the hint of blackmail and violence, the implied threat to health or reputation. In the early years, says the associate, he was also 'a dickhead who made illogical decisions under pressure.'

The politician is a long way from Carlton now, but he must have felt a guilty pang of relief when news filtered through to him that his old university dope contact had done his last deal. While Condello was alive, there was always the chance he would try to call in favours if he was desperate enough. In fact, anyone who knew Condello would imagine he might have already tried, at some point.

Times changed but Mario Condello was trapped in the gangster life he'd deliberately chosen ahead of a legitimate profession, even if he did have rosary beads in his pocket when the end came. Right up until a gunman shot him dead in early 2006, he battled the dangerous delusion that he was the smartest guy in the room. He was a fan of drama — from Shakespeare to *The Sopranos* — but until it was too late he seemed to miss the point: that a fatal character flaw is exactly that. It can kill you.

Condello could plead neither ignorance nor circumstances. He was blessed with qualities that should have made his family the classic migrant success story. He was intelligent, good-looking, charming and well-educated — in fact, he had exploited every opportunity that his parents and many others wanted for their children when they came to Australia.

His father, Guerino, a painter and decorator from a Calabrian hill town called Anoia, was captured in Libya early in World War 2 and sent to a farm near Warrnambool to work. Like many prisoners of war, he flourished in Australia, and after the war he went home, married and returned.

Mario was born in April 1952 and his sister Frances soon after. Their mother Marina then took the children to Italy, where Enzo was born. By the time they returned five years later to live in the family house in North Fitzroy, the children spoke fluent Italian. (Mario would keep up the Calabrian connection all his life, as police would discover in the 1980s, when he tried to pull off a huge international fraud by having over-insured art prints torched in a Naples bond store.) The brothers went to the local state school and then Fitzroy High. A retired teacher recalls them as handsome children, above average in all ways.

Mario got into law at the University of Melbourne. The class of 1971 included at least one future judge and several who became prominent barristers. There is no reason why young Condello could not have become a legitimate figure in law, business or politics. No reason, that is, except the dark angels of his nature.

Some are condemned from birth to a cycle of deprivation, abuse and crime, but he wasn't. His crooked life and its violent end came because he chose to lie, cheat, steal and intimidate to make fast money. He organised marijuana crops, laundered drug money for less-sophisticated criminals, dealt heroin and would order violence — by thugs he considered as expendable as his victims — against anyone who got in his way. He preyed on vulnerable old Italians who trusted him, secretly mortgaging their homes to fund his loan shark racket, drug buys and an increasingly opulent lifestyle.

Even if — and there is no proof of this — Condello's father had unavoidable hometown links with the 'Honoured Society' that transplanted Italian organised crime into Australia, there was no reason why the Australian-raised son could not leave old hill-bandit ways behind, the way many did. He could have stayed clean and ended up in Mahogany Row; instead he wanted to cut a dash and splash cash in the Mahogany Room.

His brother Enzo became a writer, artist and teacher. Enzo's play *Shakespeare and the Dark Lady of the Sonnets* was staged in Melbourne the year before Mario's murder and was on the VCE drama list. Enzo Condello told a reporter then that Mario 'loves drama', especially *Julius Caesar*, *Macbeth* and Dante. It showed. A fellow law student, now a Queen's Counsel, recalls the young Condello as a charismatic figure who always wore a long coat, drank expensive wine and schmoozed relentlessly.

'If Mario visited your house, he would bring your mother flowers,' he recalls. 'But even at uni, he had acolytes — people who followed him around. Later on, the Calabrian attitude obviously sunk deeply into his psyche. When he went to jail (a decade later) I realised Mario lived another life I didn't understand. But I said a prayer for him today.' When the budding QC went to Condello's 21st birthday party at the family Fitzroy home, he was struck by the time and culture warp.

'It was like a scene from *The Godfather*,' he says. Another QC who knew Condello said he delighted in quoting sinister lines from the mafia film, like 'Leave the gun — bring the cannoli' and

'Pauly — you won't see him no more'. He would sweep into rooms in his camel hair coat, acting the mafia don.

For someone who couldn't fight or shoot and didn't like blood, especially his own, he had some bad habits. 'Mario had a lot of front if he met you, but he was windy (frightened),' says a policeman who investigated him in 1982. Big but not tough, he compensated by being ruthless and often reckless, hiring 'heavies' prone to gratuitous violence. His criminality was exposed when police linked him to a marijuana crop on a farm near Ararat. A secret taskforce, Operation Zulu, uncovered a web of arsons, bashings, frauds, standover and loansharking, for which he served six years jail.

At his funeral, Condello's daughter Vanessa said her 'scary' father had prayed for forgiveness for actions that had hurt their family. Perhaps he should have prayed for other families who had suffered to keep his own in ostentatious luxury.

Such as the family of Richard Noel Jones. Jones, 36 and a father of three, was asleep with his wife in their Box Hill house in 1982 when two gunmen burst into their bedroom and shot him in the stomach with a shotgun. He would have died then, but was saved because feathers from their doona plugged the huge wound and slowed the bleeding. His wife was so traumatised she developed rheumatoid arthritis and could hardly walk. It destroyed their lives.

Jones' 'crime'? He had legally registered a lapsed business name, annoying the business owner, who ran a printing supplies firm. Instead of negotiating, the businessman called Condello, the wannabe standover man, who stupidly sent the armed thugs, who stupidly shot the man instead of getting the desired result by frightening him. A literature-loving, rosary-carrying lawyer should have known better. Condello beat the rap for the shooting, but wasn't so lucky on several other charges. In court, he hissed 'you're dead!' in Italian to an Italian detective.

In prison, he met more violent crooks. After one was released, detectives raided his house and found a high-powered rifle, documents with the surnames of two detectives who had investigated Condello, and a coded hit list. The policemen's families were put into protection.

Since Condello's death, more secrets have been revealed. One is about a current judge who, as a prosecutor in the 1980s, needed police protection after Condello's 'soldiers' visited his house at night to intimidate him. And then there was the old businessman, a returned soldier, who in the mid-1990s borrowed $600,000 from Condello to shore up his failing business.

He repaid most of the loan and put his Bulleen house on the market to meet the demand for $200,000 interest, on threat of death. But he was so terrified that he committed suicide with a samurai sword.

When news of Condello's shooting broke, a retired detective's wife, who had spent almost a year living in fear of Condello's threats against her family, said: 'It's about time.'

AS is usually the case, the murder victim was remembered as a kind family man with a generous spirit and a passion for life. There were 600 at the church to say goodbye to Condello. Many were sincere mourners and devastated family members, but some there were drawn to what has become a peculiarly Melbourne event — a gangland funeral. Others were there to show solidarity, not with the dead but with the living — fellow Carlton Crew member, Mick Gatto, who delivered the eulogy.

The message to enemies real and imagined was that if you pick off those close to Mick in the hope he would be left exposed, then think again. There will always be others prepared to step up.

In front of the mourners in the packed church, Gatto spoke with eloquent compassion and composure. It was no surprise.

With the number of associates and allies he had lost violently in recent gangland violence, he has had plenty of practice.

'To know this noble gentleman was to love him. I say goodbye to Mario Condello, a man among men who I'll miss more than words can say.'

But on the other side of the country, there is a man with a new name and a new life who has different memories of the slain underworld figure.

It was in the early 1980s and Condello's right-hand man already suspected he was being set up when he decided to check the case that he was about to deliver in exchange for 200 kilograms of top-grade cannabis.

The case was supposed to contain $150,000. The men who were to make the deal were from a serious Italian crime family in South Australia — they were known to turn nasty if they were ripped off. But when 'Reggie' checked, he found that more than half was counterfeit and some of the notes were so bad 'they glowed in the dark'.

'I would have ended up with my brains all over the ceiling,' he recalled, just days after Condello was killed.

Instead, Reggie called Condello to a house in Fawkner and several times gave the practising lawyer the chance to pull out of the set-up. 'All he kept asking was when was the deal going down.

'I gave him three chances. That was enough.' Although Reggie was smaller, he was tougher, and he beat Condello so badly the young gangster ended up in hospital. It was the end of their business dealings.

Condello was then a young lawyer with an office in Carlton. But he was open to all offers, including trafficking drugs, organising frauds, franchising arsons and laundering money. 'He was just a very greedy man,' Reggie says.

Condello retaliated over the beating by bringing in a gang of five heavies and offering a bounty to find Reggie. Before they got to Reggie, the heavies found his brother. They tortured him so badly that more than 20 years later he has still not recovered.

One of the men present recalls that each gang member was wearing balaclavas during the operation. Then Condello arrived wearing a leather face mask favoured by bad-boy wrestlers and S&M aficionados. 'He got it at a sex shop for sure. He was wearing gloves with the fingers cut out. It was all we could do not to burst out laughing.'

According to the insider, Condello stalked around the room, punching one fist into the opposite palm and urging his team on, but leaving the actual brutality to the experts.

When the men had finished, Condello kept suggesting the victim should be taken to a friend's place, 'up north'. He was referring to a pet food factory where criminals had previously disposed of victims through the industrial meat mincer.

The rule was the gang could slip in at night as long as they were gone before 6am, when the first of the morning shift arrived to feed more than 600 kangaroo carcasses into the mincer.

But that night the gang had no intention of killing the man. They were just after information, and once they had it, they dropped him at hospital, where he was admitted and treated.

Eventually they found their target, Reggie, in a Flemington motel and abducted, then beat and shot him. But he survived. That was the gang's first mistake. Then Reggie escaped. That was the second.

Reggie never forgave Condello for ordering his brother's torture. Eventually he became a police witness and the star of Operation Zulu, the police taskforce that ended Condello's legal career in 1982 and resulted in him being jailed for six years.

According to the head of Zulu, Tom McGrath, Reggie turned on Condello after the beating. 'He stood up under the pressure and gave evidence that was pivotal in several trials involving Condello and his associates.'

For the police, Reggie would prove to be the perfect insider. Through the late 1970s and early 1980s, he and Condello had been ideal business partners: Reggie had the marijuana contacts and Condello the money. 'He wanted me to do other things but I told him I would run the green. All I asked was that if he knew the roof was about to fall in to tell me first.'

Condello bought a farm in Ararat on a $30,000 deposit to run a marijuana plantation. 'He bought 4500 sheep as well. He wanted goats too.'

It sounded like a good idea, but the livestock ate half the cannabis crop. It was typical Condello, pushing for the extra dollar that can destroy the best-laid plans.

Reggie acknowledges, though, that he did other jobs for Condello, including torching seven businesses as part of an insurance scam syndicate.

But there were things he says he would not do. 'He wanted me to do jobs for him, but he had no brains. He came to me with 10 kilos of pink rocks (heroin) and said if I cut it and got rid of it, I could have half. I told him I wasn't interested and he couldn't believe it because he said I'd be a millionaire overnight. I told him I didn't do powders.'

Another time, Reggie says: 'He told me to go to New South Wales on a job and shoot a bloke in both kneecaps. It was over handing over a business. The bloke was a judge! I told Mario to get fucked.

'He wanted people bashed with pick handles over debts. I told him to talk to people if you wanted the money back.'

He says Condello gave him two shotguns. 'I took him up the country to teach him how to shoot. He didn't have the stock up against his shoulder so when he fired he ended up with a cut finger.'

But for a man with a ruthless streak, says Reggie, Condello preferred to be in the background when it came to violence. The big man with the impressive IQ and the mean streak was right to study law rather than medicine. 'The funny thing was that he couldn't stand the sight of blood. He would faint.'

Condello was ambitious to make it, both in the legitimate and criminal worlds, he says. 'He had a plan to be a solicitor, a barrister and then a judge. He wanted to be a judge and he would have made it too. He had contacts all the way to federal parliament.'

His former close friend says Condello was always looking for powerful friends. 'I knew that when he went to jail he would end up connected.'

Reggie says Condello could be charming and kind, but he was selfish and violent underneath.

'There were two Marios. There was the good Mario, but the bad one would win out every time.'

23

GOING THE DISTANCE

He knows his name has been
whispered in relation to
unsolved murders and that he
remains a person of interest
to Purana.

MICK Gatto is personable, friendly and charismatic. He is a master networker who is as comfortable talking to battlers at the boxing as to property developers at a multi-million-dollar building site. As he told a Supreme Court jury in 2005, when he was tried (and acquitted) for the killing of hit man Andrew Veniamin: 'I like to know as many people as I can.'

But while he has no shortage of acquaintances, his circle of close friends is shrinking. Eight months after beating the Veniamin murder charge, he buried one of the closest of all, Mario Condello, his trusted friend and fellow member of the so-called Carlton Crew, gunned down in yet another Melbourne underworld execution.

Condello himself was convinced that previous attempts on his life related to his close links to Gatto. He says Williams' Crew was determined to destroy Gatto's inner circle. In the late 1970s and early 1980s, the former heavyweight boxer, who was then building a reputation in Melbourne's illegal gambling world, came into contact with some shady and sinister people — some of whom became friends for decades.

But many didn't get the chance to grow old gracefully. At last count, Gatto has known at least sixteen men who have died violently on Melbourne streets.

Back in 1982, he placed a small death notice to mark the passing of standover man, Brian Kane, who was gunned down in a Brunswick pub in an underworld war that now looks like a skirmish compared with the events of recent years.

A four-line death notice in *The Sun* newspaper on 29 November that year said: 'Farewell to a good friend. You will always be remembered. Mick Gatto and family.' It was one of the first public signs that he enjoyed the company of colourful friends who would die just as colourfully.

There were others. Those who were loosely connected received a Gatto death notice with the message, 'Sorry to see you go this way'. Others were remembered with messages such as, 'You knew it was coming, you just didn't care.' But as the murder list grew, the victims became men much closer to Gatto — including mentors and lifetime mates. There was Graham 'The Munster' Kinniburgh, who was shot dead on 13 December 2003, and then Lewis Moran on 31 March 2004.

Kinniburgh was Gatto's friend and confidant. The former boxer referred to the former safe-breaker as 'Pa', and was a pallbearer at the funeral. The death hit him hard. In the now-compulsory *Herald Sun* death notice, he wrote: 'I love you Pa and I will never ever forget you.'

Lewis Moran was a friend but not in the same league. The last line in Gatto's death notice was, '(Say) a big hello to Pa.'

In April 2005, he lost another long-time friend, Ron Bongetti, who broke the pattern by dying of natural causes. Bongetti had been having a late lunch at La Porcella Restaurant on 23 March

2004, when Gatto shot Veniamin dead in a back room, in what a jury later found was self-defence. Bongetti was unable to help police with their inquiries.

Even when Bongetti was seriously ill, his tough-guy image meant everything. When it was suggested that he might have moved house because he feared he was on an underworld hit list, he approached one of the authors to dispute the claim. 'If anyone wants to find me, they know where I am. I'm not scared of anyone,' he said.

But while those around Gatto have fallen, he remains, at least outwardly, unworried.

The industrial troubleshooter, it would seem, is not a troubled shooter. With Williams finally in jail, Chief Commissioner Christine Nixon went as far as to say the underworld war was over. In a piece of unfortunate timing, Mario Condello was shot the very day she made her declaration.

After the hit on Condello, Assistant Commissioner of Police, Simon Overland, admitted that Gatto 'is at risk and possibly is at greater risk as a consequence of what's happened'.

Police approached Gatto days after the murder and offered him protection, an offer he declined with a polite, 'I can look after myself.' While in jail awaiting his trial over the Veniamin shooting, he was put in maximum security, but told the authorities he was happy to be in the mainstream as he was certainly not frightened of anyone inside or outside jail.

No-one doubts Gatto's bravery. He has what police and crooks alike describe as 'dash' — loads of it.

For a man in his line of work, reputation is everything. If he ever agreed to police protection, his influence would vanish because he could hardly persuade people that his point of view was compelling.

For decades, Mick Gatto has gone about his business quietly and efficiently. He moved seamlessly from using brawn to using brains and after running protection for elements of the illegal gambling industry, he eventually took a share of Melbourne's (then) lucrative two-up school.

The two-up game and Melbourne's illegal gambling houses collapsed when more legitimate businessmen rudely muscled in when the government finally legalised gaming machines and licensed Crown Casino.

The crims who used to meet to bet big in darkened warehouses and small rooms at the back of cafes have now become regular visitors at the casino's high-roller rooms. Not that police mind. The casino's state-of-the-art security camera system provides more accurate criminal intelligence and beats the odd informer who hands over third-hand gossip about second-class crooks.

When a known crim is betting big, it is a fair bet he has been up to no good.

One policeman who regularly raided the two-up school maintains a grudging respect for his old adversary.

'We could smash doors or walls to get in and Mick would always remain calm. If anyone acted up, Mick would put one hand up and say, "Shut up, these blokes are only doing their job", and that would be the end of any trouble.'

The policeman said that when the inevitable bribe offer was made and refused in a Lygon Street coffee shop, Gatto instantly turned the rebuff into a positive, saying: 'I didn't think you would, but I had to try.'

When the homicide squad chose a pasta and red wine lunch in Little Italy to farewell detectives who had transferred to other positions, Gatto was dining at the same restaurant. He did not intrude, but when he was leaving he placed two quality bottles of red on the table without comment. One detective suggested they should not drink the unsolicited gift. He was outvoted. The corks were immediately removed, silencing any further discussion.

Police refer to most subjects of their investigations by their surnames, or full names. Occasionally, the notorious ones may be known by their nicknames. But Gatto has always been known as just 'Mick'. There has always been respect.

While Gatto was well-known in select circles for many years, he was smart enough to keep a low public profile — until the underworld war made him headline news.

When he sold his house, it made the news and property sections. When he bought a new one, neighbours were publicly welcoming but privately troubled about the big man who kept odd hours.

A high-profile footballer began to wonder if he had made a blue in building his dream home nearby with a view both of the Heidelberg Golf Club and Gatto's backyard. He would remind anyone who cared to listen that his name was Nick, not Mick.

Unlike many of his dead friends who installed electronic security but were too lazy to maintain it, Gatto knows the value of precautions. Items in the backyard have been positioned to thwart a sniper from the golf course, the closed circuit television system could protect a bank and, it is rumoured, gas masks are kept handy in case of a chemical attack.

The day after Condello was murdered, the media pack headed for Mick's home looking for a fresh news grab.

They nearly got more than they bargained for when, in a scene straight out of *The Sopranos*, the usually unflappable Gatto strode out onto his manicured front lawn in a dressing gown and began to throw eggs at the fourth estate.

It was a temporary hiccup from the master negotiator before normal transmission resumed. The following day, in a mutually-agreed compromise, he walked outside his home to allow photographers and camera people to take pictures and film so they would then leave him in peace.

Recent fame has achieved what twenty years of policing could not. The so-called head of the Carlton Crew has moved his social and business headquarters from Lygon Street to avoid being annoyed by well-wishers and crime groupies.

Gatto moved to the classic Cafe Society in Bourke Street where, up until the Condello murder, he was the watcher rather than the watched.

He could be found upstairs with serious men talking serious business or downstairs occasionally indulging in a long luncheon.

In late 2005, one of the authors popped in to provide Gatto with the highly-valued first edition of *Underbelly 9*. It was considered a wise move as it contained a chapter on the Veniamin shooting and Gatto's subsequent acquittal.

The author arrived and a female staff member explained that Mr Gatto was upstairs.

The author went upstairs and was surprised to see a large number of large men playing cards in the middle of a workday afternoon. It appeared that it must have been a rostered day off for body builders. They stopped playing cards and stared. The author was relieved when Mick welcomed him warmly. The body builders returned to playing cards. The author and Gatto went downstairs. Mick ordered a peppermint tea and the author a coffee, although there was little chance that he would fall asleep.

The author handed over the book and was invited to sign it, which he did, scrawling, 'To Mick — always remember the best defence is always self-defence.'

Gatto laughed. The author was relieved.

One of the card-playing muscle men came downstairs, saying he had won and offered to buy Mick a stiff drink. Mick suggested the author should have one too. The author declined. Mick, at his persuasive best simply said, 'I insist.'

The author said, 'That would be lovely.'

As always, he was a generous host, describing the author as

'very fair'. The meeting ended with a regular Gatto farewell, 'You are a gentleman.'

Much of the 30 kilograms he lost through shadow boxing in solitary confinement had been found again at various business lunches and social dinners. When he spotted Victorian Opposition Leader Robert Doyle walking past the restaurant from Parliament House, he organised for someone to ask for an autograph, even helpfully handing the politician a pen.

As Doyle went to sign, it exploded. It was a joke, but one with a message. Gatto later said: 'That was for naming me in the House.'

Gatto left a different sort of message in the death notices of the *Herald Sun* after Condello's murder.

'I was honoured to be your close mate and will remember the wonderful times we shared.'

And in what might have been a message to others: 'Your passing has left a great void in my life, but life goes on and I know you would expect me to keep punching.'

If Gatto thought he could drift back into the shadows, he was to be disappointed.

The underworld war had made him headline news and while he might have been able to distance himself from his rivals, the media proved harder to shake.

When Gatto was acquitted of the murder of Andrew Veniamin, he would have hoped that he would not have to return to the witness box, but just twelve months later Big Mick would again head to the Supreme Court.

This time, he was a witness in a messy wrongful dismissal case involving the even bigger end of town.

Ted Sent had been the head of the massive retirement-village developer Primelife Corporation until he was sacked in 2003 from the $850,000-a-year job running the firm he had originally founded.

In the wrongful dismissal case, it was revealed that Sent had paid Gatto a monthly retainer to be his 'eyes and ears' in the hope of encouraging industrial harmony on the company's building sites.

The payments began at $4400 a month and rose to $6600. Each payment, although most were made in cash, included the mandatory ten per cent for GST.

Mick pocketed $220,000 over three years from the grateful Sent. The money was paid over during a monthly lunch — usually at La Porcella — the restaurant where Benji permanently lost his appetite after trying the .38 diet.

During cross-examination, Gatto revealed he had been hit with a back tax bill of $1 million but had settled the bill for $200,000.

'The tax is up to scratch if that's what you're looking for,' he declared.

'I was investigated by the ACC (Australian Crime Commission), dragged through a Royal Commission ... Prior to me giving evidence they raided my home, they took every mortal thing, photos, receipts, God knows what, documented everything and took it away. They went through me like Epsom Salts ... they spent $100 million, and found nothing.'

It was revealed that during the long and entertaining lunches Sent would slip over and hand the cash-filled envelope to Mick.

The invitation usually began with a quick call where Gatto would simply say, 'It's that time of the month, mate.'

Lunch would usually rely on the chef's special. 'We'd sort of have something to eat, whatever was on the menu that day, could have been a pig or whatever,' Gatto recalled.

'There would be a big group of us there just to laugh and joke. And then (Sent) would pull me aside and we would have a little chat in relation to building issues or things that were troubling him at the sites or whatever.

'He would just pull it out of his pocket and say, "Here", and I would give him the invoice,' Gatto said. 'He would always do it in private; he'd never do it in front of anyone else.'

Shortly after his two-day cameo appearance in the Supreme Court, he was again in the news.

This time the colourful and somewhat eccentric former federal policeman and barrister Kerry Milte was behind the story.

For decades, Milte lived on the fringes of Melbourne's crime, police and legal worlds.

He was big, smart and impressive, but many saw him as a Walter Mitty character who loved nothing better than a complex conspiracy.

When he was a Commonwealth policeman, Milte led then Federal Attorney-General Lionel Murphy's 1973 raid on ASIO's former Melbourne headquarters. It was said that when Murphy arrived he said to the big policeman, 'What the fuck have you got me into, Kerry?'

Milte offered to provide information on organised crime in Victoria to Chief Commissioner Christine Nixon during the underworld war.

But his involvement became a public embarrassment when he was charged with criminal offences, including bribery.

In an interview with police, he claimed the secretary of the Electrical Trades Union, Dean Mighell, had been 'threatened by Gatto with death, and he came to see me via a politician'.

When the claim was made, both Gatto and Mighell denied the allegation.

Gatto went public to slam Milte and the claims.

He said he had not threatened Mighell. 'It's made me sick, really sick, because there is no substance to it whatsoever. (There is) not a skerrick of truth in it. Not a skerrick of truth. The man is a friend. The man is a man that I have dealt with for years,' he said.

Mighell said Gatto had 'never threatened me with violence. I have never had reason to approach the police'.

Gatto admitted he had been a criminal, but said he was now legitimate. 'I haven't done anything. My conscience is clear.'

He knows his name has been whispered in relation to unsolved murders and that he remains a person of interest to Purana. Sour grapes rather than fresh leads, he says.

'I always thought that our system of justice and common fairness required that if someone with a colourful past decides to go straight, it is something which is to be encouraged rather than sabotaged.

'It seems that some people and the media do not want people to go straight or just want them to try but fail. Well, I did try, I did so successfully and I intend to continue to do so.'

While many of his friends and enemies have fallen, Big Mick may be the last man standing — legitimately.

In 2007 he sat for a young painter who wanted a portrait of a high profile figure to enter in the Archibald Prize.

Gatto sat patiently and later remarked he thought it had a good chance. When the modest artist said it would be difficult to win Australia's most prestigious art award, Gatto smiled and replied, 'I'll make a couple of calls.'

He was joking. We think.

24

MARRIED TO THE MOB

The men live fast and die young
or rot in jail. Their women face
the mess left behind.

THE last time Sylvia saw him alive, he was standing at the door of their daughter's flat, head cocked, looking at her in a way that didn't match the tough-guy talk. It was as close to wistful as a sociopath gunman and drug dealer gets.

'You don't look happy,' she said to him — sympathetically, she thought later, considering how cruelly he'd treated her.

'I'm all right, love,' he said. 'But I got a $100,000 contract on my head.'

'Why not go overseas?' she asked, then added, 'Oh yeah, I forgot: you gotta make a million dollars first.'

A flash of gangster bravado returned. 'I'm not running away,' he snarled. 'No one will touch me.' But then he stepped forward and kissed her on the forehead. It was the most tender gesture he'd made to her in twenty years. She knew it meant goodbye.

Two weeks later, Nik 'The Bulgarian' Radev was dead, shot seven times in a Coburg street, murder number sixteen in Melbourne's underworld war, which would end up with double that many casualties. Police believe he was set up by criminals he knew well, lured by the promise of a lucrative drug deal. The hit man thought to have done it, Andrew 'Benji' Veniamin, was himself shot a year later in a restaurant by Dominic 'Mick' Gatto, subsequently acquitted on self-defence.

Sylvia didn't go to her ex-husband's funeral. She had never liked gangsters and, at 39, she was free of them at last. She felt sorry for their daughter at losing her father, but for herself, she mostly felt relief. She thought she could finally get on with the life the bullying Bulgarian had hijacked when she was seventeen.

But it's not that easy to put the pieces back together, patch up fractured family ties and lead a normal life when people stare and whisper and call you a gangster's moll.

This is how it goes for those married to the mob. The men live fast and die young or rot in jail. Their women face the mess left behind.

IN 2003, Roberta Williams was an unknown nobody. In less than a year she became the best-known nobody in town. She of the toothy smile, pugnacious attitude and sharp tongue was a compulsory inclusion in media coverage of Melbourne's underworld shootings.

While the gangland war shot a lot of Roberta's male acquaintances to death, it shot her to a sort of fame. She professed to know nothing, of course, except that her chubby hubby Carl Williams didn't do it. Carl, who has a baby face, no visible means of support and a lot of dead associates, is now doing 35 years on multiple murder charges.

But back when Carl was first arrested, Roberta did the talking in the Williams family. While wiser heads in the underworld stayed low, she was a dial-a-quote for reporters. There she was, on the court steps, standing by her man. And again, praising Carl's slain bodyguard, the terminally tattooed 'Benji' Veniamin, her 'best friend'. Next, she was holding court at her daughter's 'christening' party — at that well-known place of worship, Crown Casino. Then she scuffled with a cop as the cameras rolled. Roberta said she and Carl were just normal folks minding their own business. What that business was, a court decided, was drug dealing and murder. The fact is that Roberta got to star in her own grubby soap opera and seemed to love it, while the nation looked on, bemused.

Not everyone with a deprived and troubled childhood ends up as a foulmouthed gangster's moll, but there are reasons for the path Roberta chose, reasons outlined by the judge who sentenced her to jail in October 2004 for assisting Carl to traffick drugs in 2001.

Justice Murray Kellam said in part of his lengthy sentencing remarks:

1. Whilst it is true that your plea of guilty was entered only on the day before your trial, I accept that your circumstances were bound up with those of your husband and that for reasons of loyalty and other reasons it was difficult for you to enter a plea until such time as it became apparent that your husband intended to plead guilty to more serious charges. That said however, there is no evidence before me of any expression of real remorse on your part for your involvement in the crime.

2. I have been told something of your personal history and your circumstances. You are aged 35 years, having been born on 23 March 1969. You have four children, three from a previous marriage. These children are aged 17, 12 and 10. You have a fourth child from your marriage to your co-accused, Carl Williams. That child is aged three years. Your counsel spelt out your background before me in some detail. You are one of eight children. Your father, a truck driver, was burnt to death in a trucking accident when

you were eight months old. Following that, your mother had grave difficulty coping with eight children. She was engaged in two de facto relationships following her husband's death, and both such partners, I was informed by your counsel, were physically violent both to you and to your siblings. You became a Ward of the State at age 11 and you were placed in Allambie where you remained for some three years before being transferred to Winlaton and then subsequently accommodated at a hostel in Windsor. You now have no relationship with your mother. I accept that you have a background of childhood and adolescent deprivation.

3. You formed a relationship with your first boyfriend at age 16, and by age 17 you had given birth to your first child. You later married him and had a further two children by reason of that relationship. However you separated from your first husband in 1997 after you suffered considerable violence from him. You met Carl Williams in 1998 and in March 2001 you gave birth to your youngest child, a daughter. I accept that you have a close relationship with Carl Williams.

4. You have admitted before me to prior convictions which in general relate to offences of dishonesty and an offence of causing injury recklessly between 1987 and 1990. No doubt those offences are reflective of your troubled youth and are of no relevance to my task of sentencing you today. Of relevance, however, is the fact that you were convicted of trafficking in amphetamines at the County Court on 9 April 1990 and sentenced to be imprisoned for six months, which sentence was wholly suspended. That suspended sentence was reinstated by reason of a breach thereof and you served three months' imprisonment in respect thereof.

5. In November 2000 you were convicted at the Magistrates' Court at Sunshine of being in possession of ecstasy and cocaine. You were sentenced to a term of imprisonment for three months, such sentence suspended for a period of 18 months. The event which brings you before me is clearly a breach of that suspended sentence and it can be anticipated that you will be dealt with for that matter in due course. The significance of that matter is that notwithstanding the fact that you had been given a suspended sentence, you were

still prepared to engage in the criminal activity which brings you before me.

6. A number of medical reports have been tendered before me by consent. In particular, a report from Mr Jeffrey Cummins, consulting psychologist, in relation to his examination of you on 21 September 2004 provides a detailed history of your background and your psychological state. I will not repeat that detail here but I have taken the matters contained in that report into account...

THE judge saw beyond the defiant, publicity-hungry woman in court — and on television and in the newspapers — to the scarred, scared child she had been.

If Roberta is a type whose fate is to 'star' briefly in a grubby crime soap before fading back into the inevitable oblivion, then a co-star in the same tear-stained drama is the tragic Judy Moran, a gangster gran from central casting whose blonde mane has stood out in a sea of men in black at the funerals of her two sons and two husbands.

At the height of the gangland war, both women became media celebrities in their own right, feeding off the insatiable public interest in those at the centre of the action.

Rarely a week went by where they failed to rate a mention in the media. Roberta was even the subject of a long profile in a weekend newspaper magazine.

The plot thickened with the appearance, centre stage, of a new 'love interest' for Carl Williams, in the best soap opera tradition. When Williams first entered his guilty pleas on several murder charges in early 2007, a 'mystery woman' appeared at court. Her name was Renata Laureano, she was young, attractive, and wore a conspicuously large diamond ring, all of which enraged Roberta, whose temper was uncertain at the best of times.

Asked about this on a television current affairs program, one of the authors said, poker-faced: 'It's the next best thing to the

Melbourne Cup. We don't get the academy awards here — we have the Supreme Court.'

He was referring to the fact that Roberta, upset at seeing the other woman steal the limelight — and that copies of her husband's letters from jail had been published in the *Herald Sun* — had shouted obscenities at Renata Laureano.

No wonder she was unhappy. In the letters to his estranged wife, Williams boasts of his new love.

Furious that the letters had made their way into print, Roberta arrived at court spoiling for a fight. Before Williams had even arrived in the courtroom she expressed disappointment that he'd be locked behind a glass partition.

'If I could spit in his face, I would,' she snarled. No one doubted her.

During the lunch break, she followed Williams' parents, George and Barbara, shouting obscenities at them in and outside the court as a huge media contingent looked on.

That afternoon, she was banned from attending court, and Renata Laureano took police advice to stay away.

But the gap was filled by Judy Moran. Dressed to kill, she attempted to use the courtroom to launch a tirade at Williams over the killing of her two sons and her ex-husband, Lewis Moran.

Invited by Supreme Court Justice Betty King to provide a verbal victim impact statement, the angry widow began: 'Carl Williams, the evil person that you are' before being called to order by the judge, who insisted she keep emotion out of her testimony.

Judy Moran continued: 'You have all but destroyed me, ripped out my heart'. She did not mention how many people her sons and husbands had hurt or killed.

SO what is it with women and gangsters? Roberta Williams and Judy Moran mightn't know Lady Macbeth from a Big Mac, but Melbourne psychologist Alex Bartsch, a former homicide detective, says both women remind him of the 'Lady Macbeth' stereotype. He says there are three other types of women who get mixed up with crooks — 'risk-takers', 'Florence Nightingales' and 'helpless dependants'.

'Criminals' wives can be pretty much like celebrities' wives,' Bartsch says. 'They fall into definable types with different motives.' The Lady Macbeths chase power and influence. Risk-takers are attracted by danger and the reflected 'glamour' of being with lawbreakers. The Florence Nightingales graduate from saving wounded birds and stray kittens to rescuing wounded men. Some like being in emotional control of a man — 'the caged beast' who pines for them in prison in a way that usually dissolves when he gets out.

Then there are the doormats, helpless dependants often found in ethnic crime groups where marriage within the group is common and traditional gender roles are not questioned. They cook, clean and bear children, keep up appearances and don't ask hard questions. 'Their entire sense of worth is tied to having a relationship,' says Bartsch.

Writers have always known about the allure of the outlaw. The bandit prince, the pirate king, the highwayman, the gunslinger, the bushranger and the modern gangster are prototype characters of drama. The mix of predatory appetites, reckless courage and offhand generosity has always attracted people, but more especially the opposite sex. Where you've got tough guys, you've got dolls, as Damon Runyon might have said.

There's a bit of Runyon's Broadway — and Al Capone's Chicago — in modern Melbourne. Two early casualties of the recent shooting outbreak highlight the sex appeal of gangsters.

Right up until Alphonse Gangitano killed him in early 1995, a good-looking gunman called Gregory John Workman had always been attractive to women. A senior policeman's daughter who went to Preston East state school with Workman recalls how proud she was when he walked her home when they were twelve. He was the best-looking boy in school — and he had 'dash', the word both crooks and cops use for the charismatic blend of courage, poise and recklessness valued on either side of the law.

Workman's killer was less courageous but more calculating. Some called the narcissistic Gangitano the 'De Niro of Lygon Street', but he fancied he looked more like the actor Andy Garcia in *The Godfather III*. As a private school boy, Gangitano attracted girls, though boys remember him as a bully. 'He was smooth and well-dressed, and when he turned eighteen he drove a flash red car,' one former admirer told the authors. 'He used to play cards in my mother's garage with his mates. He was always charming to girls but he had a complete fantasy about New York mafiosi.'

Gangitano courted his future partner, Virginia, while she was a schoolgirl at the upmarket Genazzano College ('We grew out of him but she didn't,' says the ex-admirer), but that long-term relationship didn't stop other women seeking his company when he became a serious gangster with the 'Carlton Crew'.

Before Gangitano was gunned down in his Templestowe home in 1998 he was close to several women, notably bail justice Rowena Allsop, who risked her reputation with such an unlikely friendship. At Gangitano's funeral — the biggest underworld event in Australia in years — Allsop gave a gushing eulogy that ranged from Big Al's taste for poetry to his Dolce & Gabbana aftershave.

Gangitano's presumed killer, Jason Moran, condemned his own children to grow up without any male family figures by mating inside Melbourne's tightknit painter and docker crime 'family'. His partner, Trish, is the daughter of Les Kane, a standover man murdered by rivals in 1978. Jason's half-brother Mark Moran was killed in 2000. Jason was shot in 2003 and his father Lewis Moran was killed later. Meaning the Moran children have lost their father, their uncle and both grandfathers to the gun.

Why would any woman risk that for her children by marrying a gangster?

'I WAS a little Italian virgin, innocent and gullible,' Sylvia Radev sighs, nodding at the framed photograph of her teenage self: a touchingly pretty girl headed for heartbreak. 'I'd never even seen a penis when I met Nik — let alone one with a tattoo on it,' she says. 'He had "TAXI" on his — because it "went everywhere", he told me.' She parodies her former husband's strong eastern European accent, giving it a sinister twist. No wonder. Even among bad men, his evil ways stood out.

He once held a gun to her head, suggested prostituting her and taunted her that he married her only to get an Australian passport.

How a respectable convent girl ended up with a monster is a cautionary tale. Her parents and sisters are ashamed and still frightened to be linked to Radev, and Sylvia worries that her neighbours will hold it against her. His malign power reaches from the grave.

She lives in a modern brick veneer in a new suburb southeast of Melbourne, not far from the shopping centre that inspires *Kath & Kim*. It's a small, neat house with a small, neat Japanese car in the drive, comfortingly anonymous.

A huge picture of a tiger hangs over the couch and prints of zebras and other animals are on the walls. At 40, wearing jeans and with her ash blonde hair short, Sylvia looks years younger. People sometimes mistake her and her 21-year-old daughter, Raquel, for sisters. But Raquel is painfully thin and looks older than her years because, her mother says, she has 'seen too many bad things'.

After moving 'maybe 30 times' in 22 years, Sylvia craves stability. She never again wants gangsters or police in her home. Police once found a pistol taped under a cabinet in Raquel's bedroom.

Radev had hidden it, but forced his daughter to lie that another criminal, by then conveniently dead, had put the gun there.

Sylvia doesn't want her two young children (to her new partner) to be exposed to the things Raquel has seen and heard. She doesn't swear or smoke in front of them and spells out words like 'K-I-L-L' and 'G-U-N'.

Sylvia's parents migrated from Calabria in the 1950s. Her father, now retired, was a driving instructor who paid off a big eastern suburbs house. Her two older sisters married young and have led law-abiding lives. Which is how Sylvia's would have gone, too, if Nik Radev hadn't trapped her.

At seventeen, she was an apprentice hairdresser working for a Bulgarian woman involved in bringing 'refugees' to Australia. The woman, who called Sylvia a 'rich Italian virgin nun', read tarot cards and predicted Sylvia would marry a man from 'far away'. Sylvia was fascinated. Soon afterwards, two young Bulgarians turned up at the salon. They spoke poor English, but one spoke Italian. They were new arrivals, known to Sylvia's boss. After they left, she asked Sylvia which one of them she liked.

Neither, Sylvia said. But if you had to choose, the woman pressed, which one? Sylvia shrugged. The sporty-looking one, she said, meaning the one who spoke Italian and was 'well-dressed' in a white tracksuit and runners.

What she didn't know was that under the tracksuit, apart from a fit wrestler's physique, were 'jail tatts'. At 21, Radev had already served time in Europe. Far from being a genuine refugee, she later found out, he had worked the system to get to Australia. But in 1980 all she knew was that he kept coming to see her. The first time he brought her violets — not a bunch of flowers, but the whole plant in a pot. She didn't know he'd probably stolen it.

Radev manipulated her. Sylvia didn't fancy the Italian boy her parents wanted her to marry. To her, Nik seemed better than an arranged marriage. It wasn't love, but she wanted to escape her family's control, and marrying him looked like a way out to a teenage girl. Radev charmed Sylvia's parents, speaking Italian and listening attentively. He knew the rules: that courtship must lead to engagement.

One day he got permission to take her out. He took her to a motel room in St Kilda.

'I thought it would be like the Rod Stewart song *Tonight's the Night* — all romantic,' Sylvia recalls. 'It wasn't. He virtually raped me. He hurt me. Then he said, "Now you'll have to marry me. No one else will have you".'

The honeymoon was at Wrest Point Casino in Hobart. He gambled; she stayed in their room. Within days he made her ask her parents to send money: he'd blown their wedding-present cash.

At five months pregnant, Sylvia was hurt in a car crash. She lost the baby, a boy, but Radev, who had been driving the car, didn't come to see her in hospital. The strongest feeling she had for him was fear. 'He didn't have to bruise me — he terrified me,' she says. 'It was mental cruelty. I was conditioned.'

Radev worked for only a few months — in a pizza shop, then a factory — before turning to crime. 'He didn't often involve me in what he was doing,' says Sylvia, 'but he would come home with money or stolen clothes.' And he started carrying guns.

Radev ran with the 'Russian mafia'. Drugs and prostitution were their main rackets, but Radev was up for anything, from burglary and armed robbery to extortion, fraud and blackmail. 'He had no fear and no shame,' says Sylvia. 'It was just a power thing for him. He wanted to be like Al Pacino in Scarface.'

He could be charming but was driven by forces she did not understand. 'He was in his own world. He would go out in the afternoon, doing his things, and stay out all night. He could say he was going to the shop and then disappear for days.' She didn't ask questions.

If he did bring associates home, they didn't discuss 'business' in front of her 'because I was a squarehead. And that was good.'

Sylvia, still hairdressing, borrowed to buy a house in Hampton Park in 1983, the year her daughter Raquel was born. In 1984, when Radev was charged with armed robbery, he demanded she sign papers to sell it: he wanted money to flee the country before the trial.

She didn't want to sell. 'He held a gun to my head while I was holding the baby and said if I didn't sign he would kill me. It traumatised Raquel because I was terrified and holding her so tight. I signed. I was crying so much I left drips on the paper.'

They sold the house and all their possessions but Radev was arrested at the airport. When he went to jail, Sylvia was relieved — but she couldn't share her troubles with friends. 'I didn't tell anyone except my parents and my sisters that he was in jail. We told everyone he was overseas. Even my bridesmaids.' She warned Raquel never to tell people — at kindergarten and, later, school — that Daddy was in jail.

She moved into a flat, started going to a gym, landed a job as a public relations assistant — and filed for divorce. 'He didn't really care because he had got Australian citizenship and a passport.' But she still visited him in jail so he could see his child. When he got out, he turned up at her flat. Unable to confront him, and helped by a female friend, she fled to a women's refuge, then rented a flat in Windsor.

'That's when my life really began,' she recalls. She worked and went out. Whenever Radev was back in jail, she was happy. 'I didn't need a man around.' But when he got out, he always found her and came and went as he wished. She had a boyfriend, but Radev bashed him and 'threatened to put him in the boot'.

She was aware of his criminal activity, but ignored it. 'Nik never told me any of his criminal plans and I never asked.' In 1998, he brought a friend from jail, Sam Zayat, later killed in the underworld war. 'Nik said Sam was a murderer but he wouldn't murder me unless Nik told him to.' She never knew whether to believe him.

Two things stick in her mind. One is that he told her that when he was a child in Bulgaria, he pushed an old man from a third-storey balcony just to see what it was like to see someone die. The other was his boasting that when he died, everybody would know about it. As he predicted, his murder and his funeral made front-page headlines. Radev's gangster friends buried him in a gold-plated casket worth $30,000. But when Sylvia took their daughter to see his grave later, there was no headstone and the plot was covered in weeds. They left a cigarette on the grave and haven't been back.

MARIA Arena was in the kitchen with her younger son when she heard the shot that ended 25 years of marriage. By the time they reached her Joe he was dead, shot from behind as he put out the garbage bin.

It was midnight. The Arenas had just got home to Bayswater, an outer suburb in the foothills east of Melbourne, from a wedding in Footscray. Maybe the killer had known where they'd been, knew when their Toyota would pull into the drive.

A year before, there had been another big Italian wedding when the Arenas' daughter Lisa married. Almost certainly, among the 450 guests at the lavish reception in Brunswick was someone who plotted her husband's execution. That thought still gnaws at Maria.

Of all the wedding guests, those who ate and drank and kissed the proud parents, only a few comforted the stricken widow and children after Joe's funeral. The rest, she said bitterly in a newspaper interview at the time, 'dropped off like flies', as if the whole family had been buried with him. If that is the Calabrian way, she said then, she wanted no part of it.

That was nearly twenty years ago. Time has dulled her anger but hasn't solved her husband's murder. Police believe Giuseppe 'Joe' Arena was tied to the Calabrian crime group, the Honoured Society. As an insurance broker and financial adviser, they say, he helped launder cash for marijuana growers in Griffith and Mildura.

Police say Arena was anointed by the secret society's Godfather, Liborio Benvenuto, as his successor. But, after Benvenuto's death in June 1988, rivals jostling for power in the society decided to kill him and take over. Police think Arena, only 50, sold up his moderate business interests after Benvenuto's death as if he expected a fresh source of income.

But his widow disputes that he was setting up as the new Godfather: 'He might have known these people [the Honoured Society] but it was only through business clients.'

Nothing about Maria Arena or the way she lives hints that her husband was anything other than what she claims: a hard-working family man who had paid off a house and made small investments. 'We were comfortable, but a lot of our friends had bigger houses than we did,' she says.

Certainly, Maria seems an ordinary suburban grandmother. She opens the door of her small unit wearing a striped pinafore over sensible trousers and a blouse. She looks as if she has been baking cakes in case the grandkids visit.

A gangster's wife? It seems ridiculous. She doesn't fit any stereotypes. Not the faded glamour girl with the big hair, the winter tan, plastic surgery and loud jewellery. Nor the traditional Italian widow in black. She looks like a middle-aged department store assistant — which she is, at a shopping centre up the road.

Maria Arena is short, in her late 50s, with golden-brown eyes, rosy cheeks and fair skin. Her mother's family was from Subiaco, near Rome, and her father was Yugoslav, so she is not tied by blood or custom to the tightknit Calabrian clans she married into. Having arrived in Australia as a five-year-old, she speaks English as if born here. Her children have Anglo names. None of them now has much to do with the Calabrian community.

The way she tells it, her marriage was just another modest migrant success story — apart from the ending. It started when she was seventeen, and began work for an Italian-run concreting firm at Lilydale that needed an office girl fluent in both English and Italian. Joe, eight years older, was her boss's cousin. He worked at a cafe where she went for coffee, and nature took its course. Within a year, she was engaged, pregnant and married, in that order. They were to have three children in four years.

They opened a dress shop that failed. Joe worked three jobs to pay off the debts so he wouldn't be known as a bankrupt,' Maria says. He worked shifts in a factory, mowed lawns and started selling insurance and real estate on the side. They tried a fruit shop, but Joe was so good with insurance and real estate that he took it on full-time.

'He had the gift of the gab and he was likeable,' she says. 'He always had time for old people and they trusted him.' Trust was vital: many older migrants spoke little English and were illiterate. They trusted Arena to handle their affairs and he became an influential figure in the Italian community.

Maria fetches a framed snap of Joe. It shows a dark, nattily dressed man with the signature smile that led the media to dub him 'the friendly Godfather'. He was so gentle, his widow says, that the only time he spanked their younger son — for setting fire to the garage — 'he felt so sick about it he went to bed'.

She tells other stories. Once, a jealous colleague at the insurance company he worked for tried to undermine him by complaining about his spelling. The workmate received a memo from the boss saying, 'If you were as good at your job as Joe Arena is at his, you wouldn't have to worry about spelling.' The rest of the memo was deliberately misspelt to make a point.

Jealousy is a recurring theme. Maria doesn't speculate about who ordered Joe's murder but she suggests he was too popular for his own good — that maybe others thought he was currying favour with certain people.

But he did not just inspire jealousy, he could be jealous himself. Asked if he had ever been in trouble, Maria gets tears in her eyes. 'We had a bad patch in our marriage once,' she quavers. It is the only reference she makes to the fact Joe was convicted of manslaughter in 1976 for killing a man he thought was her lover. He served two years in jail.

He was, she says, an intelligent man whose life was governed by his lack of education. Had he been educated, 'he could have been a lawyer or some other profession'. She means he would also still be alive.

Maria says she is not rich. She lives on her small wage and rent from an investment property. Joe's superannuation is invested to leave her children. Her greatest pleasure now is to be 'Nonna' to her grandchildren.

The youngest is only four. He is bold and cheerful and reminds her of the grandfather he will never know. 'Sometimes I look in his eyes and say, "Are you in there, Joe Arena?" '

Her eyes are bright with tears again.

25

....

PLAYING WITH SNAKES

```
Hardnosed detectives gaped
when Garde-Wilson answered
  the door with the snake
  draped around her neck.
```

IT'S lunchtime in the legal quarter and Zarah Garde-Wilson, a country girl before she turned herself into a city lawyer, looks after the livestock first, the way they do things back home on the farm.

A little earlier, she had taken a frozen mouse from a refrigerator hidden in a sleek cupboard in her sleek office in the heart of the Melbourne CBD. Now she crouches elegantly beside a long glass tank under the window, long legs tucked under her on the gleaming black floor, and works the latch on the lid.

Inside on a bed of litter is a fake rock, hollowed out underneath. She lifts it, speaking softly. To anyone eavesdropping on this private moment, it sounds as if she is saying 'shivers' ... and anyone who hasn't seen her pet might well shiver when they do. In fact, she's saying 'Chivas', a play on the name of her favourite top-shelf liquor.

In fact, the object of the glamorous Garde-Wilson's affections is a snake — a Queensland scrub python, sometimes called a diamond python because of the shape of the head and the vivid yellow pattern on the dark gun-metal skin. 'Hello, darling,' she murmurs, but the sleepy snake maintains the right to silence.

It's the perfect in-joke. Here, across the street from the back door of the Victorian Supreme Court, lives a cold-blooded reptile that preys on vermin: the ideal pet for a criminal lawyer whose clients, past and present, include several notorious names from Melbourne's underworld war. A lawyer whose own double-barrelled name has become entwined with gangsters' in the public imagination — and whose supposed *femme fatale* persona has scriptwriters sharpening their pencils and their wits.

The farmer's daughter in Garde-Wilson likes animals, but you won't catch her being gooey about them. Where she comes from in rural New South Wales, snakes were shot rather than petted. 'King browns would get their heads blown off if they came near the house,' she observes with a faint smile. She admits that she used to get quite fond of half-tame goannas when she worked a holiday job at Fraser Island to help pay her way through law school in the 1990s. But she says what she really wants is a cobra and maybe that tells you something. The cobra is exotic, fast and deadly — the reptile world's version of a hooded killer.

Of course, Chivas the sleepy python isn't venomous and is relatively harmless except to rats and mice. Not that her mistress would give her live rodents. 'Her skin is like silk. Cornered rats will fight and they'd scratch her,' she explains. 'Besides, it would be cruel.' To the rats and mice, that is. No matter what impressions strangers might form of Zarah Garde-Wilson the 'gangland lawyer', she is not cruel. The opposite, in fact.

She bought the snake from a pet shop at the Victoria Market — a shop stocking spiders, lizards and other exotic pets of the sort that police often find when they raid drug dealers' houses.

Amateur psychologists might see the impulse to buy the snake as being linked to the sort of feelings that makes a 'nice girl' take in an edgy, tattooed loner with a taste for drugs and violence.

Whether the pet snake is an ironic joke, a prop or just provides quiet, low-maintenance company in her owner's smart but eerily spartan office, is hard to say. But the reptile occasionally earns her keep. Once, when the Victoria Police anti-gangster taskforce, codenamed *Purana*, came calling, hardnosed detectives gaped when Garde-Wilson answered the door with the snake draped around her neck — 'she was like Eve,' one quipped later.

The hyphen with the python stole the scene.

Of course, sexy-woman-with-snake is so like something from a James Bond film that it verges on an Austin Powers caricature, and Garde-Wilson must know that. A cynic might see the python as a theatrical touch to go with her heavily stylised look — long hair often dyed jet black to match the slinky clothes that display her lithe bikini-model frame and big bust in ways the legal profession notices but has increasingly not approved of.

Of course, a lot of perfectly respectable people keep unusual pets, though not usually at the office. Where Garde-Wilson lives, in an inner suburb of Melbourne, she has another pet — one that *can* bite. It's a tan pit bull terrier bitch she calls Taser, after the stun-gun police use. 'Good for security,' she says cryptically. She rarely uses a dozen words if two will do. And she knows the value of silence — a conversation with her can be a series of pauses as she weighs up what to say, if anything at all.

A client gave her the pit bull bitch in lieu of paying a hefty bill. This doesn't happen much for tax lawyers or patent attorneys and it tells you something about Garde-Wilson's clients and how close she is to them. It also shows she's a soft touch for a hard luck story, and has a tendency to befriend those she sees as in need of help. Whether they all repay her kindness is a moot point. But, regardless of the fact that she got Taser in lieu of an unpaid fee, she is fond of the dog — one of few friends she can trust, it seems.

Some are dead, some are in jail and others have faded away in the aftermath of the underworld war that transfixed the nation, earning Melbourne a backhanded accolade as some sort of latter-day Chicago where opposing crime 'families' hire gunmen to mow each other down.

Talking about her dog, Zarah drops her guard a little. 'He (the client) showed me a picture on his phone of this little pup and that was it,' she says. As she speaks, the watchful coolness vanishes and her poker face breaks into a big smile. Cruella turns into Pollyanna as you glimpse the freckly, country kid pictured in her boarding school year book in 1995 — a diligent girl determined to study law, escape the pressure to marry a suitable boy on the land ('you know: "Fred" next door,' she grimaces) so joining the slow slide into genteel rural poverty she saw around her as she grew up in the New England area of New South Wales.

She turned her back on all that by the time she left school. Now, like her python, she is a long way from home. She still thinks she made the right choice — but others are not so sure.

LET'S get it straight: Zarah Garde-Wilson has not asked for this, to be the subject of a story that inevitably shoves her back into the spotlight, a target of public curiosity, professional criticism and private gossip too salacious and nasty to repeat.

In fact, when a stranger calls, she is at first not just cautious but hostile, and with good reason: her career is in the balance. What she says or does could weigh against her.

When speaking to the author in 2006, she was waiting on the result of an appeal by the Director of Public Prosecutions against the leniency of a conviction-without-jail she had previously received for contempt of court. She was charged for refusing to testify against two men accused of killing her boyfriend, on the grounds she feared for her life — fears that a judge acknowledged were not groundless, given the identities of the two notorious men implicated in her boyfriend's murder.

Still pending at that stage were charges over an unregistered pistol that a criminal-turned-informer claims he picked up from her place. Then there were four counts of giving false information to the Australian Crime Commission. No wonder she seems jittery when the author comes calling.

'I don't trust journalists,' she says in the first minute after sitting down to a light lunch and a big coffee near her office. She makes the same generalisation about not trusting most police and some lawyers — particularly prosecutors — but she is wise enough to add quickly that she respects the Melbourne legal establishment 'enormously'.

She is bitter at the way she has been portrayed in the previous two-and-a-half years, and there is no reason to think she has changed her mind since. She is furious at a Sydney magazine heading a story 'Thug-a-bye baby' in 2004. She imagined she would be treated with dignity after discussing her application to have sperm taken from her murdered partner's body and stored in the vain hope she could one day have his child. It was a vain hope in both senses of the word, some would say. Not only was the gesture doomed to fail because of legal barriers, but some cynics would see an element of vanity and publicity-seeking in her attempt to have a test-tube 'love child' fathered posthumously by her killer lover.

One thing seems certain: if Garde-Wilson had never met the dashing killer who variously called himself Lewis Caine and Sean Vincent, the odds are that few outside Melbourne's gossipy legal circles would ever have heard of the solicitor with the Sloane Ranger surname.

Apart from her reputation for annoying the bench, distracting prosecutors and attracting a certain macho type of criminal clientele by wearing plunging necklines, high heels and tight skirts that often fail to hide her suspenders and stockings, she would be just a hard-working young lawyer trying to survive in the piranha pool of criminal law. On ability, she should have prospered — but, as the cliché goes, she found love (and friends) in the wrong places and it threatened to torpedo her career. It still might.

For a conscientious solicitor, Garde-Wilson is vague about dates but it seems she met the man who called himself Lewis Caine soon after she arrived in Melbourne in mid-2002 with the now defunct firm Pryles & Defteros, after West Australian authorities had closed down its Perth branch office.

Caine, who was facing a drink-driving charge at the time, hired Zarah Garde-Wilson's employer, George Defteros. Defteros was a well-known criminal lawyer and one-time Northcote pub bouncer, who has since stopped practising because of charges, later dropped, that he was part of a gangland murder conspiracy.

Defteros introduced Caine to his hard-working junior and she fell for the would-be gangster, who had not long been out of jail after serving a long sentence. Most lawyers say that declaring herself willing and able for Caine was Zarah's second mistake. The first was working for Defteros, who had apparently thrown her into criminal legal work with little supervision or guidance about the fine line between lawyer and client. Defteros may simply have been distracted by his own heavy workload but there can be little doubt that in most criminal firms lawyers dating clients is frowned upon.

Garde-Wilson insists she has no regrets about choosing to work for Defteros ahead of a job offered by the West Australian Prosecutors' Office, and it's easy to believe her. She says her heart was always in defending the under-dog.

The trouble was that her new love interest Caine was more an attack dog. He had served twelve years for kicking a stranger to death outside a nightclub in 1988. Born Adrian Bligh, the estranged son of a senior Tasmanian policeman was a martial artist with a mean streak. In prison, he relished being a standover man in the high-security divisions. Most who met him after his release saw trouble looming.

But the then inexperienced young solicitor saw a tender side to the hard man who, at 37, was thirteen years older than she was. He was, she says, 'my first and only true love', a claim at least one of her relatives thinks is literally correct — suggesting that the studious Zarah had not had a serious sexual relationship before.

Ask her about Caine and she says, 'You can't help who you love.' She adds, 'There's not much I can say on the record.' She does not say much more off the record, and no wonder.

Raking over a lost love, a tarnished reputation and the odds of a ruined career isn't easy. Her eyes fill and she falls silent. It's hard to tell if she is masking emotion, using the lawyer's trick of buying time to frame careful answers or deciding whether to say anything at all.

After a long pause, she excuses herself to go to the bathroom. She returns, composed, and talks a little of her two years with Caine. She uses the sort of ready-made phrases heard in soap operas — 'we were soul mates' ... 'I still feel him here with me' ... 'he totally supported my career' ... 'it was all good' — but, to do her justice, sounds as sincere as any grieving partner would in such circumstances.

She won't be quoted about supposedly ugly scenes with Caine's relatives, who have criticised her over the semen harvesting, saying they believed he did not want children. She says she has more idea of his wishes than people who had hardly seen him for years, a reference to her claim that Caine was bitterly estranged from his family.

In her defence, she says Caine was not her own client, he had served his time and his debt to society, and their personal relationship was no-one else's business. She paints a picture of a genuine love match — albeit with a man who predicted he would not live past 40 and had no visible means of support other than the dole and gambling. It is this that has made people question her judgment, although it is not the only reason.

Others, not only police and prosecutors but fellow defence lawyers who routinely act for criminals and are comfortable in defending their right to do so, describe Caine in terms of a manipulative sociopath using a vulnerable young woman for his own selfish ends. Less obvious, perhaps, is the possibility that she subconsciously used *him* to rebel against her sheltered, establishment family background; her own Caine mutiny, so to speak.

When the film-maker Geoffrey Wright based a version of *Macbeth* on the Melbourne gang war, he modelled Lady Macbeth on Garde-Wilson rather than the 'usual underworld wives' because of what he saw as her glamour and complex motivations. She was 'sensual, smart, sensitive and dedicated' yet chose to 'swim with sharks' and tried to save them, he told the author.

'Zarah, like Lady Macbeth, represents the complete collapse of a moral perspective in a quest for hopeless love,' he concludes. 'The triumph of misplaced emotion over intellect.'

Why? Wright guesses at some psychological conflict that makes her 'committed to "her man" no matter how bad he is.'

Garde-Wilson is oddly ambivalent about her past and scoffs at the idea that it could have any bearing on her adult life. Perhaps the lady protests too much. She says she is not estranged from her parents (now in Queensland) but adds, 'I have always been self-sufficient, always been on my own little plane, always fought my own battles. I love my family, but we are on different levels.'

She projects an image between cool professional and romantic maverick that comes across in photographs and film footage of her, but in the flesh, a whiff of the obsessive loner hovers over her. At a distance, and through a lens, she might appear to be a languid, privileged amateur filling in time slumming it with the cheaper people and indulging in rough trade, but that is not quite right.

The fact is that in many ways Garde-Wilson is as self-made as the next person and more than many in her profession. She has had to overcome obstacles and achieved her goal through hard work and self-motivation, starting from a low base. She got into law at James Cook University at Townsville in 1996, worked hard and switched to University of Western Australia. She did not make a huge impression on her fellow students or lecturers there but did the work to get good results. She recalls topping property law one year ('the guy who marked it said it was better advice than you get from the Crown Solicitor's Office') but set her heart on crime work 'because it's about defending people's liberty'. Some would call it a romantic streak.

As a senior student she worked voluntarily at Pryles & Defteros, which had represented notorious Perth crime figures like John Kizon and Coffin Cheaters motorcycle gang members, among others. She worked hard and the shrewd Defteros offered her a job after she returned from a six-month scholarship in England in 2001. She was thrown into the deep end of criminal defence work, sink or swim. She swam, at least for a while.

For someone accused of naivety and being conned, Garde-Wilson has no illusions about some crooks. She is scathing about the Perth scene 'because it's run by Coffin Cheaters and bent police'. Once, after representing a wealthy gangster (not Kizon) she stepped into a courthouse lift with him and he leered and said, 'Do we rape you now?' Her face hardens at the memory. 'Who says *that* to a 22-year-old?'

The answer is: the sort of people who run gangs and strip joints, deal in drugs, guns and vice, and corrupt others and use violence to get their own way. The sort that the best criminal lawyers end up defending.

On the day the author interviewed Zarah Garde-Wilson, a middle-aged man in a new silver Mercedes sedan was parked in the street outside her office, waiting to see her. It was George Williams, father of Carl Williams, the western suburbs drug dealer who used to be, with Tony Mokbel, Garde-Wilson's biggest client until he was sentenced to 35 years for his part in planning a series of murders. She has been close to the Williams family. Too close, according to lawyers, police and many people in the media. One of the black marks against her is that after Caine was killed, she moved out of the city apartment, shattered, and went and stayed with the notorious Roberta Williams, outspoken estranged wife of Carl.

Why? 'Because I had nowhere else to go,' she says with a shrug. 'These people were the only ones who extended a friendly hand.' She seems to mean it. But did the crooks? Or were they just using her? Tough questions.

A senior Melbourne barrister who regularly appears in Perth met Garde-Wilson there in her first year with Pryles & Defteros. Later, he would be amazed at the transformation in her when she came to Melbourne after the firm was forced to close its Perth office in 2002.

'The change was unbelievable,' he recalls. 'In Perth she was slightly pudgy, outdoorsy, more casually dressed, but in Melbourne she'd lost a lot of weight and wore high heels — and those clothes.' Everybody knows what he means by the clothes: plunging necklines, skirts always tight and often short, a penchant for black.

The inference was she was hell-bent on impressing Caine and dressed in a way that appealed to men like him. She got what she wished for. Caine, being hell-bent on living fast and dying young, got his too.

The lawyer and her lover moved in together at a sharp building called Leicester House in Flinders Lane — a smart address, but they were renting a one-bedroom flat and 'sitting on milk crates', a neighbour recalls. 'It was no penthouse but it was a big step up from what he (Caine) was used to,' he adds, referring to Caine's previous lodging being a prison cell.

The neighbour would meet the odd couple in the lift — the well-spoken, private-school girl and the cocksure ex-crim who could not disguise the jailhouse swagger and edgy manner, somewhere between pimp and pugilist. Of Caine, he says, 'My wife was bringing her mum in with some shopping some day and he was all polite and helpful, asking if he could carry it up for them. But you wouldn't trust him. All these blokes are the same. I know the type — charming up to a point but they turn on you in a flash. You give them a big hello but keep walking.'

In early 2004 a private detective drinking at the Plough and Harrow Hotel in Carlton on the city's edge saw Caine with a notorious former prisoner and a known gunman. The detective sensed something about Caine and mentioned to friends later that he seemed 'a cocky young fella, up on his toes' and looking for trouble. If so, he soon found it.

On May 8, 2004, a Saturday night, Lewis Caine's bleeding body was found dumped in a Brunswick street — and was instantly labelled victim number 25 in the underworld war. Ten days later, armed police swooped on the gunman, known as The Journeyman, who was seen drinking with Caine at the hotel days before. It was a big arrest, and one that would have reverberations for a long time as the Purana Taskforce and prosecutors unravelled the tangled and treacherous web of criminal connections surrounding the 'war'.

The bloodsoaked end of Caine's relationship with his lady lawyer — and its bizarre postscript — pushed the then unknown

Garde-Wilson towards centre stage of the biggest show in town. Caine's murder (and the leaked sperm story) made a private peccadillo into a public 'scandal'. The social and professional gulf between the doomed lovers gave it a dramatic frisson that caught attention all over Australia.

With her piece of rough trade shot dead, Garde-Wilson was suddenly the Lady Chatterley of Little Bourke Street; the tragic love interest in a drama with real bullets, real blood and a test-tube of real semen. Her reaction to being thrust into the public eye caused problems that have dogged her ever since.

No-one could doubt her devotion to the dead killer. Having just set up her own firm, she added his name to make it 'Garde-Wilson & Caine' — a lapse of judgment and taste later quietly remedied, probably under pressure from the Law Society. The name on the frosted glass door was, by 2006, a more conventional 'Garde-Wilson Lawyers' but for the legal establishment the damage was done. And still is.

A detective who investigated Garde-Wilson's underworld connections says Caine's murder should have flagged the danger of mixing the personal and the professional, but it actually pushed her more offside.

She could have pulled back, 'maybe even gone interstate and started again,' he says. Instead, she shed any pretence of professional detachment by staying with Roberta Williams —a convicted drug offender, media junkie and, for a while, a key player in the gang war.

What was described in court later as effectively joining a criminal 'tribe' appalled other defence lawyers and dried up lingering sympathy among police and prosecutors. Her explanation is that she was friendless and had nowhere else to go — but it looked like cuddling up to drug-dealing killers. At best, it was professionally reckless and personally naïve.

'She's intelligent and a good solicitor but completely devoid of common sense,' says the detective. 'There's some sort of imbalance that makes her attracted to these people.'

To which a defiant Garde-Wilson adopts the missionary position: that she is entitled to befriend and defend people who society despises. 'Someone has to do it,' she says.

The funny thing is she probably means it. To understand why, you have to know where she came from.

PEOPLE around Armidale, NSW remember Greg and Judy Wilson's skinny little girl as polite and well-behaved but determined. If the young Zarah inherited a stubborn streak of altruism it should not surprise anyone. She descends from one of the most eminent but offbeat establishment families in Australia, distinguished by dedication to community service. She has respectable relatives all over Australia who must be bemused by their blood ties with Melbourne gangsters' pinup lawyer.

Zarah's great-grandmother, Dr Ellen Kent Hughes, the oldest of a tribe of children of a leading Melbourne surgeon, succeeded in a male-dominated profession in a man's world. She practised medicine under her maiden name almost until she died at the age of 86 in 1979. She was a local councillor for 30 years and received an MBE, at least partly for her fierce advocacy for the Aboriginal fringe dwellers around her adopted hometown of Armidale — a worthy cause, but not always a popular one among the less enlightened in the middle of last century.

The doctor's younger brother, Sir Wilfrid Selwyn Kent Hughes was one of the most remarkable Australians of his or any other generation; the sort of man who could conceivably have inspired a film like the British classic *Chariots of Fire*. He was an Olympic athlete, Rhodes Scholar, a hero in two world wars (a young lighthorseman in the first and a prisoner at Changi in the second), a successful author, Cabinet minister and driving force behind the Melbourne Olympics in 1956. Until his death, at a great age, he was a familiar figure at Melbourne's Anzac Day Parade, in which he rode an officer's charger in his light-horseman's uniform.

A sister, Gwenda, was a respected Anglican, committed communist and educational reformer who taught at one of Melbourne's oldest private schools and bequeathed scholarships to young Aboriginal students. It was that sort of family, of free spirits and strong minds.

Zarah's great-grandmother Dr Kent Hughes was no delicate Edwardian debutante. She published *Observations on Congenital Syphilis* in 1919, two years after graduating from Melbourne University. Like the great-granddaughter born just before her death, she fell in love with an older 'unsuitable' man at the age Zarah was when she met Lewis Caine.

Ellen Kent Hughes raised eyebrows by hurriedly marrying Paul Loubet, a French divorcee who died tragically just three months later. She gave birth, apparently to the Frenchman's son, moved to Queensland with the baby to work in a hospital in 1918 and two years later married Francis Garde Wesley Wilson, a returned soldier and auctioneer.

After moving to Armidale in 1928, the Wilsons started a local dynasty. The middle name 'Garde' was handed down each generation and the family stock and station business was called Garde Wilson for 65 years until it was sold in the early 1990s.

Zarah's grandfather Bill Wilson was a much-loved stock and station agent — his grazier clients included New England's famous Wright family, related to the poet, Judith Wright. One of Bill Wilson's long-time clients sums up the three generations pithily: 'Old Garde Wilson was pretty bloody tough, Bill was a gentleman and Greg had a few kicks and bucks.' Greg was the Wilson who would become Zarah's father. He stayed in the family stock and station business but took a punt in the 1980s by leasing extra land and running sheep on it. His wife Judy Kemp, known as a local beauty, was (and is) a good horsewoman. She rode in shows and Greg played polocrosse. They had two children: a boy and Zarah, who was named after a Malaysian aunt. Zarah, like her mother, rode well and won ribbons at local shows.

For a while, all went well. Greg and Judy Wilson bought land to grow more wool. Zarah moved from Martins Gully primary school to New England Girls School and her brother went to boarding school in Tamworth. But when drought hit in the early 1990s, they faced spending borrowed money to feed sheep worth less every week, gambling that rain would eventually save them. They lost.

Some debt-stricken farmers handled it the only way they knew how: they shot themselves. Greg Wilson didn't do that but he shot 2000 merino sheep in one day, which left a financial and emotional burden that affected the family a long time. For a start, it changed their life outwardly as well as inwardly. Zarah moved from the New England private school to O'Connell High School. Her uncle, Greg Kemp, thinks the experience must have left its mark on both children. Of Zarah, he says, 'She was quiet, but I think it (the drought losses) motivated her to succeed and make a bit of money.'

One night, probably in late 1993, Zarah's brother argued with his father, got drunk, took a vintage army pistol from the farm's gun safe and drove off in a rage. About 1.30am, he pulled into the BP roadhouse at Uralla, about twenty kilometres from Armidale, and filled the car. He then produced the pistol, ordered the attendant into the car and drove west. It might have been a cry for help but it promised to end badly.

By the time the alarm was raised at 5am the roadhouse owner, Reg Buckley, thought he would not see his employee alive again. But, around dawn, the now sober teenager realised the gravity of what he'd done. He apologised to the attendant and let him out at Boggabri, shaken but unhurt, and turned himself in to police soon after. Meanwhile, a distraught Greg Wilson had turned up at the service station, looking for his son and dreading the worst.

'Greg was a real gentleman,' recalls Buckley. 'He apologised and he handled himself better than anyone else about it,' in contrast with some other citizens in Armidale who later pressured him to 'call off' the police investigation, he says.

Buckley, relieved at the outcome, did not attend the subsequent court case and isn't sure if young Wilson ever served time for the hijacking. Wilson later worked as a jackaroo and is now married with children and working in a government job in outback Queensland. But, back then, the incident capped off a bad couple of years for his parents. They sold out and moved over the border to Murgon to start a bed and breakfast business.

In 1994 Zarah went to boarding school in Toowoomba, where she was enrolled under the full family name of Garde Wilson, with a hyphen thrown in. Perhaps that was the first sign that she was inventing herself a new persona who would become a successful lawyer.

WHEN Fairholme College's class of 1995 had its reunion a decade later Zarah Garde-Wilson wasn't there but a ripple of third-hand gossip about 'the underworld' went around. Few 'old girls' could recall much about her but they had heard about the dramatic events in Melbourne and that one of their own was somehow involved.

In her two years at Fairholme College, the quiet girl from Armidale had made little impression. She was neither a star student nor raving beauty. In the 1995 yearbook, her name is misspelt twice, perhaps a sign of her fringe status.

She arrived in year 11, when friendships had already formed and weren't easily gatecrashed. She played 'fair' A-grade hockey alongside a future state player, Renae Van Schagen, who recalls her as 'an independent person who got on with everyone — but I wouldn't say she had a best friend'.

One Fairholme girl, Angela Keogh, knew Zarah because they were both from Armidale and had shown horses together. Angela's mother Robyn recalls her as 'slim, well-proportioned, very controlled and a bit different. And very competitive — she rode to win,' she adds, with a faint trace of disapproval.

Zarah, though not 'daggy', was well-behaved and studious. There were rebels among the provincial private schoolgirls but Zarah wasn't one of them, surprisingly. She was never the one caught smoking, sneaking out of bounds or even wearing her uniform too short. Robyn Keogh sometimes wished her own daughters were less 'adventurous' and more like the more studious Zarah.

Things change, and so do people. A decade after leaving school, Angela Keogh was working in Melbourne but when her mother asked her if she had caught up with Zarah, she said she hadn't. Angela knew they now moved in different circles.

Zarah was in the fast lane with some of the biggest speed merchants around. One was Carl Williams, the man who was at the heart of the underworld war and who will be in jail for decades. The other was Tony Mokbel, the multi-millionaire drug baron and punter who skipped bail in March 2006 to avoid facing fresh charges, and was recaptured in Greece a little more than a year later in possession of an illegal wig.

After Caine's death, Garde-Wilson could pass for a star-crossed lover who had made a mistake but the Mokbel connection exposed by police surveillance shredded her reputation. Deliberately, some would say.

When she appeared in court on the contempt charges in November 2005, a police investigator testified that she had indulged in an 'on-again, off-again' sexual relationship with Mokbel — who already had a wife, a mistress and a penchant for prostitutes, as well as a lot of racehorses he raced in other people's names, and a lot of relatives and friends who seemed ready to 'mind' money and property for him. Police sources said Zarah had been seen in a Queensland casino with Mokbel, and used houses and cars that he and his associates owned.

Besides suffering this humiliating publicity about what she describes as irrelevant and deliberately damaging material on her private life, she was refused witness protection and found guilty of contempt. Asked why she wouldn't testify against two gunmen over her boyfriend's murder, she wept in the witness box and said she didn't want 'my head blown off'. Apart from being convicted — in itself a serious matter for a lawyer — no penalty was imposed.

At the time her barrister told the court she was suicidal and that the prospect of losing her certificate to practise law could destroy her. Two years on, she was trying to stare down notoriety and an uncertain future in the face of moves by lawyers' professional bodies to have her practising certificate revoked.

Talking with her, it's tempting to look for the note of regret, an intention of a new start, but she won't bite. She is controlled, but traces of bitterness and bravado colour off-the-record answers to questions about the path she has taken and the way she has been treated.

Ask other lawyers about her and responses range from harsh criticism about 'provocative clothes' and 'obvious conflicts' to grudging sympathy. But two common threads run through the responses, at least from male barristers: that she is naïve and has lacked a mentor to guide her through the hazards of dealing with wealthy, violent and manipulative criminals.

One of Melbourne's wiliest criminal lawyers, who was taught his craft by the legendary Frank Galbally, says Garde-Wilson 'has ability' but is trapped because she won't seek advice and has burned bridges with potential mentors. He is more generous than many of his peers. 'I feel sorry for her. We are a conservative, judgmental profession, too quick to bag people. Her response is to stand back and shrug it off.

'She doesn't speak to people around the traps. We all learn at the expense of our clients but some of us forget that. But the fact is she hasn't distanced herself from criminals sufficiently. And her mode of dress is a cry for acceptance. I think she's got guts, but it is misplaced. She has capacity, works hard and fights for her clients.'

But he warns that those who 'cross the line' and flout ethical rules don't last. 'If you lose the respect of the bench, the future is bleak.' Because once the courts lose trust in a lawyer, clients soon catch on, too. The bigger the crook, the better the lawyer they need. 'You're not better than them but you have to remain objective, and a good crook understands that. Good crooks will drink with shady solicitors but they won't use them when it matters,' he says, sharing a conclusion he has drawn after 30 years dealing with criminals.

Several senior counsel wrote references for Garde-Wilson's court appearance in 2005. These stressed her youth and inexperience, praised her diligence and skill at preparing briefs. But within a year none of the referees was keen to talk about her. One says there is 'room for criticism'. Another says 'the kindest thing I can do is make no comment', then makes several pithy comments. 'Do not glorify her,' he says.

So much for the prosecution. Margaret Cunneen, NSW Deputy Chief Crown Prosecutor, switches hats to run a defence of female lawyers in general, that she feels might apply to Garde-Wilson too: 'Women have something against them that men don't ... all the other women. It's doubly hard for women if they don't toe the line completely. If they don't they are slapped down.'

'Slapped down' is how Leigh Johnson feels about the way she has been treated in Sydney courts. Johnson's chequered legal career and personal style foreshadowed Garde-Wilson's by a couple of decades. Leggy, blonde and known in her prime for small skirts and big statements, she was often accused of getting 'too close' to notorious criminal clients, among them one of the Anita Cobby murderers.

Johnson, once memorably described by colourful barrister Charles Waterstreet as suffering the 'tall, blonde poppy syndrome', leaps to the defence that Garde-Wilson feels she cannot publicly make for herself: 'Women are taught to fall in love. She did and she chose the wrong guy — but who doesn't? Most people who get married, for a start.

'The law is male dominated. Until recently women who succeeded in it dressed in nondescript, sexless clothes and emulated men. A real woman with a good pair of legs is seen as somehow suspect. Attractive women are attacked and judged — and other women are the worst oppressors. It's been horrendous. People spread rumours all the time. I don't want to repeat them because that will only encourage it. I have threatened to sue over the things people say.

'I know of male lawyers who have had relationships with female clients in prison, and it never causes a ripple. But if a female lawyer smiles at a client then she's bonking the whole jail ... It's almost a tribal mentality in the legal profession: 'how dare that tribe touch our white women' sort of thing. The whole Zarah thing is salacious. The fact is she was in fear of her life if she gave evidence. She looked around and everyone's being killed so she did not want to. Everything else is her own business.'

Proving the point that other women can be the toughest critics, a well-known practitioner who has seen Garde-Wilson at work has little sympathy. 'She is so not a naïve, poor taken-advantage-of newcomer. It is hard to practise criminal law as a female but you have to be sensible. Would I travel interstate and stay with someone like (Mokbel) while under surveillance? You are inviting a nightmare into your life. It is partly arrogance, like some of the crooks. They splash it in your face and have a catch-me-if-you can attitude. You can't drive around in flashy cars without having jobs and not expect some backlash from the authorities.' And any lawyer who takes the same attitude can expect trouble, too.

'A magistrate tried to talk some sense into her but ... she's a very difficult person to get to know, shy and aloof — unless you are a crim, apparently.' She then quotes a well-known criminal lawyer, Alex Lewenberg, who advises young lawyers: 'Your duty to your client ends at the court steps.' Another way of saying: don't get too close because criminals are often narcissistic men with adolescent impulses who get crushes on their female lawyers.

'I liken it to being twelve years old on the tram,' laughs the lawyer. 'Blokes in custody develop crushes on you. It goes with the dependency on you while they're inside. It can be passionate but it sure ain't love. Maybe Zarah is attracted to that. And the TV cameras chasing you down the street can be fun the first time but why would you want it after that?'

An ABC reporter, Josie Taylor, had a ringside seat during court hearings on the gangland war and takes a gentler view. Originally from rural NSW, Taylor is of similar age and background to Garde-Wilson and built a natural and genuine rapport with her. During the contempt of court hearing in 2005, she persuaded her to do an exclusive television studio interview.

It was a big test for both. Taylor, then still relatively inexperienced, prepared thoroughly and asked a series of insightful questions, and Garde-Wilson did her best to answer them. Afterwards, Taylor was wondering how the lawyer would react to the robust professional encounter. Oddly enough, she recalls, Garde-Wilson's only real concern was whether the studio lighting had flattered Taylor more than her. Appearances do matter, but in ways other than make-up, clothes and lighting. There are many tough judges in the law, not all of them in robes and wigs, and it's not necessarily the clients you have but the company you keep that influence the judgment they make.

At the time of writing, Garde-Wilson is still fighting what could be a losing battle for her right to practise law. She is under attack by a conservative profession and an outraged police force that agree that she crossed the line — not only of prudence, but of the law itself.

In June 2007, the Supreme Court dismissed her application for a judicial review of the Legal Service Board's original decision to withdraw her licence to practise. But she was still able to practise pending the outcome of proceedings before the Victorian Civil Administrative Tribunal. Three months earlier, in March, she had been committed to stand trial for giving false evidence to the Australian Crime Commission (in 2004) and for possessing an unregistered Mauser .25 calibre pistol 'lent' to her boyfriend Lewis Caine by a crooked gun dealer. The dealer, who became a police informer after being caught with a cache of illegal weapons bought from a South Australian pornography king for the ill-fated Mario Condello, took part in a police operation to trap Garde-Wilson, who had asked him to take away the handgun Caine had left behind when he was killed.

Most insiders would say she has only herself to blame for her troubles but, for the general public, the jury is still out on the solicitor who plays with snakes. The defence sees a vulnerable, shy and lonely girl marooned behind a brittle facade, too proud to ask for help; the prosecution damns her as a calculating, streetwise chancer with a perverse streak, riding for a fall.

The truth, rarely clear in legal matters, is probably somewhere in between. But it's clear she has toned down her act to suit new circumstances in which the high-flying gangsters in her professional and personal life are either dead, in jail or broke. Maybe there's a message in there for Zarah Garde-Wilson. 'Every time I see her picture in the paper lately,' notes one observer drily, 'she's wearing more clothes.'

In court, that might be true. But the system has not quite beaten the maverick instincts out of the girl from Armidale. In late 2007 she astonished the editors of the *GQ* glossy men's magazine by offering herself for a provocative picture spread at no charge. Her outfit included a Jersey dress valued at $4355, Mary-Jane shoes valued at $1125 and Voodoo fishnet stockings that were priceless. Happily, the lighting was excellent.

Postscript

While her own fate was still in the balance, Garde-Wilson was still practising at the time of writing. On November 23, 2007, she appeared in Melbourne Magistrates Court for two brothers charged by the Purana Taskforce for trafficking methamphetamines, possessing $67,000 cash — and an illegal handgun. Carl and George Williams are locked up, Tony Mokbel is facing charges and most of her other clients are behind bars or dead. But the drugs, guns and money go on.

26

ENDPLAY

'You are a killer,
and a cowardly one who
employed others to do
the actual killing.'

CARL Williams spent years successfully avoiding an assassin's bullet only to commit legal suicide while giving evidence in the days leading to his final sentencing in the Supreme Court.

Stubborn to the end, the baby-faced killer turned his back on a sweet legal deal by ignoring his lawyer's advice to shut up and at least pretend to be sorry for launching a bloody vendetta that cost more than a dozen lives.

Williams was found guilty by a jury of the murder of Michael Marshall in October 2003. When he finally realised that the prosecution case was overwhelming, he pleaded guilty to the murders of Jason Moran (June 2003), Mark Mallia (August 2003) and Lewis Moran (March 2004). He also pleaded guilty to the 2004 conspiracy to murder Mario Condello.

In agreeing to plead guilty, Williams cut a deal that literally meant he got away with murder — many times.

He also killed or was connected to those who killed Mark Moran (June 2000), 'Mad Richard' Mladenich (May 2000), Willie Thompson (July 2003), Nik Radev (April 2003) and Victor Peirce (May 2002). He was directly responsible for the death of Pasquale Barbaro, who was shot dead by one of Williams' hit men while murdering Jason Moran.

Williams is also suspected of ordering the murder of Graham Kinniburgh, who was shot dead outside his Kew home in December 2003, and has been linked to several more gangland killings.

Paranoid, frightened and self-deluded, he survived and prospered by surrounding himself with a gang of soldiers whose loyalty he won with a combination of drugs, money, power and women.

But once he was in jail, his trusted subordinates began to waver. One by one they broke the code of silence and became prosecution witnesses. Key members of the Williams camp crossed the floor leaving the man who called himself 'The Premier' without the numbers to survive.

So why then did the prosecution accept a plea and do a deal with the multiple killer? Why didn't they convict him again and again for the murders he committed?

Because it would have taken up to ten years and cost millions of dollars.

It would also have given Williams the public platform and the media attention he craved. By locking him away they condemned him — as he declared himself — to a life of 'Groundhog Days'. As it turns out — 12,783 of them.

Williams first made noises that he might be prepared to do a deal as early as November 2006. He implied he had information that could help crack the murders of police informer Terence Hodson and his wife Christine, shot dead in their Kew home in May 2004.

Detectives believed rogue police were responsible for the double murder so if Williams could provide information he would have been able to demand a big discount on his sentence.

But he was teasing. Williams did end up making a statement that seemed to implicate a former detective, but later he deliberately destroyed his own credibility so he could never be called as a prosecution witness.

During the long pre-trial process before Williams was due to face the court for murdering Jason Moran and Pasquale Barbaro, his lawyers asked Justice King: If he pleaded guilty, would the sentence be 'crushing'?

While no promises were made, they were told Williams could expect to see some light at the end of the tunnel.

Justice King is no bleeding heart. She is a common sense judge who made her ruling on the basis of hard legal precedent. The former hard-hitting prosecutor and senior member of the National Crime Authority was well aware of the case law surrounding guilty pleas.

Some examples. Paul Charles Denyer is a serial killer who stalked and murdered three women in Frankston in 1993. He pleaded guilty and was sentenced to life with no minimum by Supreme Court Justice Frank Vincent, but on appeal he was given a minimum of 30 years on the grounds he should receive a discount for his guilty plea — no matter how reprehensible his crimes.

Leslie Alfred Camilleri, who killed two Bega schoolgirls in 1997, pleaded not guilty and was given life with no minimum. His partner, Lindsay Hoani Beckett, pleaded guilty and received a minimum of 35 years.

Justice King knew that if Williams pleaded she would be required to set a minimum sentence. The maximum of life was never in doubt.

Williams said he wanted a sentence that would give him some chance of getting out by the age of 70. Purana Taskforce police said they would push for a lighter sentence if he was prepared to become a witness in subsequent trials.

They wanted him to turn on his former role model, multi-millionaire drug boss Tony Mokbel, who fled Australia in March 2006 only to be recaptured in Greece in June the following year.

Mokbel allegedly paid Williams to organise the murder of Michael Marshall and police claimed he was also linked to the murder of Lewis Moran. They wanted Williams to become a star prosecution witness.

While Williams may be many things, he remains an old-school crook who believes in the code of silence. And while many of Williams' old pals turned on him, he remained determined to stay staunch.

After he decided to plead guilty he pretended to co-operate, but anything he said was carefully crafted to lack real evidentiary value. He made sure no-one would do jail time on the basis of what he said.

So, without a promise to become a Crown witness, Williams' negotiating position was weakened. The final deal struck was that prosecutors would not demand a crushing sentence and would not oppose a move for Williams' father, George, to receive a suspended sentence for pending drug charges.

In effect, sentencing was to be left to Justice King without the prosecution lobbying for the longest jail term possible.

When Williams finally agreed to the deal on 28 February 2007 — just days before the jury was to be selected — the prison van taking him back to jail was called back so the papers could be signed and the plea formally entered before he changed his mind again.

In the minutes before the court was convened, his mother, Barbara, urged him to abandon the deal and take his chances before a jury. He would have been stupid to listen. With the open and shut case against him, it was virtually certain he would have been convicted and given life with no minimum. George, whose own legal fate rested on his son's decision to plead, remained silent.

Once he pleaded, the rest should have been easy. He was to attend court for a public showing of *mea culpa*. He was to sit behind glass with a sad face and moo-cow eyes while his lawyers said how sorry he was. They would say he thought the Moran family was out to kill him; that he would leave jail as an old man and would miss seeing his daughter Dhakota grow into an adult; and that he should receive a hefty discount because of his remorse.

But, against legal advice, Williams insisted on giving evidence. The move was so stupid that his own legal team made him sign a waiver that he was doing it against their expert advice.

For just about an hour he gave ridiculous testimony contradicting known facts. He denied ever being paid money for the Marshall hit by Mokbel and tried to discredit Crown witnesses who were to give evidence against some of his mates.

Perhaps Williams' attempt to protect Mokbel was motivated by more than mateship. The runaway drug boss had been paying his daughter's private school fees after Williams was locked up. He also knew that when Mokbel was caught, the convicted drug dealer would still be a major influence in the prison system. Carl knew Mokbel could be a good friend and a bad enemy.

Williams' testimony could not remain unchallenged. In the 90-minute cross-examination, prosecutor Geoff Horgan, SC, filleted him to protect the integrity of future Crown cases. Certainly, Justice King questioned whether Williams was showing any remorse for his actions.

Williams left the court smiling. His lawyers weren't. But the self-confessed killer was fully aware that his two hours in the sun would probably cost him another two years in a dark cell. He told friends later he was 'proud' of his performance.

He wanted his fellow prisoners to know he didn't dob anyone in to save himself.

Williams is not stupid. A psychiatric report declares him of 'high average intelligence'. He is not mentally ill. The report declares him to be broadly normal. He was educated to Year 11 at Broadmeadows West Technical School and had a series of short term labouring jobs before being employed as a supermarket packer. He acquired a minor criminal record but soon aimed higher — by 1994 he had embarked on a career as a full-time drug dealer. By the time he married Roberta in January 2001 he had dreams of dominating the underworld.

He plotted revenge against the Morans and then felt he had to keep killing anyone connected with them to remain alive. It was always going to end with him dead or in jail for most of his life.

So where to for Williams, who at 36 can only hope he lives long enough to be released as an old man?

After the brief excitement of the sentencing, he returned to the maximum security Acacia Unit in Barwon Prison where he socialises with a few loyal henchmen.

The minimum sentence will help prison officers control him. If he behaves badly in jail his eventual parole would be threatened, leaving him facing life in jail. Prison officers say indefinite sentences destroy inmates because the dream of release is taken from them.

Eventually, when threats die down, Williams will be transferred to the mainstream and, if he behaves, he will eventually move to a more comfortable jail.

But he will always be a name. As he gets older and physically weaker he will become a target. Even the toughest long-term inmates end up at risk of being bashed or stabbed.

Some time in the future, a violent young offender might attack him just for the bragging rights.

As the years pass, he will become institutionalised. His wife Roberta will have moved on (several times), his parents will have passed away, his daughter grown up and the glamorous blonde Renata Laureano, who pops in to jail to visit him, will have found a life.

Carl Williams may have got away with murder but there is one thing no one can beat — time. It eventually wounds all heels.

The final curtain

DURING underworld murder hearings in Melbourne's Supreme Court, we saw many sides of the no-nonsense Justice Betty King. We saw compassionate Betty, scholarly Betty and stern Betty. But for underworld killer Carl Williams when he was finally sentenced on 7 May 2007 it was definitely a case of Ugly Betty.

Justice King cuts a far more elegant figure than most on the bench but by the time it came to handing down a sentence, she had clearly had enough of Williams, who sat behind bulletproof glass looking by turn relaxed and bored as he listened to the reasons why he could not be released from jail until he was a pensioner.

Williams still hoped for a minimum sentence of around 33 years in exchange for his guilty plea, so he would be released before his 70th birthday.

He was being optimistic. His evidence during his plea hearing was so clearly bogus that any chance of that discount collapsed.

Purana Taskforce police believe Justice King had no choice but to revise her sentence upwards by at least two years after he showed no signs of remorse.

At law, a guilty plea is rewarded with a discounted sentence, and that discount can be increased if the accused shows sincere regret.

When addressing Williams as she sentenced him to life with a minimum non-parole period of 35 years, Justice King said: 'I find that the evidence that you gave in the main was unbelievable, even incredible at times ... I find that the manner in which you gave evidence was arrogant, almost supercilious and you left me with a strong impression that your view of these murders was that they were all really justifiable and you were the real victim.

'You are a killer, and a cowardly one, who employed others to do the actual killing ... you should not be the subject of admiration by any member of our community.

'You were indeed the puppet master, deciding and controlling whether people lived or died.'

Minutes before the court convened, Williams showed no sign that he understood he was about to lose the best remaining years of his life. He laughed and chatted with his mother, Barbara, who sat in the back row with Williams' father, George, and Carl's new blonde friend, Renata Laureano. It was as if Barbara Williams was farewelling her son on a ten-day Mediterranean cruise rather than three decades down the river. She will never see him as a free man again.

A photographer was given access to take a picture of Williams behind the glass. He smiled as if he had just won the blue ribbon for growing the biggest pumpkin at the Show.

As he sat, flanked by seven big security guards, the woman whose family he had destroyed stared at him. Williams was pleading guilty to killing Judy Moran's son, Jason, and husband, Lewis. He had faced a charge of killing her other son, Mark, but it was dropped in exchange for his guilty plea.

The Moran matriarch stood and glared from the front row at Williams for four minutes before Purana detective Senior Sergeant Stuart Bateson persuaded her to sit down: 'Don't fire them up,' he gently advised.

She then sat and chatted with Purana detectives, who had spent years investigating her sons and husband.

Most Purana investigators in court wore their squad tie, which carries a small Hindu motif. It was a reminder of the ancient Indian proverb from the words of a Purana: 'For the salvation of the good, the destruction of the evil-doers, and for firmly establishing righteousness, I manifest myself from age to age.'

Judy Moran was dressed head to toe in black — complete with an extraordinary cowboy hat and Darth Vader style wraparound sunglasses she wisely removed inside the court. But despite her apparent fashion hints, lynchings have gone out of style.

Judy Moran and Roberta Williams had their routine pre-court spat where they sniped at each other on issues of etiquette, dead relatives and fashion tastes. On this day Mrs Williams contrasted Mrs Moran's black look with a white beanie, as she had recently shaved her head.

Their robust discussions were limited to the court foyer, as Mrs Williams was banned from the court after previous outbursts.

She waited outside for the final sentence.

Mrs Moran said repeatedly the death penalty should be returned and Williams executed. She was not such a strong advocate of capital punishment when her Jason had been accused of the murder of Alphonse Gangitano a few years earlier.

Three former heads of Purana — Inspector Phil Swindells, Superintendent Andy Allen and Inspector Gavan Ryan — were there to see the legal last rites delivered on team Williams.

A film producer and screenwriter slipped in, as did members of the public. One was quickly reminded that sunglasses perched on top of her head may be acceptable at the races but not in the Supreme Court.

Williams wanted the big finish. He planned to read a prepared statement he had in his blue folder. When he asked if he could address the court, Justice King firmly said 'No'.

'I expected nothing less of you,' Williams told her. 'You are not a judge. You are only a puppet of the police.'

Williams was taken from the court — his statement unread. He was already yesterday's man. His departing words — 'Aah, get fucked' — were hardly a match for Ned Kelly's exit line, 'Such is life'.

It is unlikely even immature footballers would tattoo Carl's words on their tummies. But you never know.

Superintendent Allen later spoke outside the court praising his team; pointedly reminding critics who had declared police would never smash the code of silence that they were wrong.

The Purana team and the prosecutors went for the traditional celebration meal that had seemed so unlikely in the dark days of the underworld war.

Justice King, out of her wig and gown and back in civilian clothes, wandered off for lunch. Her work was done and done well. Now she was just Hungry Betty.

The judgement

Excerpts from Justice Betty King's sentencing remarks, 7 May 2007.

Carl Williams, you have pleaded guilty to three counts of murder and one count of conspiracy to murder. The maximum penalty for each of those offences is life imprisonment.

These offences occurred during an extraordinary time in the history of this city, in that there was an almost unprecedented level of very public murders of known or suspected criminals. This was ultimately referred to in the media as the 'gangland war'. The perception of these offences was that there was a distinct war being carried on between rival gangs, firstly, over control of the illegal drug trade, and also on what could be described as a 'tit for tat' basis, as reputed members of various gangs were executed in their homes or on the streets of Melbourne. The first of these recognised murders was that of Alphonse Gangitano in January 1998 and they continued on relentlessly with up to 29 persons murdered, although it is apparent that in respect of some of those murders there may have been motives other than gangland warfare.

On 13 October 1999 you were shot in the stomach by Jason Moran in a park in Gladstone Park. Mark Moran was present at the time that this occurred, and even upon your own evidence, one of the consequences of this occurring was a high degree of animosity between the Morans and yourself. It is also clear that you and Jason and Mark Moran were competitors in the selling of illegal drugs, which would have done nothing to decrease the animosity that you bore towards each other. I accept that you had a degree of apprehension in respect of the Moran brothers also, which once again is not surprising having been shot by them at close range, and undoubtedly with a warning of some description. I am unable to say whether that shooting and possible warning related to the drug trafficking business in which you were both competitors, or whether it was a more personal basis. It is unnecessary for me to determine that matter.

You went to hospital and were interviewed by the police as to your knowledge of the person or persons who were responsible for the shooting and you refused to provide any information to the investigating officers. You maintain that was because the Morans had told you that they had a police officer in their pocket, and you did not believe it would be investigated properly. I do not accept that was your reason for refusing to cooperate with police investigators, but rather your reasons related to the supposed code of silence of the criminal milieu in which you lived.

On 10 November 2000, shotgun damage was observed on the front door of your Hillside home and on a Mercedes Benz parked in the driveway. The prosecutor opened that you believed that the Morans were responsible for such shooting and it is apparent from your evidence that you did blame the Morans for that shooting.

There is no doubt, on the basis of your own evidence, that you were actively looking for Jason Moran so that he could be murdered, you equally did not dispute the role of your advisor in the Jason Moran murder by providing you with information to help locate Jason Moran and assisting you to plan the killing. In the ensuing months various plans were formulated by you and those you had recruited to assist you in the murder.

The driver in the Jason Moran murder and the shooter in the Jason Moran murder were ultimately recruited by you to carry out the murder together.

I heard you give evidence in chief and be cross- examined over a period of some hours. I find that the evidence that you gave, in the main was unbelievable, even incredible at times. It was, in my view, designed to ensure that it would provide no evidence against any person other than those who are already dead, convicted or have pleaded guilty to various offences. You denied any involvement or knowledge of involvement of Mokbel in the murder of Lewis Moran or Michael Marshall.

Not only do I consider you a most unsatisfactory witness, virtually incapable of telling the truth, except for some minor and largely irrelevant portions of your evidence, I find that the manner in which you gave evidence was arrogant, almost supercilious, and you left with me with a strong impression that your view of all of these murders was that they were all really justifiable and you were the real victim, having been 'forced' to admit at least some of your involvement, by the statements of other members of your group who had cooperated with police.

You do not get to be Judge, Jury and Executioner. These were not vigilante killings, they were matters of expediency to you, these people were either in your way as competitors, or persons that you believed may be vengeful towards you because of other activities you had undertaken, or because of some animosity that you bore towards them. Your reasons for killing were not justifiable; you acted as though it was your right to have these people killed. That theme constantly came through in the evidence you gave before me.

In terms of the chain of command I find that you were at the top of the chain of command of that gang, and that is entirely consistent with you giving the orders for these people to be killed, whilst not taking an active part in the physical execution of these people. As the counsellor and procurer you were indeed the puppet master deciding and controlling whether people lived or died.

I sentenced you on 19 July 2006, for the murder of Michael Marshall, after a plea of not guilty and conviction by a jury, to a period of 26 years imprisonment; one year of the sentence you were then serving was made cumulative. Making a total effective sentence of 27 years, with a non-parole period of 21 years.

Your crimes occurred as I said during a time of what has been referred to as the "gangland" or "underworld" killings. All of those murders, whether charged or uncharged, carry similar hallmarks to these murders. They are invariably executions; a firearm is usually used; they are often in public places such as streets, hotels or places where ordinary citizens would be going about their normal business. Those murders invariably have significant connections with crime or gang-related activity and whilst no ordinary member of the public has been killed or harmed during these killings, those killings have clearly engendered a level of fear within our community as to potential harm of innocent persons, and equally, a concern relating to the degree of lawlessness into which Victoria, as a community, has been plunged. You were responsible to a very large degree for that fear.

There has been intense media coverage of these murders in Melbourne, and whilst you were considered a suspect by many, including the police, the evidence of your involvement was not able to be found, due to the fact that you distanced yourself from these crimes by using others to do the killings and arranging alibis. It was not until the criminal code of silence was broken that those who knew about your involvement began to talk to the police. The sentences imposed on those persons reflect the significant discounts that were given to them for the risks they took by making statements about your involvement. Whilst you were a suspect and being referred to in the media it was apparent that you were enjoying the game of 'being famous'. You gave interviews outside court, and appeared prepared to give your views of a variety of matters, and unfortunately the media to a degree pandered to that.

I have a concern that some younger members of the community who are involved in petty crime may be looking to you as some sort of hero. You are not, you are a killer, and a cowardly one who employed others to do the actual killing, whilst you hid behind carefully constructed alibis. You should not be the subject of admiration by any member of our community. You have robbed families of people they love, of sons, brothers and fathers.

I just want to make it clear to all who may look at this sentence that you are not someone to be admired in any way.

I have taken into account the suffering that the families of these victims have endured, as well as the suffering of other innocent people such as Ms Sugars and the owners of the Brunswick Club, also the parents and children attending Auskick, but acknowledge that whatever sentence is imposed, they will probably feel aggrieved as nothing will return their loved ones and no sentence imposed will ever feel sufficient to them.

Your prior convictions are limited in nature and do not relate to any matters of violence. You were convicted in May of 1990 of handling stolen goods, failing to answer bail and possession of stolen property and you were fined a total of $400. In March of 1993 again, at the Magistrates' Court, a charge of criminal damage and throwing a missile for which you were placed on a non-conviction community-based order with conditions of 150 hours of community work, which you breached, but no further action was taken as the order had expired. Finally, in the County Court in December of 1994, attempting to traffic in a drug of dependence, being amphetamine, for which you were ultimately sentenced by the Court of Appeal to twelve months imprisonment with six months suspended for a period of two years. I place no reliance upon the earlier two matters and I place limited reliance upon the latter matter only as indicating that at that stage an involvement in the criminal milieu in which this offence occurred.

Your now ex-wife has three children from previous relationships, a son, aged around 18, and two daughters, approximately 13 and 14. Together with your ex-wife, you have a daughter, called Dhakota, who is aged approximately six, having been born on 10 March, 2001.

Your parents are separated. Your mother has never been in trouble with the law and your father has no convictions. Your father has had significant health problems, particularly in the last few years.

You were educated to Year 11 at Broadmeadows West Technical School and thereafter it was reported that you had a number of short-term labouring jobs. You had a series of labouring jobs, followed by opening a children's wear shop with your wife, which became non-profitable and closed ... You then were working as a semi-professional gambler from that period until being banned from the casino.

You were working as a drug trafficker up to and including the time of the murders.

The circumstances in which you have been held and will in all likelihood continue to be held for a substantial period are of relevance in mitigation of your sentence. You are currently held in the Acacia high security unit at Barwon Prison, which is the maximum security unit of the state penal system. The conditions at Acacia are quite different to those from mainstream prisoners. The visits from family are severely restricted, particularly in terms of contact visits, access out of cells during the day, mixing with other prisoners, and access to phone calls all are severely restricted. This is not what the average sentenced prisoner has to endure by way of conditions of serving a sentence. It is how you have been held, both as a person on remand and as a sentenced prisoner. It is equally evident that this will be the manner of your incarceration for some substantial time.

There are many reasons why persons are in that unit, and in your case, a major part of it is ensuring your safety. You have been in a gang war with other criminals and the issue of revenge being taken by those other persons is not far-fetched. Equally there are many within the prison system that may have a desire to make a name for themselves by causing you harm. Equally those persons who have elected to give evidence against you must be protected from you.

You have also made a statement to the police, which I have had the opportunity to read. You offered to give evidence in respect of that statement but the prosecutor has informed the Court that since you have given evidence in the manner that you have in this case, they would not consider calling you, as they do not consider you a witness of truth. That concurs with my own observations of your evidence. Accordingly, whilst there is some benefit to you by the provision of the statement, it is of little significance when compared to your criminality.

... You have uttered words of remorse in response to questions asked of you by your counsel but I find that you have no real or genuine remorse for the victims of your crimes, only remorse that you have been caught and lost your liberty.

However, I do intend to impose a minimum term, but that is on the basis of one significant factor only, which are your pleas of guilty to these offences. Whilst I find that you do not have any genuine remorse for the crimes, I am still obliged to take into account in your favour that you have entered pleas of guilty. It is pragmatic and utilitarian to give you a discount for entering those pleas, for by doing so you have prevented this Court from spending anywhere between five to ten years hearing your trials and the appeals from those trials. Equally you have released the police officers involved in this taskforce to move on to other pressing cases that need investigating, and enabled those in the Office of Public Prosecutions to pursue other prosecutions. The amount of money that has been saved as a result is considerable. That behaviour must be encouraged. It must be made clear to all charged with offences, of whatever type, that if they do enter a plea of guilty to the offences that they will receive a real and significant discount. Without your pleas of guilty I would not have imposed a minimum term for these offences, even allowing for the other mitigating material upon which your counsel relied.

Accordingly, I sentence you as follows: on

Count One, the murder of Jason Moran, you are convicted and sentenced to be imprisoned for life.

Count Two, the murder of Mark Mallia, you are convicted and sentenced to be imprisoned for life.

Count 3, the murder of Lewis Moran, you are convicted and sentenced to be imprisoned for 25 years.

Count Four, the conspiracy to murder Mario Condello, you are convicted and sentenced to be imprisoned for 25 years.

I further direct that you serve a minimum term of 35 years

imprisonment before becoming eligible for parole. The sentence will commence from this day.

I have already taken into account the fact that you have been in custody since 2004 when determining the appropriate minimum and the sentence and I intend that the new minimum term that I have imposed commences from today. To make it absolutely clear: what I intend is that you are to serve 35 years imprisonment from today before you could be considered eligible for parole.

27

THE SUMMING UP

```
Policing is not sausage
making. Success or failure
can't be judged by what comes
out the end of the machine.
```

SO what happened?

For twelve years, gangsters played out a Hollywood movie in Melbourne streets, but with real bullets and real blood.

As with the perfect storm or a hundred-year flood, conditions had to be perfect for disaster to happen. In hindsight, it is clear there was not one reason but many.

The first is history. The Melbourne underworld is notorious for using bullets and blades to settle its differences. Gangsters have been shot on the docks and in court buildings, dumped in the bay, stabbed in prison or have simply 'gone on the missing list.' Wars have started over something as simple as the price of tomatoes (the Market Murders, 1963-64); a share of money (Great Bookie Robbery, 1976) or a dispute over sausages (Pentridge Prison Overcoat Gang, 1970s).

The second reason for the war is police apathy. From the 1980s, Victoria Police came under pressure to spend taxpayers' money efficiently. 'Key performance indicators' were imposed, setting artificial goals such as set numbers of random breath tests or patrol hours. Police were expected to cut crime rates and lift solution rates while boosting training and fixing the gender imbalance.

Achieving such goals came at the expense of gathering crime intelligence. Policing is not sausage making. Success or failure can't be judged by what comes out the end of the machine. Investigation of organised crime requires identifying the next big thing. If police can identify new players before they become entrenched, it solves tomorrow's problems today – but that requires a large, flexible, committed and expensive intelligence section.

Former Chief Commissioner Mick Miller built the Bureau of Criminal Intelligence and surrounded it with specialist squads but he insisted that when detectives were promoted they returned to uniform to share expertise – and to cut the risk of corruption created by staying too long in crime squads.

But the Miller model was eventually let slide. Specialists such as the stolen-car squad were disbanded and the drug squad was denied resources and not supervised well. Despite conventional wisdom that police should only be allowed to stay in high-risk corruption areas for limited time, detectives were able to make careers in the drug squad. It was a recipe for disaster.

Tackling potential crime bosses requires expensive taskforce policing, so the force ignored the problem until it was too late. The trouble is that budding gangsters get to grow stronger and harder to deal with.

The perfect example: Andrew 'Benji' Veniamin. Vicious, callous and cunning, in 1999 he was identified as a man ready to use guns. But little was done. Soon, Veniamin had done his first paid hit, killing Frank Benvenuto in Hampton. He would go on to complete six more contract killings before being shot dead.

When the Purana Taskforce started, investigators were stunned at how little was known about Veniamin and others. Purana's first head, Phil Swindells, was to spend months gathering vital intelligence before he could move against the gangsters.

THE war might not have started without police corruption. The murders of Terence and Christine Hodson and the ambush killing of Shane Chartres-Abbott have been linked to police – allegations deemed credible enough for two taskforces to be formed to investigate. But there was another link to corruption that created the environment for gangsters to kill.

Three drug squad detectives directly involved in prosecution cases against high-profile suspects including Tony Mokbel, Lewis Moran and Carl Williams were themselves facing charges. The cases against the suspect drug dealers could not be heard until the police cases were dealt with, which would take years. As a result Mokbel, Moran and the others were granted bail, which meant rival drug dealers were on the loose at once, fighting over the same patch.

Nine of the murder victims were on bail when they were killed and Carl Williams was on three sets of bail while ordering murders. Tony Mokbel was on bail when he fled overseas. Nothing has been done to review the bail system. In fact, when a senior policeman suggested it he was pilloried by the legal profession.

THE war was funded by massive drug money, used to pay hired guns. At least fifteen criminals were paid to kill or played supporting roles in murder plots.

Drug money undermined an already under-resourced drug squad that was tainted and out of its depth. But in the end, the easy money meant some crooks began to believe their own publicity. Old-school criminals like Graham Kinniburgh and Lewis Moran knew the value of a low profile but the cashed-up 'cowboys' made the mistake of courting publicity, ignoring the fact it would inevitably bring political pressure to clean up organised crime.

As Dino Dibra said before he was shot dead, 'Mate, I've just watched *Reservoir Dogs* too many times.'

Elements of the media polished the 'glamorous' images of some gangsters, treating them as equally credible sources to police.

At one stage, it was the gangsters who held the press conferences and the police who said 'no comment'.

Some of the taped conversations between reporters hungry for a quote and killers looking for a public relations boost would embarrass both parties if ever released.

Some of the gangsters seemed to think Purana was just another gang. One was foolish enough to write an obscene 'verse about it while in prison, beginning with the lines:

'Fucking Purana Squad,
Youse are a fucking joke,
Why pick on us?
We're nothing but good blokes.'

IN the end, the war showed that most gangsters made basic mistakes and acted without considering consequences. The Morans shot Williams without considering he might fight back. Williams started a war without considering it must end with him in jail or dead. 'Benji' Veniamin killed so often he knew he must die.

They pretended to live without fear, yet autopsies showed that several were using anti-depressants and sedatives. Mark Moran considered suicide. Many privately sought counselling.

Caught in a world of their own making, some could see no way out. Gangitano had not made enough money to invest in a straight business and lacked the character to turn his back on crime. As a result, his children lost their father.

Others were apathetic: three murder victims had security systems that didn't work. Others kept predictable routines that made it easy for killers to track them. Two did not use their secure garages, preferring to park in the street – with fatal results.

Several rejected chances to start new lives: Gangitano and Jason Moran returned from overseas only to die. Several refused police protection.

THE turnaround came because finally police got resources denied to investigators for years. They were given time, money and surveillance gear: in fact, 75 percent of the force's phone tapping and listening devices.

Many politicians and media experts predicted Purana would fail but they were wrong. For the first time in memory the underworld code of silence was smashed.

But while law enforcement has learned that organised crime needs to be constantly attacked, history shows that immediate problems get the resources at the expense of long-term solutions. Eventually, the extra effort needed to mount a Purana-type campaign will be too hard.

Meanwhile, there will always be a supermarket shelf-stacker who wants to be the next Carl Williams, a milk-bar owner who wants to be Tony Mokbel and a schoolyard bully who wants to be Alphonse Gangitano.

The Underworld War is over. Until the next one.

The hit list

1 Gregory John Workman
Shot dead by Al Gangitano on February 7, 1995.

2 Alphonse John Gangitano
Shot in his Templestowe home on January 16, 1998, by Jason Moran.

3 John Furlan
Died from car bomb on August 3, 1998.
Suspect: the late Domenico Italiano.

4 "Mad Charlie" Hegyalji
Shot in garden of his South Caulfield home on November 23, 1998. Alleged killer later shot dead.

5 Vince Mannella
Shot by unknown man as he returned to North Fitzroy home on January 9, 1999.

6 Joe Quadara
Shot dead as he arrived at work at a Toorak supermarket on May 28, 1999.

7 Dimitrios Belias
Body found in a pool of blood below a St Kilda Road office on September 9, 1999.

8 Gerardo Mannella
Shot as he left his brother's North Fitzroy home on October 20, 1999. One person close to him knew he was about to die.

9 Frank Benvenuto
Shot in Beaumaris on May 8, 2000.

10 Richard Mladenich
Shot in a St Kilda motel on May 16, 2000.

11 Mark Moran
Shot outside his house near Essendon on June 15, 2000.

12 Dino Dibra
Shot outside his West Sunshine home on October 14, 2000.

13 George Germanos
Shot in an Armadale park on March 22, 2001.

14 Victor George Peirce
Shot in his car in Port Melbourne on May 1, 2002.

15 Paul Kallipolitis
Shot in his West Sunshine home in October 2002.

16 Nik 'The Bulgarian' Radev
Shot in Coburg, on April 15, 2003.

17 Shane Chartres-Abbott
Shot June 4, 2003, in Reservoir. Alleged corrupt police involvement.

18 & 19 Jason Moran and Pasquale Barbaro
Shot in hotel car park in Essendon North on June 21, 2003. Gunman jailed and now a police witness.

20 Willie Thompson
Shot dead in his car in Chadstone on July 21, 2003.

21 Mark Mallia
Charred body found in a drain in West Sunshine on August 18, 2003. Carl Williams pleaded guilty to his murder.

22 Housam 'Sam' Zayat
Shot during in a paddock in Tarneit on September 9, 2003.

23 & 24 Steve Gulyas and Tina 'Bing' Nhonthachith
Shot at their Sunbury property on October 20, 2003.
Prime suspect overseas.

25 Michael Ronald Marshall
Shot outside his South Yarra house on October 25, 2003. Carl
Williams convicted of his murder.

26 Graham 'The Munster' Kinniburgh.
Shot outside his Kew home on December 13, 2003.

27 Andrew 'Benji' Veniamin
Shot at a Carlton restaurant on March 23, 2004.
Mick Gatto acquitted of murder on self-defence.

28 Lewis Moran
Shot dead in the Brunswick Club on March 31, 2004.
Hit man pleaded guilty; now a police witness.

29 Lewis Caine
Shot in Brunswick on May 8, 2004. Gunman jailed and now a
police witnesses.

30 & 31 Terence and Christine Hodson
Shot dead at their Kew home on May 15, 2004. Suspected corrupt police involvement.

32 Mario Condello
Shot dead in garage of his East Brighton home on February 6,
2006. Suspected gunman identified.